PRAISE FOR DENISE HUNTER'S P~~~~~~ ~~~~~

"No one can write a story that grips the heart like Denise Hunter . . . If you like Karen Kingsbury or Nicholas Sparks, this is an author you'll love."

— Colleen Coble, author of *Alaska Twilight* and *Abomination*

"[*Finding Faith*] kept me in tears as the characters struggled to find truth. A captivating story that will touch every woman's heart."

— Diann Mills, author of sixteen books, Writing Coach

"You absolutely have to read *Mending Places* . . ."

— *Dancing Word*

"Gritty, powerful, and thought-provoking."

— Carol Cox, author of *To Catch a Thief*

"*Saving Grace* kept me turning pages from the minute I opened the cover and kept me up way past my bedtime . . . A story of triumph over heartache."

— Deborah Raney, author of *A Nest of Sparrows*

"Denise Hunter handles tough subjects with a deft hand and biblical wisdom while giving readers a novel they won't want to put down."

— Kathryn Mackel, author of *Outriders*

"In *Finding Faith* Denise Hunter once again brings me to tears with her thought-provoking story. For depth and emotion, this author always hits her mark."

— Kristin Billerbeck, author of *What a Girl Wants* and *She's All That*

"*Saving Grace* grabs hold of the heart, forcing readers to think about God-challenges in their own lives. I loved it."

— Lois Richer, author of *Shadowed Secrets*

"Denise Hunter skillfully paints a story of desperate choices with dire consequences."

— Diann Hunt, author of *Hot Flashes and Cold Cream*

"It is so nice to read a romance story [like *Blind Dates*] with God at its core."

— Jane Deskis, heartlandreviews.com

Surrender Bay

DENISE HUNTER

THOMAS NELSON
Since 1798

NASHVILLE   DALLAS   MEXICO CITY   RIO DE JANEIRO   BEIJING

Published in Nashville, Tennessee, by Thomas Nelson. Thomas Nelson is a trademark of Thomas Nelson, Inc.

Thomas Nelson, Inc. titles may be purchased in bulk for educational, business, fund-raising, or sales promotional use. For information, please e-mail SpecialMarkets@ThomasNelson.com.

Library of Congress Cataloging-in-Publication Data

Hunter, Denise, 1968–
    Surrender bay / Denise Hunter.
      p. cm.
    ISBN 978-1-59554-257-1 (pbk.)
      1. Teenage girls—Fiction. 2. Massachusetts—Fiction. 3. Domestic fiction.
I. Title.
    PS3608.U5925S87 2007
    813'.6—dc22

                                     2007032732

Printed in the United States of America
07 08 09 10 RRD 5 4 3 2 1

The Lord your God is with you,
he is mighty to save.
He will take great delight in you,
he will quiet you with his love,
he will rejoice over you with singing.

ZEPHANIAH 3:17

Prologue

"Why'd you wait so long to turn on the flashlight last night?" Landon asked.

Even though evening shadows crawled over Landon's backyard, Samantha Owens could see his eyes searching hers. He hadn't said anything about her delay before now, but she could tell he'd been bothered all day because he didn't once tug her ponytail.

She lifted her body out of the waist-deep Nantucket water, flipping over to land on the pier with a sodden plop. The outdoor lamp lashed to the last post spotlighted her. Her bathing suit clung to her stomach, and she pulled at the fabric just to hear the sucking sound as it left her skin.

She looked over her shoulder and saw Landon's mom through the lit kitchen window, washing supper dishes. Mr. Reed appeared just then and pulled her against his chest. She laughed at something he said, then turned in his arms. Sam looked away.

Landon splashed through the water and hoisted himself onto the pier beside her. His arms had filled out over the summer, and he'd shot up a good two inches. Sam wasn't sure she liked him changing so much.

"Did you hear me?"

Landon bumped Sam's foot under the water, and she felt him watching her. She shrugged as casually as she could. "I went to bed late. I got a book on the Red Sox. Did you know they used to be called the Boston Americans?" A breeze drifted over her wet skin, tightening it into gooseflesh.

"Your light wasn't on." Skepticism coated his words.

Changing the subject never worked with Landon. When would she learn? "I snuck in the bathroom to read. You know how Emmett is." Landon didn't know the half of it, but some things she'd never tell anyone. Not even Landon.

Sam lay back, resting her spine against the wooden planks. She closed her eyes and wished she could stay just like this all night, listening to the sound of crickets and the splash of water kissing the shoreline.

"I was worried."

His voice sounded older, deeper than she remembered. "You worry too much."

He shifted, and Sam opened her eyes. He was lying beside her, his body a plank-width away, his head turned toward her. The moonlight glimmered on his hair, and shadows settled between his drawn eyebrows. "Don't forget the flashlight again."

Sam didn't much like being told what to do, but something in the tone of his voice touched the deepest place in her as no one ever had. "I won't."

He held Sam's gaze as if testing her sincerity. After a moment, she crossed her eyes at him, watching his face blur into a double image.

"Weirdo," he said.

"Freak."

"Slime bucket."

"Geek."

A mosquito stung her neck, and she slapped at it. Her skin was already speckled with half a dozen bites, but they didn't bother her much. She was surprised Mrs. Reed hadn't come out yet with the can of Off!, but maybe she and Mr. Reed were too busy smooching in the kitchen.

Sam imagined the inside of her own house, just two doors down, and felt a shadow press its way into her soul. Her mom would be calling her in soon.

She turned to Landon, glad to see his face had softened. "Wanna have a sleepover at your house? We can decide what we want to put in our time capsule."

Landon glanced away, and Sam didn't recognize the look that passed over his face.

"We're getting too old for that."

Well, la-di-da. Maybe Landon thought turning thirteen had made him all grown up. Sam suddenly felt every day of their seven-month age gap. "Time capsules aren't just for kids, you know."

One corner of his mouth slid upward, but not quite enough to bunch up his cheek. He pulled himself upright and splashed back into the murky water. "I wasn't talking about the capsule."

She wanted to ask what he meant, but she could tell he didn't want her to by the way his head dipped low.

"Samantha!" Her mom's voice had an edge that said she'd been calling awhile.

"Coming!" Though Sam knew she should get up and go, her body lay against the boards as heavy as a ship anchor. She should have gotten out of the water hours ago so she wouldn't drip water across the kitchen floor. Too late now. At least Emmett wasn't home.

"I should go in too," Landon said, wading alongside the pier. "The mosquitoes are bad tonight." He smacked at his arm.

Why couldn't she just stay at Landon's house? If he was so worried, why didn't he invite her over?

He stopped at the shoreline, where the water licked at his feet. "You'd better go."

He'd stand there until she left, he was just that stubborn.

Sam pulled her feet from the water and walked down the pier. They crossed paths in front of his parents' Adirondack chairs. Landon turned and lifted his fingers. "Don't forget the flashlight."

"I won't." Her feet carried her across the Reeds' yard, then across Miss Biddle's. She knew by feel the moment she stepped into her own backyard. Emmett kept the grass clipped so short their lawn had turned wheat brown. It drove her mom crazy.

Sam entered the cottage through the back door, hoping she could sneak into her room and change into dry clothes before her mom saw how wet she was, but the squeak of the screen door gave her away.

"Samantha." Her mom's lips pinched together as she looked Sam over.

"Sorry, I forgot." Ribbons of water dripped from the edges of her swimsuit, carving rivers between goose bumps. They trickled over her ankles as she made a mad dash past her mom to her bedroom. "I'll clean it up," she called.

"You bet you'll clean it up. I don't know why I bother cleaning around here."

Sam rummaged through her drawers, pushing aside the nightgowns her mom had bought, and pulled out her favorite long T-shirt and a stretchy pair of shorts.

A few minutes later, Sam entered the kitchen and took a towel from the drawer, then wiped up the mini puddles. The bones of her knees knocked against the wood floor as she crept along, swiping in wide arcs.

"Why do you wear that ratty old thing? You look like a boy, Samantha."

"It's comfortable." Sam slung her wet ponytail across her shoulder.

"You missed a spot." Her mom pointed toward the door.

Sam backtracked and dried the area. By the time she finished, her mom had left the kitchen, so Sam tossed the towel in the washer and returned to her room, shutting the door. The doorknob was the old-fashioned kind, cut glass with clear angles. She'd thought it beautiful when she was little. When the sunlight flooded the room and hit the glass, it splayed prisms of light across the wall. Now she wished for a plain old metal doorknob, the kind with a lock.

Sam turned out the light and slipped under the quilt. Before she lay against the pillow, she reached into her bedside drawer and withdrew the flashlight. The switch flipped on with ease, and she set it on the wooden sill of the window. She turned on her side and tucked the covers under her chin.

She lay that way for a long time, hearing the sounds of her mom getting ready for bed. She knew it would be a while before Emmett came home, but still she listened for the sound of his car, for the crunch of gravel under his work boots. She listened until her ears were so full of silence it seemed they would burst.

Sometime later she startled awake to the sound of the front door opening. She heard her mom talking; then Emmett's voice rumbled through her closed door. "She didn't pull the weeds like I told her to." He cursed.

"Well, she can do it tomorrow." Her mom's voice was fading. "How much did you lose tonight?"

The sound of their bedroom door clicking shut resonated in her ears.

৯৮   ৯৮   ৯৮

"Get up."

Sam's arm stung with the sharp slap, and she shot up in bed. Dawn's light filtered through the window, gray and dim.

Emmett was already walking away. "Go pull the weeds like I told you yesterday. No breakfast until you're done."

"I already did." In her fog of sleep, the words slipped out.

He turned and hauled her out of bed, and her knees buckled as her feet hit the floor. Fully awake now, she realized it was Saturday and her mom was at work. "I'll do better."

He straightened, and she noticed tiny red veins lining the whites of his eyes. She looked at the rug beneath her feet. He released her burning arm.

When he left, she traded her long T-shirt for an old, faded one and set to work in the flower beds, pulling the weeds she'd missed the day before. The sun was nowhere to be seen, hiding behind a thick curtain of angry clouds. She'd emptied two bucketfuls and was back on her knees when Emmett opened the back door. The squawk of the hinges made her jump.

"Since you didn't do what you were told the first time, you can pull the dead blooms and trim the hedges too." With that, he disappeared into the house.

She sat back on her haunches and brushed the hair from her face with dirty fingers. She scanned the rows of lilies, and she pictured all the rose blooms in the front yard and the hedges lining the yard. With a sigh, she leaned forward and grabbed a dandelion, wrapping it around her hand and yanking hard. She tossed it, roots and all, in the bucket.

The rain started then, first a drop on her hand, then one on her cheek. Within a minute, a steady shower fell. She planted her knees in the dirt and began pulling wilted blooms from the lily plants. By the time she'd finished the first one, the dirt under her knees was mud, and her empty stomach twisted. She scooted toward the next plant and went back to work.

Sam didn't see Landon until he fell to his knees beside her. Wordlessly, he plucked a bloom and then another, tossing them in the bucket. When he finally looked at her, his hair hung in wet, dark strands over his eyes and a clump of dirt smudged his cheek, and Sam knew she looked no better.

His lips turned up on one side, and she couldn't stop her own smile.

They worked until the beds and hedges were done and their clothes were soaked clean through. Landon reheated the pancakes his dad had made that morning, then they watched TV with his younger brother, Bailey, until lunchtime. By then, the sun had come out again, and the threesome played all afternoon, passing a football and fishing off the end of the Reeds' pier.

At supper time, Landon headed inside, and Sam said she had to go in too. But when she got home, her mom and Emmett were gone, so she had a bowl of Lucky Charms and a handful of peanuts. When she saw Landon in his backyard again, she joined him, and they tossed his football until it was too dark to see.

Later, Landon stood at the water's edge, the cool water nipping at his toes, while she stood poised barefoot on the first plank of the pier like a 747 aimed at a runway. At the end, the light glowed against the black sky.

Even in the dimness, she saw his hard, flattened lips and knew they suppressed a reprimand, just as he knew a scolding would not stop her.

Sam smiled impishly at him, then darted forward, building speed in just a few long strides. At just the right spot, she sprang into a round-off and followed it with four back handsprings.

Her hands and feet alternately punched the boards, making a rhythmic *thud-thud, thud-thud.* She landed solidly in the spotlight four planks shy of the water. Nearly a record. She was no Mary Lou Retton or Julianne McNamara—she was too tall and big-boned to be nimble—but she didn't care so much about form.

She strode back toward Landon and stepped into the dark water, making sure to keep her clothes dry.

"I wish you wouldn't do that," Landon said before compressing his lips into a tight line again. His olive green eyes looked almost black in the nighttime shadows, and she could see the shimmering lights from the water reflected in them.

"I haven't fallen yet," Sam said as she worked her toes into the silty sand until the tops of her feet were covered.

"When you do, don't come crying to me."

Sam smirked at that because Landon knew she never cried, and if she ever did, he'd be the first one to scoop her up and sweep away her tears.

When the moon was high in the sky, Landon's mom called him in, so they said good night and Sam went home. She could hear the TV blaring in her mom and Emmett's room, so she crept into her bedroom and shut the door. After getting ready for bed, she lifted her window to invite the night breeze inside and set the flashlight on the sill.

Sam curled up on her side and closed her eyes. Sometime later, she heard her mom and Emmett talking on the back porch. She strained to hear them.

"The flower beds look nice," her mom said.

"Took the better part of the day."

Sam heard a rush of exhaled breath and envisioned the puff of cigarette smoke from her mom's mouth.

"What are our plans for tomorrow, baby?" Emmett asked.

Sam pictured her mom crossing her arms, shrugging him off.

Sam thought she must have missed her answer because there was such a long pause. Then she heard her mom's reply. "We don't have any."

There was a haunting tone in her mother's words that Sam hadn't heard before.

Their voices lowered to low mumbles she couldn't interpret, so Sam listened to the nocturnal orchestra outside her window. A loon called out over the buzz of the insects, and the water licked the shore-line. If she concentrated hard, she could hear Mom's boat knocking against the pier bumper. A breeze rattled the tree leaves and carried the sweet scent of salt-spray roses through the air. Her body began to relax. Her thoughts slowed and her breaths deepened.

⌇   ⌇   ⌇

Sam opened her eyes. Darkness blanketed her room, and outside her window, a thick fog swallowed the moonlight. A sound had wakened her. The distinctive *clunk* that sounds across the water when an oar strikes the hull of a boat. The numbers on her clock read 4:37, an odd hour for a boat to be out.

She untangled herself from the quilt and decided to investigate. When she pushed open the screen door, it squeaked, and she cringed. Very carefully, she set it against the wooden frame. Her bare feet grabbed grits of sand as she walked across the rough boards of the porch.

Sam crossed her arms against the cool air and tiptoed across the damp, stubby grass. The fog glowed under the light from their pier. She stopped on the beach and listened.

The water slapped restlessly against the piles, and the wind teased Miss Biddle's flag, making the hardware ping against the metal pole—sounds so familiar and constant that she sometimes heard them in her dreams.

Maybe she'd dreamed the sound. She sighed, and her shoulders drooped with resignation as she turned to go back.

Another sound stopped her. One that was absent from her usual backyard symphony. She stepped onto the pier and walked the length of it, feeling her heart punching her rib cage with each step. When she reached the end, she stared at the vacant spot on the water.

She tilted her head downward. The cleat that held the lines of her mom's boat was empty. She studied the water under the light and saw on its surface the remnants of a disturbance: ripples, gradually weakening as they rolled toward the barren shoreline.

I will never leave you nor forsake you.

JOSHUA 1:5

One

"You can just drop me off, you know. I'm not a baby." Eleven-year-old Caden flipped her mom a look, then stared out the passenger window.

"I like watching you." Sam pulled the Ciera into the parking lot of the Boston Academy of Gymnastics and was about to expound on the thought, but Caden interrupted.

"The other moms don't stay."

It wasn't true, but Sam had a feeling this objection had less to do with Caden's assertion of independence and more to do with her.

"Did Bridget tell everyone about me?" Sam asked.

Caden crossed her arms, her warm-up suit rustling.

"If I didn't clean the gym, we wouldn't be able to afford lessons, Caden."

Though her daughter frowned, her jaw and shoulders rigid, Sam knew the stubborn front concealed a wounded little girl. Knew it because Caden was so much like her.

"They all know now. Bridget has such a big mouth. She thinks she's so hot just because her mom owns the gym."

Sam turned off the ignition and withdrew the keys, then glanced at Caden, who made no move to leave. The clock on the dashboard read 7:02. "Honey, let's finish this later. You're late for class."

"So you're staying?"

Sam's parental pride shrank two more sizes. "By the time I got home, I'd just have to turn around and come back. I promise to sit in the back and keep my hood up to conceal my identity." Sam regretted the sarcasm instantly.

Caden discharged her seat belt, and it sprang upward, clanging against the door frame. "Whatever," she said, then exited the car, not quite slamming the door.

Sam grabbed the day's mail from the dashboard and tucked it in her purse. As she entered the gym, the familiar odor of sweaty little gymnasts assaulted her nostrils. She walked past the office and up the stairs to the balcony, where she found a seat in the back row. She smiled at a woman seated there, the mom of one of Caden's classmates. From her pantsuit and trendy heels, Sam guessed she didn't scrub bathrooms for a living or work a side job to afford her daughter's lessons.

On the floor below, a maze of mats and apparatus were spread across the blue carpet. Caden's class stretched, their legs straddled, leaning forward until their bellies touched the ground. Her daughter lay there, head resting against the carpet. The girl next to Caden whispered something to another girl and they laughed. Sam assumed the worst, and she wanted to give the girl's ear a swift tug.

Instead, she settled back into the chair and pulled the mail from her bag. Electric bill. Bank statement. Credit card bill. She'd open that one last. No sense ruining a perfectly good day. The last piece was addressed to her with a black pen. In the upper left-hand corner was a sticker with Miss Biddle's name and address.

Strange. Beyond the annual Christmas card, she rarely heard

from Miss Biddle. And even when she did, she almost didn't want to open the envelope—as if doing so would open a door from her past she'd rather leave closed.

Curious, she turned the letter over and slid her finger under the flap. She withdrew a piece of notebook paper neatly creased in thirds. She unfolded the note.

Dear Samantha,

I hope this letter finds you well. I would have preferred to call, but the number you're listed as having is disconnected. I'm afraid I have some bad news.

Just yesterday your stepfather had a heart attack at work. They tried to take him to the hospital, but he passed away in the ambulance and they were unable to resuscitate him. I know there was no love lost between the two of you, but still I hated to tell you this way.

A strange feeling swept over Sam like an unexpected wind on a still night. There was no sadness or grief, but rather an unexplained dread.

I contacted Judge Winslow (from the probate court), who will be handling Emmett's estate, and I learned Emmett had no will. Since you are his adopted child, and the only living relative, his cottage and belongings will pass to you. You might contact Judge Winslow down at the Town and County building. I'm sure they'll send you notification soon, but I thought it might be better to hear the news from me.

Sam stared at the letter, but the words blurred as her thoughts scrambled. Excitement overtook the dread. The cottage sat on the valuable Nantucket shore and was worth a fortune. It was small and old, but even the smallest shanty on the island neared a million dollars.

The thought of what she and Caden could do with that kind of money stirred something she hadn't felt in a long time.

Hope.

She finished the letter, skimming over the funeral information.

A million dollars. She could pay off her credit cards, get out of their crummy apartment, buy Caden some decent clothes, pay for gymnastic lessons. Heck, she could send Caden to a private school if she wanted. And college. Caden could become anything she wanted to be.

Even Sam could go to college. It was a thought she hadn't allowed since she got pregnant with Caden. Even now, she tamped down the thought, too afraid to hope in case this was all a dream.

But the flimsy white paper in her hands was real enough. Emmett's name scrawled in black sobered her. Memories raced through her mind at the speed of light, none of them good. The feeling of being trapped, overpowered, and abandoned all at the same time made her squirm in her chair as if to make sure she wasn't restrained.

The realization that she would have to go back there stole her breath and jarred her mind to a sudden halt. The house would have to be cleaned out. Furniture and personal belongings would have to be sorted through. The cottage would need to be readied for sale. The flower beds, if they still existed, would need tending.

How long would it take, and would Patty let her off work that long? Sam hadn't had a vacation or sick day in—well, she couldn't even remember. They'd just lost an office building to Murphy's Maids the week before, so the schedule was lighter, and Gina had been asking for extra hours.

Still, the thought of going back to the island made Sam's soul shrivel like a sun-scorched bloom. There was a reason she hadn't gone back. A reason she'd left in the first place, and nothing had changed.

Except that going back was now worth a million dollars.

Sam lifted her eyes from the letter and found Caden's class across the gym at the foam pit. Caden sprang forward into a round-off and two back handsprings, then finished with a backflip into the foam squares. The spotter never touched her. It was her first unassisted backflip. When she came out of the pit, she looked toward the balcony to see if Sam had caught the moment. Before she could give her daughter a thumbs-up, Caden looked away. When she walked by Bridget and her new cronies, they turned, an obvious snub.

Sam wanted to thump them all. They were doing it because of her, and the guilt that descended on her was as heavy as a lead blanket.

Could a million dollars buy her and Caden a new life? Sam was suddenly sure it could. And she was equally sure she could face any demon from her past for the chance to make it happen.

Two

This isn't happening. All Sam's bravado from two weeks before sank like a boulder in the Atlantic as she clutched the ferry's railing, watching Nantucket Harbor creep closer. Dozens of boats dotted the water, their empty masts poking the sky like skinny white fingers. Beyond them, gray-washed stores and cottages lined the piers and step-stoned up the hillside.

Caden leaned against the rail, the wind tugging at her hair. On her other side, a man pointed his digital camera toward the high tower of the First Congregational Church and snapped the picture.

With every inch of the ferry's progress, fear clawed up Sam's throat. She kept her eyes trained to the east side of the ferry, not ready to see what lay to the west. How would she face the Reeds? A heavy cloud rolled over the sun, casting a shadow over the town and turning the water black.

"It looks small," Caden said.

It was the first thing she'd said since they boarded the ferry. But the silence beat all the complaining she'd done before that. *Why do we have to go? I'll get behind the other girls at the gym. I don't want to leave my friends. Why can't we go someplace exciting? My life is so boring!* If she only knew that Nantucket was the last place Sam wanted to go. If Caden knew about the money the sale of the house would bring, she might have worried less, but Sam wasn't ready to handle requests for designer jeans and salon haircuts.

"It is small." Her gaze scrolled past the marina and yacht club, but an overwhelming curiosity drew it back. People mingled on the multitiered decks, sipping drinks, and a couple played on the tennis courts, slamming the ball back and forth in low drives that scarcely cleared the net. Sam had taught tennis there three years straight, but thinking of the club always dredged up that last unfortunate summer.

Her eyes landed on the lighthouse that squatted on the boulders at Brant Point. "See the lighthouse? Its original structure was built in 1746 and was the second lighthouse built in America. It's called Brant Point Light." She rattled off the tidbit like an old-timer.

Sam was rewarded with silence.

The ferry began docking, and she hated the way her hands trembled. She wanted to stay on board and sail back to the mainland. The urge to escape Nantucket was still rooted as deeply as the thick oak that grew outside her Boston apartment window, and the urge to stay away was just as strong.

Moments later, they debarked and lugged their suitcases down the cement dock and across the busy cobblestone street. When she spotted a taxi, she lengthened her steps, urging Caden along. As the driver loaded their suitcases, Sam gave him the address, then slid into the car.

Caden glanced out the window. "Are those summer people?" she asked, referring to the clusters of pedestrians crossing streets and disappearing into bustling shops.

"Mainly they're tourists. The summer people come in July."

"At least there are stores. What's with all the bikes?"

"One of the perks of a small island. Bikes are the main mode of transportation."

Caden was silent as they drove through town. Only when they eased onto quieter streets did she speak again. "Can I meet Landon? Does he know you're here?"

Caden's hope caught Sam off guard. She had been telling "Landon stories" to Caden since her daughter was old enough to talk. Lately, though, Caden wasn't interested in anything she had to say. "I don't think so," she said, choosing to let Caden interpret the answer however she wanted. Only Miss Biddle and Judge Winslow knew Sam was coming. Besides, she wasn't even sure Landon returned to Nantucket after college, though he'd talked of nothing else those last years together.

When the driver turned onto her old street, she squeezed the edge of the seat with cold fingers. "It's down just a ways on the right," she told the driver.

"The ocean is in the backyard?" Caden stared through her window, a new light flickering in her face.

"Yep." Caden's curiosity encouraged Sam, and she wondered if leaving the city was just the prescription for her daughter.

"It's two drives down. Right there, the one with the rose trellis." Only eleven years had passed since Sam last saw the house, but she hardly recognized it. The shaker shingles were weathered to ash gray, and the white paint that trimmed out the windows and porch was faded and peeling.

The cabby turned into the gravel drive and pulled to a stop. Caden was out and standing in the overgrown yard before Sam touched her own door.

Sam finally emerged and took in the house while the driver set the luggage at her feet. The window boxes stood empty, the hedges were overgrown, and only weeds sprouted from the flower beds lining the front of the house. She could still see her mom bending over the orange lilies, pinching faded blooms from the plant. She could see her on her knees, pulling up weeds and throwing them in the gray five-gallon paint bucket.

Sam's racing heart flopped. It was going to take every moment of her vacation to get the place in shape for the market. If the inside was as neglected as the outside, she wasn't sure a month was enough time.

Caden had grabbed her suitcase and pulled it close to the sidewalk.

After Sam paid the driver, she picked up her own bag. She hadn't given a thought to how she'd get in. Maybe Emmett still kept a key under the flowerpot on the back porch.

"Around back." Sam circled wide around the building, staring in morbid fascination like a driver passing an auto accident. There it was—the place she'd wanted to leave. The place she never wanted to return to. She reminded herself that she'd run from people, not the building. Emmett couldn't hurt her anymore; he was gone. It struck her as ironic that the man who'd never provided for her was now, in his death, providing her with a windfall.

She'd just have to wade through hell and back to get it.

The enclosed back porch was smaller than she remembered. They entered through the screen door, the squawk tugging her back to her childhood. The flowerpot was still there, empty except for a few inches of dry dirt. She pulled a key from underneath.

"Voilà," Sam said with more optimism than she felt.

She unlocked the door and shoved it open. A whiff of smoke and stale air greeted her.

"Ewww." Caden wrinkled her pert little nose.

Sam set their bags off to the side.

"He didn't, like, die here, did he?"

The ghost of his presence felt so real it was as if he hadn't died at all. Sam listened for the sound of his feet thumping across the floor. She shook away the sensation.

"The house has been closed up awhile. We'll open the windows and get some fresh air in."

Caden was already in the living room, only a few steps away. Sam looked at the old porcelain sink where she'd learned to wash dishes, and wash them right. In the strainer beside it, two plates leaned at a cockeyed angle, and a few pieces of silverware poked upward. A shirt hung haphazardly over a kitchen chair. She wanted to remove it between two pinched fingers and toss it in the garbage. But Emmett's things were everywhere.

"Was this your room?"

Sam followed the sound of Caden's voice. The double bed had been stripped down to the faded floral mattress, and a layer of dust shrouded the bare furniture like a flannel sheet. Other than that, it looked the same. She didn't know if she could bring herself to sleep here.

She opened the window, fighting the stubborn sash. Fresh, salty air wafted in, billowing the gauzy curtains.

"Is this where I'm sleeping?"

Sam glanced around, taking in the gaping closet door, the dresser that had Scott Burnwell's initials carved into the side, the photo of her mom hanging on the wall.

"Sure," she said.

Sam left and went to air out the kitchen. Next, she entered Emmett's room, striding toward the window. On an inhale, her nostrils filled with the smell of him. Gasoline and Old Spice and Winstons all blended together in a stench that turned her stomach. She flung up the pane and left, shutting the door behind her.

What she'd give to be staying in a hotel! Such a luxury on the island would cost a fortune she didn't have. At least, not yet.

"I'm going outside." Caden whizzed past her and out the back, the porch's screen door slapping against the wooden frame. This was a different world for Caden, and Sam could tell, despite her daughter's feigned disinterest, that she was taken with it.

Sam looked around the house and tried to see it with a fresh, unjaded perspective. The wood-plank floor, dotted with rugs, and the painted white furniture had a certain charm that her apartment lacked. For the first time, she saw it was really a quaint little cottage, a place Caden might see as homey and cute. She hadn't expected that. She'd thought Caden would feel the same way about it that she did.

But her daughter couldn't know what it had been like to grow up here. Even now the walls seemed to press in from every side, and the air seemed too heavy to breathe. How would Sam endure weeks of sorting through the memories she'd spent her life trying to forget?

Three

"How much chocolate did you give her, Mrs. Maley?" Landon Reed put his stethoscope in place and timed the beats.

"It was a piece of chocolate cake, not even pure chocolate. I didn't think it would hurt her." Mrs. Maley drew her fingers through her Lhasa apso's thick white fur.

Landon set down his stethoscope and palpated the dog's bloated belly. When Mrs. Maley brought her dog in last fall with chocolate poisoning, he explained that chocolate was toxic to dogs, but even so, she brought Fanny in again on a frigid February evening after having rewarded the dog with Hershey's squares. *She just looked at me with those pleading eyes, and I couldn't say no. I didn't give her much.*

Now, seeing the dog in misery again, he wanted to shake the woman. "What kind of chocolate was used in the cake?"

"It was the baking kind, you know, the kind that comes in foil-wrapped squares." She brushed long strands away from Fanny's face. "She'll be all right, won't she?"

Landon ignored the question while he finished the exam. The dog would be okay, he guessed. She had an increased heart rate and had vomited, according to Mrs. Maley, but he saw no signs of hyper-activity or muscular twitching.

He rubbed Fanny's belly. "Baking chocolate is the most toxic of all chocolates. One ounce of it will poison a ten-pound dog, and Fanny is barely over that weight."

Mrs. Maley fingered the salt-and-pepper hair at her nape. "I didn't know."

"I'll have Nancy get you an information sheet, but I'd like to keep Fanny overnight just to be safe. I know you love her and don't mean to harm her, but you can't give in to her begging. Once dogs have chocolate, they crave it. It's up to you to be strong for her sake."

Mrs. Maley stared at her pet. "I understand. But you think she'll be all right?"

"I believe so. But I'd rather be on the safe side."

"Oh yes, of course." Mrs. Maley caressed Fanny with long, slow strokes.

"I'll send Nancy in with some paperwork and that info sheet."

"Thank you so much, Dr. Reed."

He nodded and left the exam room. The waiting area was empty, and Nancy had locked the front doors and straightened all the magazines. After he asked Nancy to finish up with Mrs. Maley, he gave Dr. Schmidt instructions regarding Fanny's care, then went to his office to shed his lab coat and retrieve his keys. He hoped Mrs. Maley could show some restraint where Fanny was concerned. Otherwise, she'd bring the dog in sometime and wouldn't be taking her back home.

When Landon exited the clinic, his black Labrador bolted across the small fenced-in yard. Max gave a short bark and sidled up against Landon's leg.

Landon scratched behind Max's ear. "Hey, buddy. You ready to go home?"

Max's tail thumped against Landon's thigh, then the dog trotted beside him, matching his stride. Landon opened the Jeep door, and Max hopped into the back, plopping down on the seat, ears perked and tongue hanging between his sagging flews.

Landon left the parking lot and turned onto the cobblestone street. He braked in front of the Even Keel Café, allowing a group of tourists to cross the road, before continuing out of town and toward the house.

He turned onto his street, wishing he had something to do. It was unlike him to feel antsy, but then, lately he hadn't been himself. The routines he normally found comfort in were beginning to bore him, and the stillness of his house stirred a restlessness he didn't understand.

The feeling had worsened since he ended things with Jennifer, but he knew it wasn't from missing her. As beautiful as she was, inside and out, he hadn't connected with her the way he longed to. She deserved better, but telling her had been hard.

Before Jennifer, there was Tracie, who talked incessantly but never said anything, and Natalie, who only wanted to go out. He'd taken her to DeMarco's, Jared's, and Brant Point Grill. He'd taken her to the aquarium, to Nantucket town shops, to Martha's Vineyard. He hardly saw the inside of his cottage for weeks. Besides, Max didn't like her.

Lately, he'd had all the time in the world to think, and he found himself yearning for something more. If he could just figure out what.

He pulled into the drive and turned off the ignition. Max stood between the two front seats, paws propped on the console.

Landon exited the Jeep, and Max followed, then trotted toward the house.

Landon's eyes grazed past the neighbors' houses, and that's when his legs forgot how to work.

He felt as if he was trapped in a time warp as he watched her, on her hands and knees, tugging at a weed in the flower bed. With her flaxen hair pulled back into a ponytail, she was a vision straight from the past, and he blinked to make sure he wasn't seeing things. Was dusk playing tricks with his vision?

No, she was there, and it was Sam. Her movements, the way she brushed wayward strands from her face with the back of her hand. Eleven years ago this summer she disappeared, but he could've picked her from a crowd of ten thousand.

He knew all the clichés about kindred spirits and soul mates, but there were no other words to describe what he'd felt for Sam. She was the only girl who'd ever captured him, mind, body, and spirit. The only girl he would've died for. Somehow that summer changed everything between them.

But standing here, seeing her now, summoned all the summers before. Thoughtful moments on the pier, lighthearted moments on his dad's boat. Moments spent absorbing her strength and admiring her tenacity. She'd always drawn him like a blustery wind drew sailors onto the sea.

His eyes never left her form as his feet began a quiet march toward her.

⁂ ⁂ ⁂

Stupid, stupid weed! Sam pulled at the stubborn green stalk that jutted out of the ground, her legs straining. Finally, the roots gave way, and she nearly toppled backward onto her rear end.

She'd spent the afternoon cleaning the inside of the house, just for her own sanity. Even Caden had refused to shower in the claw-foot tub until the soap scum had been scrubbed away. Her stepfather had apparently lost the desire for a clean house once his personal maid departed, but at least cleaning was a job she knew.

Sam grabbed a dandelion, wrapped it around her hand, and yanked it up by the roots. It dawned on her as she sat on her knees that she was doing the same task Emmett used to assign her. The thought bothered her, but she reminded herself it was for money this time, not for the whim of her stepfather. Still, a moodiness had enveloped her since their arrival, and the irony that Caden's moodiness had been replaced by her own was not lost on Sam.

She sat back on her haunches and let the sharp wind smack her face. Seagulls cried, piercing the twilight, and she could hear the distant ebb and flow of relentless waves. Miss Biddle's flagpole pinged. Her breath quickened, leaving her mouth as dry as sand. She wished she was back in her apartment making mac 'n' cheese, or having a drink at Brewsky's, or even scrubbing floors at Havernack, Kleat, and Thomkinson's.

Sam closed her ears to the noise and plucked another dandelion, tossing it in a heap on the grass. She wondered if she should check on Caden, but she could hear the faint thudding of her bare feet on the back porch. It was getting dark anyway, and she would have to call it quits soon. She gathered the pile of weeds and stood, feeling her leg muscles stretch.

When she turned, she noticed a man's figure standing a short distance away. She started, then took a step backward, trying to discern his features in the muted light. He was tall and solid-looking. It was odd the way he stood so still, silence weaving a web around him.

Sam was a strong woman, but alarm pumped through her veins anyway. "Can I help you?" Her heart thudded against her rib cage, but she infused her tone with confidence.

He shifted then, tucking his hands in his back pockets. His head tilted sideways in a familiar move that made her stomach feel as if a dozen seagulls were trapped inside.

"It's me," he said.

The sound of his voice resurrected a wistfulness for a time that was no more. A time when play reduced the hours between sunrise and sunset to mere moments. A time when companionship validated long silences. A time when safety was as close as his embrace.

Sam had always missed him. Always when she described him to Caden, always when she stood on a Boston pier, looking across the vast ocean, but she hadn't known the depth of her yearning until now. Hadn't known the utter darkness of her world until the sudden presence of his light.

Her breath left her lungs, delivering his name. "Landon."

Four

Sam stared at Landon, the clump of weeds in her hand forgotten. They say when you die, the moments of your life play out like a movie in fast forward, and she knew what they meant now. But she wasn't about to die. She felt more alive than she ever had, and the reason was the man standing a few feet away.

"Sam. It's been a long time." He pulled his hands from his pockets.

For a moment, she thought he would step forward and embrace her, but the years slipped between them.

"Eleven years." The moment the words were out, she wished them back. Was he remembering the last time he'd seen her, at his brother's funeral? She spoke quickly as if to run an eraser across her previous words. "How are you?" It was something she'd ask a stranger.

"I'm doing all right. Graduated and came back to the island."

"Just like you always planned."

He shifted, and a street lamp flickered on, illuminating the side of his face and casting shadows over the other side. She was acutely aware her own face was in the light now, and she felt strangely exposed. She brushed back the hair that had come loose from her band.

"Just like." The corner of his mouth tipped.

Time stretched out like the shore along Madaket Beach. She wondered who he'd married, but she didn't want to know. She wondered if he ever thought about her, but she was afraid to ask.

Sam dropped the weeds, letting them fall at her feet, and brushed the dirt from her hands.

"Where do you live now?" he asked.

She heard the unspoken questions. *Where'd you disappear to eleven years ago? Why did you leave without a word?* The proverbial elephant was in the room.

"Boston." She supposed it didn't matter if he knew where she lived now. She supposed it didn't matter now if he knew she'd been pregnant when she left the island. So long as he didn't know who the father was.

He nodded slowly, and Sam knew he was wondering what the draw of Boston was. Her plans, as he well knew, had been to teach tennis for another year after high school to bulk up her savings for college. She was going to take two years at Cape Cod Community College and graduate to a bright future in environmental technology.

Now she was a commercial cleaner living in a neglected apartment with her fatherless adolescent. Wasn't life funny?

"What are you doing there? What's your life like?" He aimed a full smile at Sam, and she felt its impact. "I want to know everything."

His warm eyes tugged at Sam. "I don't know where to start." He was too young to have laugh lines, but he had them anyway. His face had matured, time carving the angle of his jawline and the planes of his face.

"Where do you work?"

Sam shrank at the inevitable question. She was a far cry from the person she'd planned to become. Once, she'd planned to change the world. Now she changed toilet paper rolls in corporate restrooms.

"I work for K&D Services, a commercial cleaner in downtown Boston." She could have stopped there but didn't. "I clean office buildings." It came out like a dare.

He searched her face, and she knew he saw right through her. She was silly for trying to pretend she was proud.

"I heard Emmett died." He cocked his head. "I didn't think you'd come back."

She was grateful for the turn in topic, even if it wasn't her favorite subject. She shrugged. "The house was left to me. I have to clean it out, put it on the market . . ."

"I figured that he would have left it to one of his buddies or something."

"He probably would have if he'd thought to say so. I guess he didn't plan on dying yet." She didn't want to talk about Emmett anymore. "How are your parents?" Guilt prickled at the thought of them.

A deep bark sounded across the lawn, and Landon turned toward it. "That's my dog, Max. He's wondering where I am."

He looked at her again and picked up the conversation. "My dad is fine. He's living in New Jersey near his brother. I'm afraid my mom passed away two years after you left."

The loss must have hit Landon and his dad hard. "I'm sorry."

He nodded. "Dad didn't want to stay on the island, so I bought their place. We're living there now."

Sam's ears hung on *we're*. Of course he was married. Probably had the appointed 2.5 children. And the dog, of course.

Sam didn't know why she begrudged him that. No one deserved happiness more than Landon; she was convinced there was not a better man alive. It wasn't like she regretted her singleness. She'd had opportunities to marry, but she knew the grass wasn't greener on the other side.

Having Landon and his brood living two doors down depressed her. He'd been the only light of her childhood, and even that was being snuffed out.

"Why don't you come over to the house? We can catch up."

She'd have to meet his family sooner or later, but she wasn't willing tonight.

Caden came tearing around the corner of the house. "Mom, when's dinner?" She stopped when she saw Landon, looking back and forth between them.

Sam swallowed. "Caden, I'd like you to meet Landon Reed." She forced her eyes to her old friend, but it was too dark to read his expression. "This is my daughter, Caden."

Caden smiled. "Hi." Sam was glad Caden didn't add that Sam had told her nearly everything there was to know about him. Except that Landon had loved her. She'd never told Caden that.

"Nice to meet you."

Sam wondered what he was thinking. Caden was small for her age, and he might think she was nine or ten. The thought relieved her.

"I'm getting hungry." Even in the dimness, Sam could see the streaks of dirt on her daughter's legs and the wet strands of hair alongside her face.

"Shower first, okay? I'll have something ready when you're done."

"All right." She left as quickly as she'd appeared, leaving an awkward silence in her wake.

"I should go in too. It's getting late." A mosquito landed on the back of her arm, and she smacked at it.

Landon took a step backward. "Sure." He kicked at the grass. "I guess I'll be seeing you around."

"Yep." She gathered the weeds she'd dropped.

"Good night." He backed away.

"'Night."

When he left, Sam let out her breath, and her body sagged onto the stoop. Landon Reed. She could hardly believe he'd been standing in front of her just a moment ago. When she'd left the island, she thought she'd never see him again. That was the plan, really, and yet here she was, back in Nantucket. Two doors down from him, just like old times, before everything became so confusing. Before that last summer.

Sam had been eighteen, and the last days of summer bore down on her with the speed of a monsoon. Landon took her out on his dad's boat for the day, but by evening an unsettling quiet fell over them.

She reeled in her fishing line and secured the hook on one of the pole's rings. Landon stared out to sea, his gaze cast in the direction of the mainland. Three more days. Her heart did that funny flop that happened every time she thought about his leaving. She set her pole on the floor of the boat and leaned back against the rail, closing her eyes. The boat rocked gently beneath her.

"I'll be back for Thanksgiving break. It won't be that long."

She'd seen him nearly every day of her life. Three months was a lifetime. Of course, it would pass quickly for him. He'd be having fun, taking classes, meeting new people. New girls.

Sam clenched her jaw until it hurt. Why should she care about that? He was like a brother. Closer than a brother. Something in her refuted the thought, but she resisted the argument.

Something tickled her bare leg, and she opened her eyes. Landon was beside her, his knee propped up on the bench, his elbow poking outward. The wind tousled his hair.

"Who am I kidding?" he said. "I can't imagine three months without—without seeing you."

Sam had never seen him so solemn. He hadn't shaved that morning, and a light coat of stubble covered his jaw. She wanted to draw her fingers across it and feel the coarseness against her hand. She turned away, his words echoing in her head.

She didn't care if he would miss her. It was his choice to go away to college. He was doing this to them. She knew he had dreams, but Sam had her own too. It wasn't fair that he got to go away while she had to stay here and work for another year to afford college.

"Sam?"

She covered her frustration, burying it deep where all her other hurts were hidden. "It'll be fine." And it would be. She was used to people leaving, just not Landon. She'd come to depend too much on him, and her weakness angered her. "I have other friends, you know. And you'll make plenty."

Landon made friends easily, and she resented it now. He was the only teenager she knew who could walk into a room of strangers and not feel the need to attach himself to someone. That confidence attracted others by the boatload.

"It's not the same, and you know it."

Why not? Just because her other friends hadn't taught her how to swim, hadn't let her beat them at Scrabble a thousand times, hadn't rescued her when Jared Garrett dumped her in the ball bin in the third grade? Why had she let him in? She shifted, sitting up and putting an inch of distance between them.

"Don't do that." His voice rode the wind. The sun was gone now, and the clouds on the horizon had turned twilight blue.

"Do what?"

"Push me away."

Her gaze bounced off him. "If I were pushing, you'd know it."

Somehow his arm had settled against the back of the railing, around her. She fought the urge to run to the other side of the boat. He was looking at her, and she could feel his eyes like a burning laser. She wanted to look. She was afraid to look. Her heart rumbled like an engine.

"I've been doing a lot of thinking this summer, and there's something I want to tell you before I go."

She was supposed to look at him now. She could hear the plea in his voice, but all she wanted to do was put her hand over his mouth and stop the words she was sure he was going to say.

"Sam. I know you're mad at me for leaving." He hooked a finger under her chin and turned her head. One look and something in her softened. How could she help it when he looked at her like that?

"I'm only leaving for college. I'll be back, I promise."

He'd been there when her dad died. He'd been there when her mom left. Who would be there when Landon left? A cool wind passed over Sam's skin, chilling her.

"I'll write. We can talk on the phone too." But he wouldn't be there to see the flashlight in the window. She hadn't thought about that in years, the way he worried about her. Especially after her mom left.

"Sam." Landon leaned closer until she could feel his breath on her cheek.

She wanted to throw her hands over her ears, because she knew what he was about to say would change everything. And she didn't want anything to change. Especially not now, when he was leaving. But her muscles refused to move.

His eyes had turned jungle green in the dimness, and a deep furrow separated his brows. "You've been my best friend for as long as I can remember. I used to pull your ponytail and hunt for worms so we could fish off the pier. I know what you're thinking before you say it, and I know who you are deep inside, where you're afraid to let anyone go."

Sam's heart kicked into third gear.

"You're more than my best friend. You're my soul mate. I'm not sure when it happened." He looked down, then back up. "But I love you, Sam. Not the way a brother loves a sister, but the way a man loves a woman."

Her throat clogged up with a big knot, and she sat, unable to move.

"I love the way you brush your hair back from your face, I love the way you don't care what anybody else thinks, I love your strength and your vulnerability and your brutal honesty."

He leaned back a bit as if to read her face. She wasn't sure what he'd find.

Her emotions wrestled on the surface, a dangerous place for them. She loved Landon, there was no doubt about that. At the moment, she was terribly afraid she loved him the same way he loved her. She was even more afraid he'd see it in her eyes. She looked away.

"You're scaring me," he said.

"I don't know what to say." She whispered the words over the wind. She couldn't tell him she loved him, even if it were true. She'd never said those words to anyone, except maybe her mom and dad when she was small, but she didn't remember for sure.

"I guess that says it all."

Sam felt him withdraw and breathed again. She could hear the pain in his voice, and she hurt for him. She glanced at him in time to see his Adam's apple bob. Why did he have to go and tell her he loved her? Why change things when he was about to leave? Last year she might have reveled in his admission, but he'd just proven he was like everyone else. All he cared about was his own goals. He didn't love her any more than her mom had. It made her angry, a feeling she was much more comfortable with.

"Let's just leave things as they are." It's what he should have done to begin with.

Five

"Miss Biddle." Sam's neighbor stood on the porch in a flowing leopard print tunic, black pants, and earrings that dangled halfway to her shoulders. Time had hollowed her cheekbones and aged her parchment skin.

Sam stepped out the door and let the woman embrace her. Miss Biddle's short jet-black hair spiked out at the nape like the tail feathers of a duck.

"Samantha Owens, just look at you." Her wrinkled hands held Sam's as she leaned back for a better look. "My word, you're a grown-up, aren't you?"

"With all the responsibilities that come with it." The last time Sam had seen her, Miss Biddle was stuffing a wad of cash in her palm and telling her to take care of herself. "Come in. Meet my daughter," Sam said loudly, remembering Miss Biddle's hearing impairment—a residual effect of her days playing guitar in a traveling band.

"Caden, this is Miss Biddle. She lives next door."

"Hi," Caden said, curling on the sofa in her pj's.

"Hi, honey." Miss Biddle turned, the tails of her tunic swaying. "She has your beautiful hair and your mom's petite size." She tsked.

They caught up over a cup of coffee, and Miss Biddle filled Sam in on the details of Emmett's death, something she could have done without. She told Sam that Emmett sold his car not long ago and had taken to riding his bike again. Sam was beginning to get antsy, when Miss Biddle announced she was late for a luncheon.

After she left, Sam cleaned up the yard, putting the old Adirondack chairs out back until she could paint them, then taking down the rose trellis in preparation to paint the house.

Later that afternoon, she found her old bike in the shed. The dark building was missing a lightbulb and had a broken door-knob—two more things for her to-do list. She repaired her old bike, pumped up the tires on Emmett's, and rode with Caden to the grocery. Sam had cleaned out the fridge the day before, tossing the spoiled milk and moldy leftover pizza.

After they shopped, she slipped three plastic grocery bags into the bike basket and one around each of the handlebars. "You ready?" she asked Caden.

Her daughter had already hopped onto her old bike and began peddling.

"Stay on the side," Sam called. She imagined Caden rolling her eyes. They pedaled past Cap'n Tully's Tavern, and she wished she could pull over and lose herself in a few beers. Being back in her old house was stirring up things she'd rather forget. A few cars dotted the tavern's parking lot, but later there would be a large Friday night crowd.

After what she'd just spent at the grocery, she had no business throwing away money on beer. They'd have to watch their pennies if they were going to stay long enough to finish the house. She'd hoped Emmett's bank account would provide her with some fast cash, but a few calls proved him to be broke as he'd always been.

"Turn here!" Sam hollered loud enough to be heard over the wind rushing in their ears.

"I know, Mom." Caden tossed the words over her shoulder, and Sam ignored her snippy tone. They didn't have much time before the Realtor arrived, and she needed to get the groceries put away.

Her legs strained the last couple of miles, and she realized riding a bike involved a different set of muscles than cleaning. When they got back to the cottage, Caden helped put away the groceries, and as Sam shoved the last can of soup into the cabinet, a knock sounded on the door.

Sam swung it open, and a familiar face smiled back. In high school, everyone had liked Melanie; it was impossible not to. "Melanie Walker?"

She drew in a breath. "Samantha Owens! Oh my goodness, how wonderful to see you." Her voice still held a Southern twang, a curiosity, as she'd been born on Nantucket, same as Sam. Melanie embraced her in the doorway.

When she pulled back, Sam invited her in and introduced her to Caden.

"I have a daughter about your age, Caden," Melanie said. "Her name's Amber. Maybe you can come over and visit sometime."

Caden looked at Sam for approval.

"It would be nice for Caden to have a friend on the island."

After her daughter went outside, Sam and Melanie turned their attention to the house.

"So you're putting the old place up on the market, huh?" Melanie scanned the room. "The housing market is good right now, so you're in luck." She smiled, showing her dimples. "What have you been up to since graduation?"

Sam shrugged and smiled. "Not much really. We live in Boston. I've only been in town a couple of days."

"You know, it seems like just yesterday we were all in high school, doesn't it?" Melanie sighed, clearly favoring the good old days. Sam wouldn't go back for anything. But Melanie always had it all together. Good grades, good girl. Not exceptionally popular, but definitely well liked. She'd dated Landon's brother briefly during high school. She was a cheerleader then, and Bailey was the school mascot, a whaler. They only went out a couple of months, and Sam always thought they'd been too much alike to be a couple.

Melanie told her she'd been married and divorced. After they caught up, she looked around the cottage, giving Sam suggestions on fixing the place up. She noted the weathered shingles, and Sam told her painting was already on tomorrow's to-do list. They filled out paperwork, and Melanie said she'd wait to hear from Sam before listing the house.

By the time she left, Sam had filled both sides of a sheet of paper with repair and maintenance projects. Her funds were going to be stretched, but she had some wiggle room on her credit card. If she could get the cottage into top-notch shape, it would fetch a good price, and she could pay off her card in a heartbeat. She just had to buckle down and get these projects done.

Sam looked around the quiet cottage. The sooner, the better.

☙ ☙ ☙

Landon tossed his keys on the coffee table and poured fresh water into Max's dish. His thoughts had been fastened on Sam all day, and the previous night he'd tossed about like a fish in the hull of a boat.

"Here you go, buddy." Max began noisily lapping water.

Landon paced the living room. She was back on the island, two doors down, one hundred yards away. Even with twenty-four hours to absorb the shock, his mind still reeled. He thought of all the times he'd tried to find her. And she'd been only hours away. In *Boston.*

The phone rang, and he answered. His friend Scott greeted him.

"Hey, how's it going?" Landon asked.

Scott told him about a show he'd watched a few nights before on common foods and plants that were toxic to house pets.

While Landon listened, he sat on the sofa and pulled the curtain back, looking toward Sam's house. All was still. He wondered if she was home. It was Friday night, so maybe she'd gone out to eat. He was the only one with no life.

"I taped it for you," Scott was saying. "Maybe you can run it in your lobby for your clients or something."

"Oh, thanks."

"Are you all right?" Scott asked. "You seem distracted."

Landon weighed whether to say anything about Sam. She and Scott had a long, complicated history. But no one knew his feelings for Sam better than Scott.

"Sam's back on the island." The connection crackled quietly in his ear before he heard Scott's muffled curse.

"What the—?"

Landon let the curtain fall back in place. "Emmett left the house to her. She came back to get it ready to sell."

"Did she mention why she disappeared without a trace?"

It was only natural for Scott to be defensive. He'd helped Landon pick up the pieces when Sam left. "She's been in Boston." He decided not to mention Sam's daughter.

"Is she married?" Landon wondered why Scott asked.

He stood and paced the room again. "I don't know. I didn't talk to her long." Max looked at him, licking his chops.

"Whatever you do, don't get involved with her again. You know she's nothing but trouble."

Landon wished he'd never mentioned Sam. Scott was incapable of being objective about her.

When Scott said he needed to go, Landon hung up and made a roast beef sandwich from the deli meat in the fridge. After that, he went outside and stood on the tiny back porch, casting glances at Sam's house. It was hard to tell if anyone was home. The sun still shone, and the curtains in her room blocked his view, though they fluttered lightly in the breeze.

Should I stay or should I go? What if Sam was married? How would it feel to find her wrapped in another man's arms? The thought carved a hole in the middle of his gut. *She never mentioned a husband, Reed.* But she hadn't said anything about a daughter either, until Caden came running around the house.

He went back in the house and washed the utensils he'd dirtied making his sandwich. "What do you think, Max?"

The Labrador stared up at him, questioning.

Landon set the dish towel on the counter and ruffled Max's ears. "You think I should wait until tomorrow, don't you?"

Did Sam want him to come over? He'd tried all day to analyze her response to him the night before. Maybe he'd caught her off guard. Of course, it wasn't like she didn't know where to find him. Besides, he'd waited eleven long years to see her again. One more night wouldn't kill him.

$\mathcal{S}ix$

$\mathcal{S}$am dipped the wide paintbrush into the five-gallon bucket, letting it soak up the white paint, then slathered it on a thirsty shaker shingle. Caden had been eager to help and enthusiastically applied herself to the job—for about thirty minutes. Now she was somewhere in the backyard, probably turning back handsprings. Hopefully not down the pier, as Sam used to do.

Though most of the island's homeowners let their shingles turn to weathered gray because of the unrelenting abrasion from the wind and sand, she knew a freshly painted cottage made for curb appeal. Melanie had agreed. Unfortunately, the shingles soaked up the paint like a sponge. She would need more paint than she had estimated, and one coat wasn't going to do the job. It was going to take twice the time she'd figured on, and she considered making Caden come back to help. Just as quickly, she scratched the idea.

Already the air was warm, and there wasn't a fresh breeze in sight. She set her brush down and pushed up her sleeves.

"'Morning."

Sam turned and saw Landon. He wore khaki shorts that revealed lean, sinewy legs, and a white T-shirt that showed off his tan.

Her heart tore off, and she blamed it on his sudden appearance. "You scared me."

"Sorry." His grin proved otherwise. "I came to see if you needed help."

She heard a bark from the backyard and Caden laughing.

"I brought Max over. Hope you don't mind."

She shrugged and wet her brush. "It's fine."

She could feel him staring at her, and a film of sweat broke out on the back of her neck. Didn't he have a family to get back to?

"Do you have an extra brush?"

A drip of paint ran off the edge of the shingle, and she caught it with the wet bristles. "I'm fine. I'm sure you have other things to do."

He must have spied Caden's brush sitting on the lid behind her, because she heard him grab it. He dipped it into the bucket. "I don't mind. I'm not doing anything else today."

"Don't you want to change?"

He shrugged. "These are work clothes."

They painted side by side quietly for a few minutes. When they reached down to fill their brushes simultaneously, she glanced at his left hand. His wide, tapered fingers were bare.

The way that revelation lifted her spirits was completely irrational. She heard Caden squeal happily and Max bark.

"Sounds like they're having a good time," he said.

From the corner of her eye, she watched his tanned arm make small swipes. He was bulkier than he used to be. Taller, too, it seemed. She was no shrimp at five-seven, and he was a good six inches taller.

Sam realized it was her turn to say something. "She's never had a pet." The apartments they'd lived in had no-pet policies, not that it stopped Caden from begging. Besides, all pets eventually died, just like Freckles had, and loss was something she longed to shield Caden from.

"Max likes her. I can tell from his bark."

Freckles had liked Sam too. When her dad brought him home, she thought she was the luckiest girl in the world. Then her dad died, and Emmett came. Freckles didn't stand a chance. She pushed the memory away.

Landon began humming a Phil Collins tune, one she hadn't heard since she hung around his house in her youth. She wondered what his life was like now. He probably wondered the same about her. Once, they knew nearly everything about each other. Now they knew virtually nothing.

He seemed to read her mind. "I have a vet business in town, did you know that?"

"I could've guessed. It's what you always wanted." Landon had always possessed clear vision and goals. So had she, but life got in the way.

"I still love it. But what about you?" He glanced at her hand. Her left one. "What have you been up to?" The unspoken question hung in the air.

Paint ran down her wrist, and she wiped it on her shirt. *Well, I got pregnant, then Emmett kicked me out, then I lived in a homeless shelter in Boston while I waitressed at a bar until Caden was born.*

"Not much," she said. "I clean office buildings and take care of Caden. I don't have time for much else."

They painted in silence for a few minutes, long enough for her to think she was free and clear.

"What about Caden's father?"

If it had been anyone else, she would have told him to mind his own business. "He's gone." She hoped he wouldn't ask her to elaborate. Some things she couldn't tell even Landon. Especially not Landon.

"Did you ever marry?"

Sam jabbed her brush at the shingle, filling in the crevices. "Nope." Let him think Caden's father hadn't wanted her and no one else had either. Why should she explain?

"Me neither," he said.

A weight lifted from her shoulders. She wondered why Landon hadn't been snatched up by some woman yet. He'd had no trouble attracting girls in high school, and she had to admit, he'd only gotten better with age. Even Caden had commented on his looks.

They painted side by side, using the rickety ladder to reach the gable, and when they finished the front of the house, it was lunchtime. Landon invited them over for sandwiches and chips, then they worked the rest of the afternoon.

Sam was amazed at the way they fell back into their old friendship so quickly. He had a way of getting around her defenses. When the sun sank low in the sky, Landon asked them over for supper. She was about to reject the offer, afraid they'd make pests of themselves, but Landon promised a game of Scrabble, and she couldn't say no to Caden's excitement.

After they ate, they set up the Scrabble game on the kitchen table. Sam sank into the wooden chair across from Landon, watching his brows furrow as he lined up his tiles on his rack. In the background, an old Santana song played.

"You're not thinking you have a chance, are you?" Sam asked him.

"There's always a first time." When she'd had a bad day with her mom or Emmett, he was the first to pull out the board game, even though he didn't like losing.

"Are you good, Mom?" Caden set the first tiles on the board. *Claps.* "Double letter on the *s.*"

"You two have never played?" Landon asked.

How could she explain that she had no time for fun and games? Earning a living and keeping the household running took all her energy.

"Mom doesn't play games." Caden found a pad of paper under the directions in the box. "Oh, look!"

The pad bore at least a dozen sheets of scores. Her name and Landon's. Sometimes his mom had played too. Bailey had always been too active to sit still for a board game.

"Those are sure old," Landon said.

"Notice who always won," Sam couldn't help adding.

Caden flipped through the pages while Landon placed a word adjacent to Caden's.

"Sheesh, did you ever beat her, Landon?"

"Mr. Reed," Sam corrected.

"It's okay," he said. "She can call me Landon."

"You call him Landon when you tell me stories, Mom."

Landon drew four tiles. "Stories?"

Judging by the heat in her face, Sam knew it was turning pink. Somehow admitting she'd told Caden their stories was like admitting he'd been the cornerstone of her childhood. She didn't know why that embarrassed her.

"Oh, sure, Mom's told me all about you. She told me about the time capsule, and about that night crawler you dug up that was the size of a snake, and about the time she rode on your handlebars and got her foot stuck in the spokes."

Sam studied the letters on her rack, carefully avoiding Landon's eyes.

"She did, huh?"

Sam picked up her tiles and arranged a word. *Coop.* "Double word score," she said.

"Did she mention I warned her about the perils of riding on handlebars?" Landon asked.

She'd only been eight or nine, and she thought it would be great fun to ride on the handlebars. Barefoot.

"She said you were always trying to talk her out of stuff." Caden tucked her golden hair behind her ear.

"He was a chicken," Sam said.

"I was cautious. And for good reason. You broke your big toe, if I remember right."

"Small price to pay," she said. "Your turn, Caden." Sam drew three tiles and arranged them on the rack.

"Did she tell you about the time she dug up Miss Biddle's flowers?"

Caden smiled. "No!"

"I didn't dig them up; I just picked them. And only the roses."

"Her *prized* roses."

Sam shrugged. "I had good taste."

"Why'd you do it, Mom? Did you get in trouble?" Caden added two letters to make the word *mob*. "Triple letter on the *m*."

"It was my mom's birthday,". Landon said.

"Miss Biddle wasn't too happy, either." When Mrs. Reed took Sam over to apologize, Miss Biddle had surveyed the mess, her eyes watering like a sick puppy's. It was the year before Sam's dad died. "Miss Biddle didn't tell my mom and dad. She always had a soft heart."

"She put a gate around her garden, though," Landon said.

Sam laughed, and it felt good. When had she last laughed?

They played until all the tiles had been drawn and no more words could be formed. It was no surprise to anyone when Caden tallied the scores that Sam had won. But Caden had come within four points of beating her.

"Caden, it looks like you inherited your mom's knack for the game."

"I guess she has." Sam helped her put away the pieces. She needed more times like this with her daughter. Back home it seemed she was forever playing the bad guy. *Caden, go clean your room. Caden, brush your teeth. Caden, do your homework.* Why was it so hard to have moments like this with her?

Max barked. He sat at the door, his head cocked toward them.

"You need to go out, buddy?" Landon stood.

"Can I take him?" Caden asked.

"Sure." Landon put the Scrabble game under the TV console while Caden left.

Sam stood and stretched, her right arm and lower back already aching from the painting. They'd finished the first coat, and she figured she'd wait a couple of days on the second coat. Her muscles thanked her.

"I appreciate all your help today," Sam said. Truthfully, work aside, it was the best day she'd had in a long time. She'd never had a friend like Landon, someone she felt so comfortable with. He knew her inside and out and liked her anyway, and she experienced a certain security in that.

He leaned over the stereo. Turning it up, he faced Sam, smiling. "Remember this one?"

It was "I Can Love You Like That." She hadn't heard it in years. Not since the week before their senior prom. Landon had planned to take Bekah Ward, a pretty girl who had a crush on him through most of high school. He finally asked her to prom, then admitted to Sam he didn't know how to dance.

"Don't be silly," she'd said. "Give me your hand." His parents had taken the boat out, Bailey was on a date, and they had the little Reed cottage to themselves.

Once she was in his arms, she swayed with the music, her feet shuffling back and forth. He was stiff as a statue.

He stepped on her foot. "Ouch," she said.

He chuckled. "I warned you."

"Loosen up. Let your knees and hips move."

"I can't." His breath tickled her ears.

"Of course you can. Close your eyes. Listen to the music. Feel it. Move with it." She closed her eyes, but instead of hearing the music, she heard his heart. Instead of feeling the music, she felt the warmth of his body.

Sam opened her eyes, looking over his shoulder but seeing nothing. Her palms grew clammy, and she swallowed. Their movements grew subtler. He was moving with her now. "That's better," she rasped. His hand settled on the small of her back, and she fought the urge to arch closer.

What was getting into her? *This is Landon. Your best friend, Sam.*

"See?" She pulled away, out of his arms. "That's all there is to it."

He thanked her for the lesson, but a week later, when she sat home thinking of Bekah in his arms, she wondered who'd learned a lesson that night.

"I guess I was a real klutz back then," he was saying now.

"Bekah didn't seem to think so." Did she sound snarky? She smiled to soften the comment. The Monday after prom, Bekah bragged about Landon's good night kiss. Sam had wanted to slap the silly smile off her face. That's when she knew she was in trouble.

Landon cocked his head, studying her. The soft glow from the table lamp turned his skin golden brown.

Sam shifted under his scrutiny and looked away, feeling her skin heat.

"I wanted to ask you, you know."

The timbre of his voice beckoned her attention. "Why didn't you?"

The corners of his mouth tucked in. "You'd been my best friend all my life, and suddenly I was thinking of you in a different way. I was afraid of what you'd think." He lifted a shoulder. "Afraid you didn't feel the same way."

What would she have said if he'd asked her? She remembered the dance they shared in this very room all those years ago. Her own feelings were changing then; she just hadn't wanted to admit it.

"I did finally outgrow my two left feet." He reached over and turned the volume up. All-4-One belted out the chorus.

Sam knew what was coming next. It was time to leave. Before she turned to pick up her purse, he spoke.

"Let me prove it." He held his hands out to her, palms up.

All she had to do was step into his arms. Put one foot in front of the other and slip her hand into his. She could lay her head on his shoulder and lose herself in the strength of his embrace. She could forget about her pile of debts and the stress of raising a child alone. She could just follow someone else's lead for a change.

Sam remembered the way she felt when she first danced with him for those brief moments. She remembered that night out on the ocean when he told her he loved her. She remembered the fear that sprang up from deep inside.

"I should be going." Sam retrieved her purse. "I have to get an early start in the morning." She turned toward the door, seeing his hands drop to his sides.

"Thanks again for your help today," she said, opening the door. Max was sprinting up the porch steps ahead of Caden, and Sam let him pass. "Time to go, Caden." She crossed the lawn, hearing her daughter's footsteps behind her, swishing through the grass as Sam fled into the darkness.

Seven

Sam was prying the lid from the paint bucket the next day when Max darted into the yard, his owner following.

"Max!" Caden called from the end of the pier. "Come 'ere, boy!" Max ran, his paws clattering across the boards. He stopped just short of jumping on Caden, and she rewarded him with a hug.

"'Morning," Landon said.

Sam stripped the lid from the bucket and set it in the grass next to the Adirondack chairs. "Good morning." He looked good in the dusty blue T-shirt and jean shorts. Too good. She'd thought about him until past midnight. The scene in his living room had replayed in her head, and because she tossed and turned, she slept in and was getting a late start.

She wiped down one chair with a wet rag to prepare it for the paint.

Landon put his hands on his hips and eyed the extra brush she'd brought out for Caden.

"I don't expect you to help, Landon. I know you have a life." She turned the chair over and wiped the underside.

"I want to."

And I want you to keep your distance. Yesterday had shown her how vulnerable she was still. After all these years, they picked up right where they'd left off. As much as the friendship pulled her, the deeper feelings he evoked made her want to hightail it back to Boston.

When she dropped the rag and reached for the brush, Landon picked up the discarded cloth and began cleaning the second chair. She filled her brush and slathered paint on the wood.

A few minutes later Landon dropped the rag and picked up Caden's brush.

"Have you considered keeping the house?"

"No."

He swiped the paint neatly along the wooden slats. "Why not?"

Sam shrugged. "My life is in Boston."

"Doesn't have to be."

Keeping the house had never even occurred to Sam, and she didn't plan on considering it now. Besides, it wasn't as if she could afford living here. "I never wanted to stay here. You know that."

He took his time trimming the edge of the chair's arm, his tongue caught between his lips. "Emmett's gone."

"The memories aren't." If she was honest, they were with her even in Boston. Landon tossed her a look, but she turned to load up her brush.

"You could make good memories here. You and Caden." When she didn't answer, he continued. "All the memories aren't bad. We had good times."

In her desperation to escape her house, the outdoors and Landon's house had been her sanctuary. He'd been her refuge, her comfort, her safety.

Then he'd left.

"Selling is the right thing. Once we get it fixed up, it'll bring a pretty penny." Then she and Caden could go back to Boston and wait for the sale. When the money came in, Caden's future would be secure.

Landon dropped the subject, and they finished painting in silence. After setting the chairs in the sun to dry, they put the first coat of gray on the small shed. When the wind blew the door shut, they discovered it locked automatically, so they propped it open with a rock. Afterward, Landon secured the wobbly porch railing while she worked on the flower beds.

Sam was tilling the soil when she heard a friendly voice call out. She turned and watched Melanie jog up the drive, cute in her baby-blue shorts set.

"Wow, the house is looking fabulous, Samantha." She wiped a dot of perspiration from her forehead, her breathing labored.

"I didn't realize you lived nearby." Sam set the cultivator against the porch rail and pulled off her gloves.

"Yeah, not quite a mile away." Melanie put her hands on her slim hips. "You've come a long way in a short time."

"You haven't seen the inside. I haven't done a thing in there."

"Hi, Landon." Melanie smiled, all dimples.

"Hi there. How's Taffy's ear?" Landon asked.

"Oh, just fine. Those drops you gave her are doing the trick." She turned to Sam. "Hey, Samantha, I was wondering if Caden would like to come over sometime. Amber loves to have friends over, and I was thinking Caden might like a change of scenery now and then."

"I'm sure she'd like that. Just give us a call when you're ready."

"Great." Melanie backed away. "Well, I'd better get back to it before I lose my energy. See ya."

Sam watched her go, her blond ponytail swinging rhythmically. Melanie would be an easy woman to dislike if she weren't so nice.

Sam put her gloves back on.

"Is Melanie your Realtor?" Landon took the cultivator and picked up where she'd left off.

Sam grabbed the hoe and began defining the edges of the bed. "Yeah."

"She'll do a good job. She handles a lot of properties around here."

They worked in silence for a while, and Sam couldn't help but think about Melanie and Landon and how suited they were to one another. She was pert and blond, and he was tall and dark. She was a warm, likable person, and he deserved someone like her. Sam wondered if they'd ever gone out.

They spent the afternoon putting another coat of paint on the house, and by suppertime, she wanted nothing more than a soft bed. Though Landon invited them over, she turned him down, only to receive a pout from Caden. Landon seemed to have won her daughter over quickly enough, and Sam wondered if Caden was starved for male attention. Would spending time with Landon be good for Caden, or would it only hurt her when they left the island?

That night Sam lay awake, the night sounds seeping through the walls. Beside her, Caden softly snored, and Sam envied her peace. She'd lain in this bed a thousand times staring up at the dark ceiling, feeling so alone she had to pinch herself to make sure she was here at all. She remembered the first time she experienced that feeling.

It was the morning her mom left, after Sam watched the ripples from her boat wash to shore. She walked barefoot back up the pier and through the damp grass, then curled up in the chair. The chill from the early morning air pebbled her skin, but she didn't move.

Time stood still.

It was barely light when Emmett hollered her name from the back porch, the sound of it echoing across the bay.

"I'm here."

Sam heard his steps across the grass. "Where's your mom?" He jabbed the words at her.

She stared down the pier, knowing what she'd feared was true.

"Where's your mom?" He grabbed her arm and squeezed, but she didn't feel it.

"She left."

He held her there, staring her down, his bushy brows becoming one. Then he let go. "Her things are gone. Everything."

A hard lump grew in her throat, but she stuffed it down.

"Except you." He laughed, but it wasn't pleasant. "Leave it to her to take everything but you."

Moments later, she heard the car's engine and wondered if he would come back. She laid her head against the hard wood. More time passed.

Sam didn't hear Landon until he slid into the other chair. She was surprised to see that dawn had morphed into daylight and the sun, peeking over the horizon, had burned off the fog.

"What are you doing?" he asked.

She stared out at the sea, watching the shadows play on the surface. "Nothing."

"Why are you still in your pajamas?"

She looked down. Her long T-shirt hung to midthigh, and she pulled the hem down, feeling the coldness of her legs through the material.

"I don't know," she said. Numbness flowed through her veins. She wondered if that was why she didn't feel cold.

"You should go inside and get dressed. You're cold."

She could feel him staring at her and heard the concern in his voice. He always noticed things other boys didn't.

"My mom left." She remembered what her mom had told Emmett the night before, about not having any plans for the day. Had she even told Sam good night? What was the last thing her mom had said to her?

"Where'd she go?"

Beyond the bay, a sailboat rode the waves, its sails billowing in the wind. "Away."

An eastern phoebe called out from the tree limbs above her, nearly swallowing Landon's reply.

"Is she coming back?"

Sam's lips were stiff, like they hadn't moved in weeks. "I don't think so." She didn't know if Emmett was coming back either. As much as she feared him, she feared being alone more, but she didn't tell Landon that.

Emmett did come back, much later, his clothes reeking of beer, his lips loosened by excess. *"Don't ever let yourself love, Sam,"* he'd slurred. *"Just soon as you do, they leave you. It's the one thing in life you can count on. Love never brings anything but pain."*

Later, she weighed his words against her own experience. She had only loved three people—her mom, her dad, and Landon. Two of them had left. What Emmett said held more than a grain of truth, and she wondered for the first time if Landon would leave her too.

Now, she looked at Caden lying beside her, the moonlight washing over her hair, and it hit her fresh that her daughter was nearly the same age she'd been when her mom ran off. So young, a tender age that carries enough of its own problems. She imagined trying to leave Caden and couldn't. What kind of selfishness brings a parent to abandon a child and never look back?

Sam's eyes burned. A stone hardened in her throat, and she pushed it down, just as she had all those years ago. She turned on her side and reminded herself the past couldn't hurt her anymore. But Emmett's words chanted at her through the night. *Don't ever let yourself love anyone. Don't ever let yourself love anyone. Don't ever let yourself love anyone . . .*

Eight

Landon fell into a new pattern the next week. Instead of savoring his work, he waited impatiently for the last appointment of the day, after which he could go help Sam. At first, she'd been resistant, but as time wore on, she loosened up. Their friendship was finding its footing again.

Thursday, as he walked toward her house, she smiled, and he felt like he'd won the lottery. Sam turned off the mower when he entered the yard.

"You should have waited," he said. "I would've done that for you."

She wiped her hands on her khaki shorts, and he followed the long line of her legs before meeting her eyes again.

"I like mowing."

Caden ran up then, her hair hanging in wet strings alongside her face. With her brown eyes and button nose, she was a miniature of Sam, and something caught in his gut.

"Can we go now, Mom? Can Landon and Max come?" Caden asked.

"I have to finish the yard first." Sam looked at him. "We're taking some food up to Brant Point." Sam lifted a shoulder. "You're welcome to come along."

"A picnic on the beach," Caden added. "Can you come?"

"It's about time you took a break," he said to Sam. "I can finish the yard if you want to grab a shower."

She quirked a brow, and he quickly added, "Not that you need one."

To his surprise, Sam agreed to the help. By the time he finished mowing, Sam and Caden had packed a bag of food and changed into bathing suits. They all piled into his Jeep, along with Max, and headed the few miles to Brant Point, where they spread a blanket on the sand. He'd been wanting to ask Sam on a date all week. He'd tried at least a dozen times, but when he opened his mouth, the words stuck in his throat. Dating would change the dynamics of their relationship. He was ready for that, but was Sam?

The sunbathers had left for the day, and the trio had the beach to themselves. After they ate, Landon showed Caden a few of Max's tricks, and she rewarded the dog with chunks of bread. When Max ran to the water, Caden peeled off her shorts, put on a fluorescent orange swimming cap, then followed Max toward the water.

"Don't go out too far," Sam called. She lifted her hand to shade her eyes from the sun and said to Landon, "I told her about rip-tides, but you know how kids are. They think they're immune to danger."

They watched Caden plunge into the cool water.

"Is she a good swimmer?" he asked.

Sam nodded. "Our last apartment had a pool. It wasn't much more than a cement hole in the ground, but she loved it. Used to turn flips off the side and scare me to death."

"I haven't seen her flip-flopping down the pier yet."

"Give her time." The wind blew a strand of hair across Sam's face, and it caught between her lips. She tucked it behind her ear. He hadn't seen her hair down since she'd come back, and he found himself wanting to draw his fingers through the length of it.

Caden followed Max into the shallow water, where Max shook, splattering the girl.

Unlike Sam, Caden was small-boned and pixie-faced, but she seemed mature for being so young. "She seems like a good kid."

He saw rather than heard Sam sigh. "She is. Lately she's been kind of snippy. I think she's going through some adolescent stuff."

"She's awfully young for that, isn't she? What is she, nine or ten?"

Sam stilled. The wind ruffled the corner of the blanket, and Landon stretched his legs, holding it down.

"She's eleven."

He looked at Sam, then at Caden. Eleven. He did the math and felt his gut clench. If Caden was eleven, Sam had gotten pregnant right before she left the island or shortly after. Either before he told Sam he loved her or after, depending on when Caden's birthday was. He didn't want to know. Had she been pregnant the last time he'd seen her, at Bailey's funeral?

He could still see her beside his brother's grave site. She hadn't looked like herself. She wore her hair down, and it was the only time he'd seen her in a dress other than at the prom. She stood beside him, and when he took her hand, it was steely cold despite the August heat. She was a sickly shade of white. He wished he didn't have to leave for college the next day, but he'd already delayed his departure for the funeral. His parents wouldn't hear of him missing the first days of college.

All this time, he thought Bailey's death had somehow shaken Sam and made her leave the island. Now he wondered if it was the pregnancy.

She hadn't even let him kiss her, yet she'd slept with someone else that summer. Someone who hadn't loved her like he had, someone without the guts to stick around and help raise his daughter.

He felt her rejection all over again. Surely Sam hadn't been in love with someone else that summer. He'd have known it. But the alternative hardly made him feel better.

Sam leaned back on her hands, her chin raised, her face set. She was an enigma. She'd been his soul mate, a mystery to the rest of the world, and yet he always had his finger on her heart's pulse. But that last summer, everything had changed. Was it his words of love or Bailey's death or her pregnancy? He wasn't sure what had taken Sam away from him, but as he looked at her now, vulnerable even with her false pride, he realized he wanted her back enough to risk everything.

Sam watched Caden play in the water but didn't see a thing. Beside her, she could feel the realization sinking into Landon. Though she sat still as the lighthouse behind them, her heart hammered.

She was about to jump up and go for a swim when he spoke. "I'm sure Caden will come around. She seems well adjusted."

He was letting Sam off the hook, and they both knew it. She leaned back on her elbows and crossed her legs at the ankles. He would ask who Caden's father was eventually, but she was relieved to let it slide for the moment.

They talked about a lot of nothing and chuckled about the old times. She dipped in just enough to wet her legs, but the chill in the water kept her from wading in any farther. Caden begged Landon to come into the water, but he hadn't worn his trunks. Sam wondered why he didn't wade in as she did. When they were kids, he'd been in the water constantly.

Sam lay on the blanket until the warm air dried her skin. The sun had set by the time Caden came toward them, shivering, and she realized they hadn't brought a towel. They packed up, and Sam shook the sand from their blanket and wrapped it around Caden. Landon drove them home and parked in his drive, then walked them back to their house, carrying the cooler.

Max ran ahead with Caden, who left him on the porch in favor of a warm bath. By the time she and Landon reached the door, Max was lying down, his head resting on his paws.

"Caden wore him out," Landon said, setting the cooler down.

"I think the feeling's mutual." She opened the door and set the sack inside. In the background, she heard water running into the tub. She turned.

Landon was closer than she realized. The lamplight from the living room washed over his face. He had bits of sand in his hair, and before she could reason with herself, she ruffled his hair, letting the grains fall to the floor. The strands were soft against her fingers, and she imagined them trailing down several inches, touching the roughness of his jawline.

He stilled, and she slowly drew her hand away. His eyes darkened as they homed in on hers.

"I had a nice time tonight," he said.

They were date words, but she didn't mind. Mainly because she didn't have a straight thought in her head. His eyes always told her so much, and now they were saying things she hadn't heard in so long. Things her barren soul soaked up like a withered plant.

"Me too."

He lifted his hand, and her skin tingled in anticipation.

"Mom, where's my shampoo?" Caden's voice was a deluge of cold water.

"Under the sink," Sam called over her shoulder.

The bathroom door snapped shut.

Sam turned back to Landon. "Well, thanks for taking us tonight," she said.

"Thanks for inviting me along." Landon straightened, letting the screen door close. "Good night."

Sam shut the door and leaned against it. She pictured the way Landon had looked at her. Her breaths fell heavily, and her mouth had gone dry. She let herself imagine what might have happened if Caden hadn't broken the spell. Landon had wanted to kiss her, and the thought put a smile on her lips.

᠅   ᠅   ᠅

Sam was inside the lighthouse, and through the tiny window she saw her mom in her boat, the current carrying her farther from shore.

"Wait, Mom! Come back!" She screamed the words.

Someone in the boat stood. Landon. Landon was leaving. She called his name, but he didn't hear her, didn't see her.

Rain battered her face through the opening in the stone, and she turned to race down the stairs, but there were no stairs. Instead, she was in the yacht club at Landon's going-away party. His parents were talking to their school principal, and his mom laughed at something.

"Someone help!" Sam called, but no one heard her. "My mom needs help! Landon's leaving!" She scanned the room for Bailey. He would help her. But she couldn't find him. Why wouldn't anyone listen?

Across the room, Emmett lounged on the arm of a chair, a drink in hand. He stared at Sam, the only one who saw her.

She ran toward him and took his arm. "Help me! They're leaving, Mom and Landon. I forgot to tie up the boat, and it's floating away." She tugged his arm, but he jerked it from her.

"I'll leave you too. Everyone will. No one hears you, and no one cares." He pushed himself off the chair and walked away.

"Somebody, help me . . . somebody, help me . . ."

꒰Ꙛ   ꒰Ꙛ   ꒰Ꙛ

Sam's eyes opened, and the sound of her own breathing filled her ears. Darkness pressed in on her. She looked around to orient herself. The window, the closet, shadows of furniture.

She trembled, wanting to leave the bed but somehow afraid to. The dream had been so real. Emmett and the Reeds. Landon and her mom. The vividness of it hollowed her stomach, leaving a void. And Bailey. Dear Bailey.

Sam stared at the ceiling, afraid to close her eyes again, afraid the dream would haunt her sleep. Beside her, Caden lay still, undisturbed. Sam turned to the window and looked toward Landon's house. From where she lay, she could see the roofline in the moonlight.

She remembered the way he looked at her earlier, but this time the memory didn't warm her. This time it chilled her skin, making her shiver under the quilt.

Nine

There was nothing on TV but old reruns and depressing news. She flicked the TV off and settled against the sofa. The nightmare had chased her from bed. While awake, she could rein in her thoughts, but sleep allowed her untamed mind to run wild. Now that she was wide awake, the quietness of the cottage haunted her.

It didn't help that the smells and sounds of this house jerked her back to her past faster than the snap of a flag. Just being here made her feel like a lonely, motherless child again. She forgot sometimes that she was a full-grown woman with her own eleven-year-old child.

A knock sounded on the door, and she jumped. The clock read 11:32. Miss Biddle would have been in bed at dark, and Sam couldn't imagine why Landon would come back. She slid her finger between the drapes and peeked out.

The porch was dark except for the little bit of moonlight, but Landon's silhouette was easy enough to distinguish. She wondered what he could want.

Sam opened the door. "Hey."

He looked up as if she'd interrupted his thoughts. "Hey. I know it's late, but I saw your TV on. Can we talk for a minute?"

Sam glanced back toward the bedroom where Caden slept. "Sure."

He stepped backward, allowing her to slip outside so they wouldn't let the bugs in. The light flooding the window gilded his face. "I was wondering if you'd like to go somewhere next Saturday."

She wasn't sure what she'd expected him to say, but it wasn't this. "Where?"

"Anywhere." He cleared his throat, then his Adam's apple bobbed. "I'm asking you on a date."

The hollow spot inside her filled with something pleasant. Hope. For an instant Sam wanted to say yes. But just as quickly, fear funneled into the spot and washed everything else away. Her nerves clanged like pots and pans in the hands of her irritable mother. She wasn't sure why or where the terror came from, but she didn't need to understand it to react. She wanted him to take back the question, to set things back where they'd been.

"We're just friends, Landon."

He looked away, and the light from inside caught his eyes. When he looked back at Sam, she folded her arms across her stomach. "Come on, you know that's not true."

Her pulse skittered. *Fake it, Sam. Come on, say something. Anything.* She grabbed onto an idea like a drowning person to a life preserver. "Maybe you should ask Melanie out."

He stared at her blankly. "Melanie?"

Sam shrugged. "You're two of the nicest people I know, and I was thinking you'd make a nice couple." Even as she said it, her heart squeezed. She told herself to hang tight. Stand firm. Soon she would be back in the safety of Boston, and this unsettling fear would be a thing of the past.

The way he was looking at her with those wounded eyes didn't help. Like she'd just slammed a two-by-four into his head for no reason.

"I don't want to go out with Melanie. I want to go out with you."

He wasn't making this easy. On either of them. She looked at the boards on the porch floor. "I don't think so, Landon. It wouldn't work."

"How will you know until you give it a chance?"

Why did his tone have to beckon her like that? She hated the clash going on inside her. Fear of saying yes versus the pain of saying no. It wasn't a fair fight. "I can't."

He studied her, and she shifted, crossing her arms.

"No reason?" His voice was steady and deep—just like he was. "Just 'I can't'?"

Sam looked at the dark fingers of the tree limbs reaching into the sky, at the bits of sand that coated the deck, at anything other than Landon's face. Her mind emptied of any rational response.

His hand lifted her chin until their eyes met. "Still pushing me away, Sam?"

"No." The word was a breath. Her insides quaked with the turmoil. She prayed her feelings weren't obvious to him.

He let go of her chin, but his attention remained fastened on her. "What are you so afraid of?"

"Nothing."

He shook his head slowly. "It's written all over your face. Just like it was that day out on the boat."

She didn't have to ask what day he was talking about. She looked away. How could she tell him he ignited the fear?

He stepped back, and the distance left an empty spot that opened a chasm. Her shoulders sagged.

"You win." His lips tucked in on one corner. "For now." He turned and left.

Sam wrapped her arms around herself, guarding against the coolness of the night.

⁊⁊   ⁊⁊   ⁊⁊

Landon paced from the kitchen to the living room and back again.
Max watched him, his forehead scrunched. Max's toy frog lay in the
middle of the floor, and Landon kicked it. From his spot next to
the recliner, Max watched it bounce against the table leg, squeak-
ing as it hit.

"Too tired to chase, huh, boy?"

He stopped by the window and looked across Miss Biddle's yard
at Sam's cottage. He couldn't believe she'd suggested he ask Melanie
out. He wasn't interested in Melanie. He only wanted Sam.

He'd wanted her a long time, since that last summer. Before that,
if he was honest with himself. Ever since Scott had dated her during their sophomore year.

His friend had wanted to ask Sam out for weeks, and when Sam
told Landon she was going out with Scott, something happened
inside him. He wouldn't define it as jealousy, more like protective-
ness. Scott was a good friend, but he was fickle when it came to
girls. Sam had been hurt enough, and the last thing she needed was
someone toying with her.

Scott and Sam went out on two dates, and it was after the second that Landon heard Scott pulling into Sam's drive. It took
everything in Landon not to get up off the pier, cross into her yard,
and see if Scott was kissing her good night on her front porch. A
full eight minutes passed before the old Ford rumbled away.

A few minutes later, Sam had joined him, sitting beside him, her
feet dangling in the water. Even in the moonlight, her face was

flushed. She sat quietly, chewing her lower lip, still nervous from the date, he supposed. He didn't know why that rankled him.

"Have a good time?" he asked.

"Sure."

He hadn't realized how weird it would be to have Scott dating Sam. *Weird* wasn't even the word. He didn't like it at all.

Sam leaned back, her arms supporting her weight. At fifteen, she'd grown into her long legs, and she'd filled out in a way that made hugging awkward. He'd bet it didn't feel awkward to Scott.

He shook the thought. He was tired of thinking about Scott and Sam and tired of analyzing his feelings. "Emmett home?"

She lifted her foot from the water and brushed a strand of seaweed off with her other foot. "Nope." A breeze blew in over the water and lifted her hair off her shoulder. She pushed it behind her ear.

It occurred to him that she'd shed her ponytail for the date. He wondered if Scott had run his fingers through her hair the way Landon longed to now.

He scooted back, taking his feet from the water. "You're quiet tonight." She didn't say anything for so long, he thought she'd let it drop.

She lay back against the boards, looking up at the stars. "Have you ever kissed anyone?"

He realized where the question was coming from, and his stomach tightened. "Sure." He'd kissed Maddie Franklin in the second grade during recess. Elena Schwartz laid one on him on the bus during a field trip to the whaling museum in fifth grade, and he pecked Camy Smith on the lips at a football game in the sixth grade.

"You're not counting Maddie, Elena, and Camy, are you?"

He smiled at her, watching her expression change as she realized he was. She jabbed him in the ribs, straight-faced. "I mean a real kiss."

He twiddled his thumbs, suddenly feeling very juvenile. It wasn't like he hadn't had the opportunity. There just hadn't been anyone . . . kiss-worthy. "Not yet." He watched the moonlight twinkle on the surface of the water.

"Scott tried to kiss me tonight."

He looked at her then. Her head was cradled in her arms, the moonlight caressing the elegant curves of her face. "Tried?"

"I turned away. Like I didn't realize he was about to kiss me."

Now, there was the best news he'd heard all week. He worked to stop the smile. A stab of guilt tweaked his conscience. Scott was his friend, after all. "Why?"

She sighed. "I don't know."

"Well, you must know something, or you wouldn't have turned away."

She pulled her feet up from the water, her square knees poking skyward, her stomach flat.

He looked away.

"I guess I was afraid."

He looked back at Sam. If Scott had done anything to hurt Sam, the guy was in for it. "Afraid of what?'

She sat up rabbit-quick, facing him and folding her legs beneath her. "What if I did it wrong?"

"Did what wrong?"

"Kissed. What if I'm bad?" Her eyes softened, their vulnerability tugging at him.

The corner of his mouth lifted. "You're not gonna be bad, Sam."

"How do you know? I've never kissed anyone, not even in grade school." She pulled at her lip with her teeth. "What if I do it wrong and he laughs at me?"

"Scott wouldn't do that." *Are you trying to talk her into kissing the guy, Reed?*

"But what if he stops liking me? I don't want to make an idiot of myself."

A good one-liner popped into his mind, but he knew better than to tease at a moment like this. Besides, she was looking at him with those fawn-brown eyes, and he forgot what he was going to say. She was normally so self-assured, he didn't know what to think of this insecure Sam except that it made him want to protect her.

"I'm sure you'll be—"

"Will you do me a favor?" She looked down at her hands, clasped in her lap. "I wouldn't ask, but . . ."

"You know I'd do anything for you." For a fearful moment, he realized how true it was.

She breathed a laugh. "This is kind of above and beyond." Her gaze ricocheted off his.

"Name it." Maybe she wanted him to talk to Scott. Tell him she was sorry or something. He could do that.

"Will you help me practice?"

She couldn't possibly mean it the way it sounded. "Practice?"

She gave a wry laugh and lifted her hands in a helpless gesture. "I know it's stupid and weird and everything, but I just thought . . ." She wet her lips, looking away.

He caught a whiff of her perfume, something light and fresh smelling, not sickeningly sweet like the perfumes other girls wore. "It's not like I'm an expert or anything."

"You have more experience than I do." She looked at him. "I wouldn't ask, except—I'm really worried about it." She looked afraid, her eyes wide, her shoulders stiff. She straightened and rubbed the back of her neck.

His heart clawed its way up his throat and throbbed there. He could do this. It was just a kiss between friends. No big deal. He shrugged. "I'm all yours." Somehow the words came out level even though his insides rocked like a rowboat in a gale.

Her shoulders drooped. "Okay." She wet her lips again. "Okay. What if you just kind of leaned over, you know, like you're Scott and you're kissing me good night."

He couldn't believe this was happening. "All right." He looked down at her lips, awaiting his. She closed her eyes. He leaned forward.

"Wait." She pulled back, her eyes popping open.

He wondered if his heart was going to stop then and there.

She folded her feet under her. "Let's stand up. I'm not sure what to do with my hands."

He stood, wondering if he'd lost his mind. "Just put them on his waist or his shoulders. If the kiss lasts long enough."

She stood inches from him, his shadow hiding her expression. "How will I know if it's going to last long enough?"

"You'll know."

"Okay, I'm ready."

His mouth went dry. "You might not want to say that to him."

"I won't, you doofus. I was just saying it to you." Her face had lost that fearful look, and her hands hung casually at her side.

Before he lost his nerve, he took a tiny step forward and leaned in until her breath tickled his face. His lips closed on hers, touching gently.

He felt her timid response and cupped her jaw with his fingers. Her lips danced with his, slowly, softly. Excruciatingly.

Her hands settled at his waist, just above his belt. He deepened the kiss. His other hand found her waist, and he pulled her closer until he could feel the heat of her body through his T-shirt.

She was soft and pliable, and he feared she could feel his heart thudding through his shirt. He pulled back, ending the kiss.

Her eyes opened, and her mouth, still moist from his lips, curved slowly. "How was that?"

About an eleven on the Richter scale. Maybe a twelve. "Not bad." He cleared his throat.

"Not bad?" She lifted her chin. "I rocked and you know it." She was practically glowing.

"You were adequate."

She waggled her head. "I was awesome. And Scott's going to beg for more."

It was probably true. "I liked you better when you were unsure of yourself," he teased.

"Bull. You probably like me more now. After my fabulous kiss." Her smile was infectious. "Don't go getting the hots for me now." She shoved his shoulder.

Too late. "You wish."

She laughed and backed away as the wind tousled her hair. "It's getting late. I'm going in now."

Landon tucked his hands into his shorts pockets. "See ya."

She turned and walked down the length of the pier. When she reached the grass, she turned. "Hey, Landon?"

"Yeah?"

"Thanks." She smiled, then turned and disappeared into the yard's shadows.

No problem. Except that he was quivering from the inside out.

Now, Max curled up at his feet, nudging his leg. He leaned

down and petted the dog, the memory of that kiss still on his lips. It was the first time he admitted to himself that his feelings for Sam had completely evolved. Somehow he managed to keep it a secret from Sam—until the summer before he went to college.

He looked out the window toward her cottage and realized afresh that she wouldn't be around long. Once she went back to Boston, his chance would be gone. And the thought of life without her wasn't a possibility he wanted to entertain.

Ten

The next day, Sam and Caden bought flowers and bushes to place in the beds. Back at the cottage, they dug in the soft, loamy dirt. Brightly colored flowers were heaped around them, their perfume mingling with the decaying smell of the soil. They'd picked purple phlox, yellow primrose, and lady's mantle, more for their ease of care than their beauty. Their cost had been a factor as well, since the bills were piling high on Sam's credit card.

"I'll plant this one," Caden announced, picking up a hosta. After she placed it in the soil and packed dirt around it, she stood and brushed the bits of soil and twigs from her denim shorts.

"Get the hose," Sam told her.

By the time they stood back to admire their work, it was nearly time for Landon to get off work. Melanie had invited Caden over to spend some time with Amber for the evening, and Sam wanted to be inside by the time Landon got home.

She fixed an early supper, then Melanie and Amber picked up Caden, leaving her alone in the house. She saw Landon pull into his driveway, so she worked inside, thinking he wouldn't come over if he didn't see her outside.

Cleaning out the attic was the job at hand, but on first glance at the piles of dusty boxes and old furniture, she was tempted to change her mind.

The heat chased her down the rickety stairs, her arms loaded with the first box. She went back for several more before she sat on the living room rug and opened them. Old football awards and war memorabilia filled the first two boxes—Emmett's things. She set them by the door to be thrown out with Wednesday morning's garbage. The next box contained yearbooks and old cards and letters. She nearly set it by the door, but the small stack of cards, yellowed and crackling with age, captured her attention. Sam lifted them out, and dust mites danced up her nose, provoking a sneeze. Her eyes watered, and she told herself it had nothing to do with the memories that played hide-and-seek in the corners of her mind.

The card on top of the stack read "Congratulations on the arrival of your new baby." She opened it and saw Miss Biddle's name scrawled at the bottom of the card. Why had her mom saved these? Or maybe her dad was responsible.

Sam didn't remember him very well, as she was only eight when he died. He'd shown her how to repair a hole in a bike tire, and he'd fished with her on the end of the pier. He smelled like leather and peppermint and made her feel important and secure. She remembered feeling lost and scared when he died. Months after his death, she couldn't recall what he looked like, and she rooted through her mom's photo album until she found a photo of the two of them together on the front porch. The photo sat on her nightstand until her mom married Emmett. One night she came into her room to find the photo missing, and she never saw it again.

Darkness enveloped the room as she sat sorting through the boxes. Not an absence of light, but an absence of peace.

The phone rang, and she punched it on.

"Mom, Amber wants me to spend the night," Caden said. "Her mom says it's okay."

Sam wanted to demand Caden come home. The house echoed with emptiness, and memories taunted her. Even as she agreed to let Caden stay, her mind raced to find a solution. No way was she sticking around here all evening.

She stood and grabbed her purse, banging open the door. Her weary legs protested as she straddled the bike and took off, but she welcomed the breeze that blew the dust of the past off her shoulders. With the wind at her back and her purse in the basket, she was free as she pedaled down the road. The scent of the ocean blew in off the bay, fresh and welcomed after the dankness of the attic.

Sam didn't know where she was headed until she pulled alongside Cap'n Tully's Tavern, and suddenly the idea of losing herself in a cold beer held more appeal than she could refuse.

Neon lights flashed on and off, and the rumble of laughter was more intoxicating than any liquor. No one seemed to notice her walk across the peanut-strewn floor and make herself comfortable at the bar. Moments later, the bartender, a Brad Pitt look-alike, set a bottle of Bud Light in front of her.

"You look familiar," he said with a flirty smile that made her sit up straighter.

Sam took a swig. She hadn't drunk a beer in ages, and the yeasty flavor stung her taste buds. "Grew up here. I've been gone for a decade, though."

A middle-aged man slid onto the stool beside her and started small talk while the bartender made a mixed drink for a woman with bottle-blond hair and too much mascara. She laughed at something the bartender said, and he winked as he set the drink down in front of her.

Sam sipped while she talked to the man beside her. Phil was peeved with his wife, and the more he imbibed, the more peeved he was.

By the time she finished her third beer, she was feeling mellower herself. The alcohol was a welcome anesthetic, numbing her pain. This place felt more like home than the old cottage.

When Phil left, the bartender opened a new bottle for her and leaned against the distressed wooden countertop. "So what's your name, gorgeous?"

She was far from gorgeous, but who was she to argue? It felt good to have the attention of an attractive man. Someone who was less threatening than Landon.

"Samantha." The name sounded more feminine than its shorter version, and she wanted to feel feminine just then.

"I'm Anthony, but everyone calls me Tully." His smile was contagious.

"As in Cap'n Tully?"

"One and the same. What brings you back to the island?"

For a moment she wondered how he knew, then she remembered telling him earlier. Sam figured she'd better make this beer her last tonight if she wanted to keep her wits. "I'm getting my house ready to put on the market . . . you know, painting and stuff." Her words came out with effort, but her tongue was loose. "I live in Boston with my daughter. It's a good place to live. Lots to do, and there's always the Red Sox."

They talked about baseball and Boston, and every so often Tully stepped away to wait on a customer. But he always came back, planting his elbows near her beer bottle. Once when Tully stepped away, a kid barely old enough to be in the bar hit on her. Tully came back and told the kid to take a hike.

Sam's third bottle was empty, and she knew she'd had enough, so she set her chin in her palm and talked. Tully's humor and charm made the darkness of the cottage and her anxiety over Landon seem so far away, she wasn't sure they were real. For a moment, Landon's face flashed in her mind, but she focused on Tully. Thinking about Landon was confusing.

When Tully asked her to go out on his boat with him the next Saturday, she was too mellow to say no. He seemed harmless enough, and a day of fun sounded like a good idea. Besides, she didn't need Landon. She just needed a distraction.

Eleven

Landon stepped around the stacks of boxes and bags on Sam's back porch, propped the screen door open with his foot, and knocked. He had the distinct impression she'd been avoiding him since he asked her out, but he wasn't going to let that stop him.

Caden answered the door. "Hi, Landon. Come on in. Mom's in the kitchen."

"How's it going?" he asked Caden.

"Okay. Is Max outside?"

Landon smiled. "Sure is. He's waiting for you."

Caden slid out the door, and Landon stepped into the kitchen, where Sam kneeled on the floor, stuffing a box with everything she took out of the gaping cabinet.

"Can I help?"

Sam sighed. "I've got it covered. Just cleaning out cabinets." She continued working, not sparing him a glance.

He ignored the hint. Landon grabbed a box and began filling it, watching Sam's back go straight like a perturbed cat's. Why did she have to be so difficult?

Most of the pans and dishes were in pretty good shape, though mismatched. He supposed that kind of thing mattered to most women. "Don't you want to keep any of this?"

"Nope."

They worked in silence for a while. Landon wondered if Sam had second thoughts about turning him down. He knew she felt something between them too. Didn't she want a relationship? A husband? A father for Caden?

As premature as it sounded, given Sam's very recent return to his life, Landon hoped to take the relationship in that direction. Even that last summer, he'd been thinking forever when it came to Sam. She was every bit the challenge now that she had been, but then, he'd never been one to give up easily when something mattered.

Maybe if it was less like a date and more like an outing, she'd be more open. He'd keep at it until she said yes. Deep down, he knew she wanted to, though he couldn't figure out what held her back. He'd never met anyone so closed. The door to her heart was like a vault door, thick and impenetrable. If he wanted to win her over, he'd better move fast, because at the rate she was emptying those cabinets, she'd be gone before he knew it. He couldn't help but take it personally.

"You've been working too hard. Why don't we take a day off Saturday? We could go to the surf side and teach Caden how to ride the waves. She'd have a blast."

Sam shifted the dish towels around in the box to make room for an electric frying pan. "I don't think so, Landon."

He waited for an excuse, like all the walls needed a coat of paint, but she didn't offer one.

"How about just the afternoon, then? We could tape and trim in here in the morning, have a relaxing afternoon at the beach, and grab a quick supper on the way home. I'll help you paint after we eat. I'll bet we could get the whole inside painted over the weekend."

Sam stood and opened an upper cabinet, shoving the filled box to the side with her foot. "I can't."

"I know you have a lot of work to do, but—"

"It's not the work, Landon."

Though she continued to empty the cabinet of glasses and bowls, he sensed hesitancy in her tone. Why couldn't she say what she meant?

He shoved a strainer into a box and stared up at her. "What, then?"

A long pause. "I have a date Saturday."

Landon watched her filling the box. He'd asked her out the night before last, and she hadn't had a date then. Or had she? Maybe that's why she'd turned him down. He found himself hoping that was it.

"Since when?" he asked.

She wet her lips. "Last night."

Nice. She'd turned him down and accepted someone else's offer. Heat crawled up the back of his neck, making the hairs stand on end. He shoved a stack of pan lids into the box, and they clattered loudly.

He felt her watching him, but he wasn't interested in eye contact. Who was it? Someone she knew when she lived here? Someone she just met? And where could she meet someone, when she'd hardly left the property since she arrived?

He folded the flaps of the box and kicked it away, then grabbed an empty one and filled it mindlessly. He was acting like a petulant child but couldn't seem to help himself. "Who with?"

She went back to work. "I don't think you know him. His name's Tully."

The name stopped him, a blender balanced in his hands. "Tully Sullivan?" His tone was sharp, but he was ticked.

She tossed him a glance. "You know him?"

He wanted to add that everyone knew Tully, or at least knew about him. The man was a player. Scott, who hung out at Tully's bar, told Landon the man hit on anything in a skirt. And Landon thought he'd been arrested several years prior on assault charges.

"You could say that," he said instead. He didn't know which bothered him worse: the thought of Sam being preyed on by that jerk or the fact that Sam had chosen Tully over him.

He latched onto the latter thought. Sure, the guy had looks going for him, but he was a jerk. Is that the kind of man Sam wanted? He shoved the blender into the box and kicked it to the side. It was lighter than he thought, and it ricocheted off the refrigerator.

He had so much more to offer Sam. She deserved better than Tully, couldn't she see that?

He tried to remember the nature of the assault charges filed against Tully. The details were vague. It seemed like a woman had filed them, though. He didn't want Sam alone with a man like that.

He attempted a calm tone. "He's not a good man, Sam." An understatement at best.

Sam lifted her chin. "He seemed nice enough to me."

"Of course he did—he was hitting on you."

"Is that really what's bugging you?"

Landon stood. "I'm not kidding. He had assault charges against him awhile back."

"Really. What for?"

He put a hand against the countertop and leaned into it. "I don't remember exactly."

Sam turned away, emptying the cabinet of glasses.

"He's bad news."

"It'll be fine. We're just going out on his boat for the day. Broad daylight."

"Doesn't really matter if it's broad daylight if there's no one around for miles."

She tucked the glasses into the box, working silently.

"And what about Caden?" he asked.

"I don't know. I guess I'll ask Miss Biddle to watch her."

She had it all figured out. He'd offer to watch Caden himself, except he wasn't about to enable the date.

♫ ♫ ♫

Sam wasn't sure how she expected Landon to respond, but this was a surprise. The way he leaned toward her, his brows shoved together, she knew he wasn't going to let up.

"Don't go, Sam. Call him and cancel."

"I'm not canceling."

"I don't trust the guy."

"Well, it's not really your call, is it?"

He clenched his jaw and looked away.

For the first time, she wondered if there was any credence to the assault charges. Nantucket was a small community, and rumors could fly faster than a jet ski, but what if it was true? Maybe being alone on a boat with Tully wasn't the smartest move. But she was eager to get out on the water, away from this place that smelled like Emmett. And she wanted Landon to forget about her. There were too many reasons they couldn't be together. Reasons she couldn't begin to explain.

Sam wasn't sure she was capable of love, and she didn't want to find out. He needed to find some nice girl who wasn't damaged by life. Someone like Melanie.

"I'm serious, Sam. I don't want you going out with the guy."

His possessiveness hit a nerve. "Maybe you should come along and be our chaperone." She was being sarcastic, but as the thought rolled off her tongue, she wondered if she'd hit upon something. "Seriously, why don't you invite someone, and we'll make it a double date." It would relieve her anxiety about being alone with Tully and give Landon a chance to go out with someone else. She congratulated herself on the idea.

A myriad of emotions flickered over his face. "What?"

"I'm sure Tully wouldn't care. You could ask Melanie—unless you had someone else in mind."

His jaw muscles twitched. He studied her until she had to look away. She put the remaining bowls in the box and set it on the floor. "What do you think?"

"Melanie and I are just friends."

Perhaps. But that could change given the right conditions. She shrugged. "Suit yourself." Sam grabbed a fresh box for the cleaning supplies under the sink, but Landon blocked her way. "Excuse me."

Landon moved aside, and she knelt to empty the cabinet.

"You're still planning to go?"

At this point, she wasn't giving in even if she was wrong. "Yes." If the word came out a little sharp, so be it. He was too stubborn for his own good. She'd given him an opportunity to fix things.

The room filled with silence except for the sounds of her loading the box. She heard Caden outside telling Max to fetch, then praising him.

"Fine. I'll ask Melanie."

It was what she wanted, so why did a pain start just under her left rib? She tipped her chin up. "Great," she said with all the enthusiasm she could dredge up.

Twelve

"Oh my goodness, it's like a yacht!" Melanie slid on her sunglasses.

"Not bad," Sam said.

Landon's prayer for rain on Saturday went unanswered. Instead, he found himself standing on the marina pier between Sam and Melanie while white puffy clouds drifted across a bright blue sky. The smell of dead fish and salt water lingered in the air.

When he called Melanie, he'd tried to make the invitation sound like a friendly outing with Sam and Tully instead of a double date, but she'd seen right through it.

"You still care for Sam, don't you?" she'd asked.

Was he so transparent? Now he felt like a fool for asking her. "I'm sorry. I shouldn't have called."

There was a moment of silence. Landon cringed. He deserved to be told off.

"I have an idea," she said. "Why don't I go along on the outing anyway? Maybe seeing you with me will make Sam see what she's missing."

And that's how the plan had been set in motion. Melanie was a sweetheart to do this for him.

Now, as he stood on the dock and watched the Ocean Alexander

Flushdeck rock in the water, his legs trembled. Memories of the night Bailey drowned flashed like an omen in his mind, turning his stomach. *Come on, Reed, pull it together.*

"Hey, everyone." Tully exited the cabin, ducking his head as he cleared the threshold. "Come aboard." Tully helped Melanie, then he took hold of Sam's hand.

The relaxed smile on her face hit Landon hard. She looked as carefree as a young girl. Why could Tully make her feel that way when he couldn't?

"Welcome aboard *Lady Love.* You can have a seat on deck or join me on the flybridge. I'll show you around once we get to Martha's Vineyard."

Landon took a seat on deck, as his legs seemed too unsteady to support him, then he put his arm along the rail. Melanie sat next to him, and Sam followed Tully up the few stairs to the flybridge.

Why had he thought he could go out to sea without the memories haunting him? He remembered the taste of salt in his mouth, the stinging of his eyes, and the feeling that his lungs would burst. He was ready to jump ashore, but the boat was already moving away from the dock.

He looked up at Sam standing next to Tully in her khaki shorts and white gauzy top. As much as he wanted off the craft, he needed to be sure Sam was safe. His conversation with Scott the day before rang in his head.

"Listen, if she wants to date a guy like Tully, why do you want her? If you ask me, they're cut from the same cloth. Forget about her, Landon."

If only he could. But she was seared into his soul, and he didn't see any way to change that.

As the boat progressed, he and Melanie talked occasionally over the rush of the wind in their ears. When they decided it was too hard to hear over the noise, Melanie settled back in the seat and turned her face toward the sun.

Landon's fingers clenched the rail behind him. He could feel his heart pounding even over the rumble of the engine. It was going to be a long day.

He looked up at the flybridge again. Sam wore her hair down, and it whipped behind her like a golden flag.

He watched as Tully left the captain's seat, trading spots with Sam. Tully leaned around her, letting her steer the boat. Landon could feel his insides heat, and it had nothing to do with the sun. Tully's hand rested on her shoulder, and she turned and laughed at something he said. Tully was shorter than Landon, but his bulky calves and biceps left no doubt that he worked out.

Why hadn't he realized how difficult this would be?

He was relieved when they neared Martha's Vineyard and Tully slowed the motor to a stop and anchored the boat. It was then that Landon wondered how they'd get ashore. He looked down at the surface of the rippling water, feeling his muscles cramp as they had that night. He'd called Bailey's name over the peals of thunder until he nearly drowned himself.

"All right, mates, let me show you around." Tully interrupted the bad memory.

The three of them followed Tully through the boat. The salon was open and bright with parquet floors. A master bedroom led out of the salon, and a galley completed the cabin. It was in good condition, and Landon guessed you could buy a house on the mainland for what the boat cost. He figured Tully's Tavern must be pretty profitable.

Tully had brought a picnic lunch for the group, and he carried the basket on deck, then prepared a raft to take them ashore.

Moments later, Landon stepped onto the bottom of the raft, a flexible rubber that gave when he put his weight on it. He reluctantly let Tully steady him by the arm and sank against the side.

What am I doing out here? He struggled to steady his breath. Melanie settled beside him, Sam sat across from him, and Tully took the back where he could steer.

Think about something else. He looked up at two seagulls soaring. Their high-pitched cries rose on the wind.

Across from him, Sam hid behind sunglasses, and he wished he'd brought his own. To hide his fear if nothing else. The boat took off with a jerk, and he braced his body with his feet. *It'll be over soon. Tough it out, Reed.*

He made it through the short trip by sheer will, but a sheen of perspiration coated him by the time they reached shore. Landon wasn't sure he'd be able to get himself back on the boat. His stomach was in knots, and he fervently hoped they would spend the rest of the day on dry land.

Somehow he managed to make conversation through the lunch, and once all the supplies were packed away, the other three stripped down to their suits. Landon spread out on the beach towel he'd brought.

"Aren't you coming in, Landon?" Melanie laid her hand on his shoulder possessively. She wore a lime green bikini that showed off her deep tan.

"No, I'm just going to hang out here." He lay back, letting his weight fall on his elbows as Melanie strolled toward the water.

A few feet away, Sam withdrew sunscreen from her satchel.

"Here, let me get that." Tully took the lotion from her, squeezed some into his palm, and rubbed it on Sam's back while she held her hair up on her head.

"You have great shoulders," Tully said. "And nice, smooth skin."

"Thanks."

Give me a break. Landon watched Tully's tanned hands rubbing in circles across her back, then kneading the lotion into her shoulders. *All right, pal, it's rubbed in.*

When he was done, Sam smiled at him and held out her hand. "Thanks, I can do the rest."

Landon was relieved when Tully headed toward the water, leaving him alone with Sam. She rubbed lotion on her legs while he watched in silence.

"Having a good time?" she asked.

"Peachy."

She looked at him, her brows lowered. "What's wrong?"

"Nothing."

"Okay."

What had he thought he was going to get when he agreed to tag along on her date? Would he have to watch Tully kiss her good night too? The thought made his lunch sour in his stomach.

"You should go out there with Melanie." Sam smoothed the lotion on her arms. "She's nice, you know."

Yeah, he knew. If he didn't know it before, he knew it now, with Sam shoving it down his throat every two seconds. He felt like an unwanted secondhand pair of shoes.

"Well, I'm going in." Sam walked down the beach and waded into the water until she was knee deep, then she dived in and came up beside Tully. The current pulled them together, lifting them gently as a wave rolled ashore. Tully's hands steadied her, then lingered on her shoulders.

Landon wanted to dive into the water and rip them apart. He didn't even want Tully looking at Sam in her swimsuit and noticing her curves or her long, toned legs, much less touching her.

He lay back against the sand and closed his eyes. Why didn't Sam see what was right in front of her? Tully only wanted to use her for his own selfish needs, and yet she ran after him. Why did Sam settle for so much less than she deserved?

Landon wasn't sure how much time had passed when he felt cool droplets of water splatter his legs. Tully spread a towel beside him and plopped down, arms braced on his knees.

"Water's fine." He watched Sam, who floated on the water, arms relaxed out to the side. "She is one hot lady."

Landon pulled himself upright and stopped a reply by biting the inside of his mouth.

"You know her long?" Tully asked.

"Practically all her life."

Landon felt Tully's eyes on him for a long minute. "Cool."

৵   ৵   ৵

It was nearly dark by the time Tully walked Sam up her porch steps. Miss Biddle's car wasn't in her drive, so Sam figured she'd taken Caden out. The sun had sucked all her energy, leaving her pleasantly lethargic. The breeze caught her damp hair, chilling her, and the night smelled of freshly cut grass and Miss Biddle's roses.

Sam reached the door and turned to Tully. He was charming and flirtatious, and he didn't dredge up emotions that made her feel threatened. She'd been able to forget the house and her past for most of the day. Only when she looked at Landon was she reminded of everything she was running from. And seeing him touch Melanie had discomfited her.

Tully leaned one hand against the door frame, trapping her against the door. "I had a great time today."

Sam's face relaxed in a smile. "Me too." She toyed with the idea of asking him in.

He looked boyishly handsome with a strand of hair falling over his forehead. He leaned in, closing the gap between them.

Sam let her eyes fall closed, waiting. Feeling nothing but pleasantly sleepy.

"Hey there."

Her eyes popped open. Tully pulled away. His arm fell.

Landon stood in the yard, hands tucked in his back pockets. She wondered how he'd seen Melanie home and gotten back so quickly. *What, did you just dump her at the curb?*

Tully turned toward Landon, crossing his arms.

Silence covered them like an itchy blanket. Landon would have to be blind to miss the fact that he'd interrupted something.

"Did you need something?" If her tone was sharp, so be it. Landon had already tagged along on her date. Did he want to hang around and watch Tully kiss her good night too?

"I remembered I promised to look at your faucet. Thought now was as good a time as any."

Sam's eyes narrowed. "It can wait until tomorrow."

"I don't mind." He stood as fixed as Sankaty Head Lighthouse.

Sam shifted.

Tully took a step back.

In the distance, the water lapped the shoreline, and the wind made the tree leaves flutter.

"I should be going anyway," Tully said. He shot Landon a look, then leaned forward and pecked her lips.

She barely felt the kiss under Landon's paternal watch.

After Tully got in his Mustang and drove away, she turned and opened the door, ignoring Landon.

"Wait." He was on the porch before she could shut him out.

"What now, Landon? Do you want to come in and make sure I don't hurt myself flossing?"

"That's not fair."

"You intruded on a private moment."

"I was worried about you."

"You're jealous."

The words hung in the silence. She wished she could take them back. Especially when she met his eyes and they softened, drawing her to him like a riptide.

"I can't believe you kissed him," he whispered.

Her insides stirred, warming her. She hadn't meant to hurt Landon, but she could see that she had. She'd hurt him all day long. She regretted it now.

His fingers cupped her chin, and he drew his thumb across her lips as if to rub away any trace of Tully. The gentle sweep of his thumb affected her more than Tully's kiss. Her legs felt weightless, as if a gentle breeze could blow her over. She knew if he leaned down and brushed his lips across hers, she would let him. And she also knew Landon's kiss would be unlike Tully's. This one would turn her world upside down.

Instead of kissing her, Landon stepped back. He said good night, then turned and walked away as her heart splattered on the board porch. It wasn't until the next morning that she remembered he'd come to fix the faucet.

Thirteen

The next night, Sam and Caden ate supper alone. Landon had left after helping paint the living room's wicker furniture in the backyard while Sam sorted through drawers and closets.

"Why can't we eat at Landon's? It's more fun over there."

Sam spooned a heap of macaroni and cheese onto her plate. "There's no more to do over there than there is here."

"He has games."

"We have games at home, and you never play."

"I can't play them alone." Caden stabbed the hot dog with her fork and dipped it in mustard.

"Caden, you know I have a lot of work to do. It's not easy being a single parent." She hated justifying herself to her child. How could her daughter understand all her responsibilities?

"You should get married. Then I'd have a dad, and you wouldn't be gone all the time."

Sam breathed a laugh. "It's not that simple."

"Bridget's mom just got remarried, and now she has a new brother."

Sam stabbed a piece of macaroni and aimed her fork at her daughter. Why did Caden think she had all the answers at the ripe old age of eleven? "Hey. It's not like I'm not trying. I have dated, you know."

Caden harrumphed. "Yeah. Jeremy."

"There was nothing wrong with Jeremy." Other than the way he called constantly and showed up at their door every day, invited or not. It occurred to Sam that Landon did the same thing, yet it didn't leave her feeling smothered.

"He only talked to me when you were in the room."

Sam had noticed that, but she wasn't going to admit it.

"I went on a date yesterday, remember?"

"Amber said he owns a bar and has dated everyone except her mom. Sounds like a real winner."

Sam clamped her mouth shut. Why did it seem like Caden got along with everyone but her?

"Why can't you date someone nice like Landon?"

Sam wasn't sure why it surprised her that Caden had thought of it. "He's just a friend. Besides, I'll find my own dates, thank you."

They finished eating in silence, then she sent Caden to take a bath and decided to tackle the few remaining boxes in the attic. The sooner they finished, the sooner they could leave this place. Somehow, the thought left Sam disquieted.

She was surrounded by a pile of junk when Caden came in from her bath, smelling like a fresh and clean baby. Her daughter settled on the floor somewhere behind Sam. She wondered how long their silence would last.

The box in front of her held items unfit for a secondhand store. Sam shoved it to the door, then opened a bag of Christmas lights and decorations. They smelled musty. When was the last time anyone had put up a tree in this house?

"Mom, look!"

She hadn't heard so much excitement in Caden's voice in months. Caden was looking at a picture. Sam scooted beside her to see.

Sam's mouth went dry. It was a photo taken right before they'd left for the prom.

"It's my dad, isn't it?" Caden asked.

Sam had given Caden a picture of her father when she was old enough to ask about him. It was cut from the yearbook Sam had taken from the island, and Caden kept it in a silver frame on her nightstand.

Caden's lips curved into a wide smile. She looked back at the photo taken in Landon's front yard. Caden's father stood between the two of them, his arms curled around Landon and Sam.

"Did Landon know my dad?"

Sam's mouth worked silently. She was unprepared for this. In the photo, Caden's father wore his wide, charismatic grin as easily as he wore the black tux. He stood as tall as her in the flats she insisted on wearing. After the photo, they went their separate ways.

"Mom?" Caden's brows were pinched. "Did he grow up here with you? Did he live around here? Do I have grandparents here?"

Caden's questions came too fast, a tidal wave in speed and intensity, and Sam wondered if there was any way of stopping it now. If she told Caden, Landon would find out, and she couldn't stand the thought of that. Maybe she couldn't stop what was happening, but she could put it off.

"I want to answer your questions, Caden. But I'm going to ask you to wait. Wait until we leave here. When we get back to Boston, I'll tell you everything. I promise."

Her face fell. "That's not fair."

"I have my reasons. Good ones." Sam ached inside and wished she'd left Caden in Boston so they wouldn't be faced with this dilemma.

Tears flooded Caden's eyes and spilled over. "I deserve to know about my dad! Why won't you tell me? You're just being mean!"

"Caden, if I told you now, other people would—" She stopped, not wanting to say too much.

"Other people would what?"

"No one else can know. If I told you, it would be too hard for you to keep it a secret."

"I can keep a secret." Just then Caden reminded Sam of herself at her age, with her wet blond hair hanging in strings around her face. She'd kept secrets at her age. Things she still had told no one.

"I'm not a baby."

"I know you're not." Sam wet her lips, giving herself a chance to back out of this, not at all sure she wasn't being foolish. If Landon found out . . .

Sam saw the sincerity in Caden's expression. "All right. There's something I never told you because—well, I didn't think you'd ever need to know. I never planned to come back here, never planned for you to meet Landon."

"What? Tell me, Mom." Fear glimmered in her eyes, dread of what her mother was about to say.

"It's nothing bad; it's just . . . you have to promise you won't tell Landon."

"Landon?"

"I know that's a big thing to ask of you. We'll be here for a couple of more weeks. Do you think you can do that?"

She nodded, wiping her tears. "Was my dad a bad person?" She looked at the photo.

"No, Caden. He was a good guy. The best. He . . . he was Landon's brother. We grew up together, just like Landon and me."

"And you were in love?"

Hope brightened her face, and Sam couldn't dispel it. "I loved Bailey very much." Caden needn't know Sam had only loved him as a dear friend.

"Then Landon is my uncle?"

Her childish delight brought a smile to Sam's lips.

"And his parents are my grandparents!"

Fear stabbed Sam. "Wait, honey. Yes, Landon and his dad are related to you, but his mom passed away, and his dad doesn't live here anymore. And don't forget what I said about it being a secret."

"I don't understand. Why don't they know about me?"

"I have my reasons."

She glared and shoved the box away. "That's not fair."

She was right. So much surrounding her life hadn't been fair. Bailey's death hadn't been fair, either—to any of them.

Caden rose to her feet. "I finally have a family, and you won't let them know about me!"

"You already have a family, Caden. We're a family."

Her daughter blinked hard, but a tear escaped. "Some family." She ran to her room and slammed the door.

Sam closed her eyes and sighed. It had been a mistake to tell her. But it was too late to take it back. She knew better than anyone that second chances were a myth.

Fourteen

"How was Saturday?" Scott asked Landon on Monday afternoon. Landon pulled off his white overcoat, cradling the phone between his shoulder and ear. "Like the date from hell." When Scott chuckled, Landon wanted to slug him. Scott had been around a long time, but sometimes Landon wondered if they were too different to remain friends.

"Sorry, man. I tried to warn you."

He'd about had it with Scott's warnings. He picked up the file for his last patient, a golden retriever named Jackson. "I can take care of myself."

"It's real simple, Landon. Just stay away from her. You keep going over there, helping her, and she's just playing you."

"You don't know her, Scott."

"I know her better than you think. You're too good for her."

Landon pressed his lips together so he wouldn't say something he regretted. His friend didn't understand Sam like he did.

Scott laughed. "I don't know what you think you see in her, but you didn't see her at the tavern last week."

Landon's breath caught in his lungs. He opened his mouth to ask. *Don't ask. Maybe you don't want to know.*

"She was flirting with all the men. Including Phil Henderson. Sat talking to him for a good hour. You know he's married, right? Has like six kids."

"It's not a crime to talk to someone in a bar."

"Open your eyes, man. She's interested in every guy who isn't you. You're getting hung up on her again, and she's going to leave just like she did last time. I don't want to watch you go through it again."

His words bounced around in Landon's mind. He remembered the way she pushed Melanie on him, and the way Sam rejected him, and the way she accepted Tully's kiss. But he also remembered the way Sam looked at him when he smoothed his thumb over her lower lip.

And he remembered things Scott didn't even know about. Like the way Sam stood stoically at her dad's funeral, and the way she stared vacantly across the water the day her mother left. Sam's young heart was shattered, and she built a thick wall around it to protect herself. He loved her like no one else could, and she knew it. If only she would let him in, he would spend the rest of his life proving he would never leave her.

꒰ꜛ   ꒰ꜛ   ꒰ꜛ

Amber called the next day and invited Caden over for the afternoon. Judging by the glare her daughter leveled at her over her bowl of chicken noodle soup, she was happy to escape Sam's company.

After she left, Sam tarped the kitchen floor and pushed the table and chairs away from the wall. Paint fumes from the day before still hung in the air and filled her nostrils. At least the potent smell covered the odor of Emmett.

With the trim work done, she figured she could roll all the walls today and apply a second coat tomorrow. The sooner she finished, the sooner she could get the house on the market and escape this cursed place. The thought of Caden's stricken face the night before worried her. What if she told Landon? Sam couldn't bear it if he found out she'd run straight into Bailey's arms after Landon told her he loved her.

Even now, she wondered what she'd been thinking. It was stupid to leave Landon's party that night, but a tidal wave of pain crashed into her, driving her to run.

She pried off the paint lid easily and set it on the kitchen counter. The roller and pan still lay in a bag in the shed, so she went after them. Outside, the air was thick with the smell of rain, and dark clouds gathered. The wind whipped her ponytail against her face, stinging her cheek.

She jogged the rest of the way to the shed, hoping to make it back inside before the rain fell. In her hurry, she tripped on the rock they used to prop open the door, jamming her bare toes. She limped the two yards to the back of the shed.

She strained to see in the darkness. The familiar odor of dirt and old garden tools took her back fifteen years. Her hand fumbled along the rough shelves, and she made a mental note to buy lightbulbs on her next trip to the store. The cheap beach ball she'd bought Caden bounced away as the back of her hand connected with it, then she touched the cool, hard edges of the paint tray.

Just as her fingers closed around the aluminum pan, the door slammed shut. Darkness enveloped her. She whipped around, her thoughts flying fast. She'd kicked the rock just far enough to move it out of the door's path.

Sam took two steps and groped for the knob. Her hand grasped it and turned, but it didn't give. She jiggled the knob frantically, straining to see in the darkness. She shoved her body against the door fruitlessly.

Think, Sam, think. Don't panic.

But the darkness of the small space took her back to days she'd spent her life trying to forget. Days when she sat huddled in the corner of her closet, waiting for Emmett to let her out.

Sam put her hand over her heart as if she could still it. *You're in the shed, and Emmett is gone. You're fine.*

She looked around at the windowless walls, hoping for a sliver of light that would reveal a possible escape. Emmett had built the shed himself, and she cursed his meticulous carpentry. She could imagine him looking at her now from beyond the grave, taking malicious delight in her predicament. She could almost hear his drunken laugh.

Stop it, Sam. She put the brakes on the thought, but her legs trembled. Outside, the wind picked up, howling across the ocean and shaking the tree limbs.

Maybe she could bust the door open with something. Her vision had adjusted to the darkness as much as it would, but she still had to grope to find the sawhorse that sat in the corner. She grabbed it, heedless of the sticky cobwebs, and pulled. Everything that sat on top of it clattered to the cement floor.

With the sawhorse braced in her arms like a battering ram, she drove the wooden end into the door as hard as she could. The steel door seemed as sturdy as a brick wall, and the force of the impact rattled her. She swung the sawhorse back and rammed again. Nothing.

The rough wood cut into her palms, but she kept driving the sawhorse into the door. Finally, she set it down and leaned heavily against the wall, her chest heaving. It wasn't going to budge.

Sam straightened and reached for the shovel that was propped against the wall. Her fist closed around a handle, but when she slid her hands to the bottom, she felt the sharp tines of the rake. She set it down and moved on. The heaviness of the next rod told her she'd found it.

She carried it the two steps to the door and felt for the knob. Judging its approximate location, she brought the shovel's blade down, and it connected with a clang. Without pausing, she lifted the shovel and brought it down again and again.

Sam stopped when her heart threatened to burst from her chest. She threw the shovel to the floor and dug her hands into her hair. She wasn't going to be able to get herself out of here. The place was as sturdy as a mausoleum, and it was beginning to feel like one.

If only Caden were home. Melanie said she'd call later in the afternoon before she brought Caden back, but Sam wouldn't be inside to answer the phone.

Miss Biddle was her only hope. A very slim hope. If she was home, she'd be hard-pressed to hear Sam even if the wind wasn't howling. If Miss Biddle hadn't heard the clanging of the shovel against the doorknob, what were the chances of her hearing anything? Still, what other choice did Sam have?

Sam pressed her mouth into the corner of the doorsill, sucked in a deep breath, then yelled for her neighbor as loudly as she could. She called out several more times, then stilled, her ear pressed against the door. Somehow the screaming had sent a surge of panic through her veins. She was hyperventilating, and the beating of her heart shook her body.

Outside, the branches of a tree scraped the side of the shed and sent a shiver up her spine. She turned into the wall and slid down it until she crouched on the cement floor. The cool hardness of it took her back to the first time Emmett locked her in her closet.

It was the night after her mom left. Sam waited all day for him to come home. She wondered what would happen if he didn't. She'd heard about orphanages and foster care, and the thought of leaving home was scarier than the thought of staying.

Emmett got home after dark, and when he walked in the door, it was as if he didn't see her sitting on the couch. He went straight to the refrigerator, and she heard the sucking sound of the door opening and the clanking of bottles.

Sam pulled her knees to her chest and held them tight. It seemed like an hour before he came back into the room. He stopped short when he saw her, like he'd forgotten she lived there.

He cursed. "She's not back, but you're still here. She probably ran off with some man, but she left her spawn, didn't she?" He gestured toward her with the brown bottle.

Sam pulled her legs closer and looked down at the white fabric of her long T-shirt stretched across her knees. She had sat on the porch as it got dark and wished on the first star she'd seen. A futile wish, probably. Still, she asked.

"Will she come back?"

"What do you think?" The loudness of his voice shook her skull. "She took every last thing that mattered to her."

He smirked at Sam, and she knew what he meant. "That's not true."

"Then why are you still here?" He swore again. "I wish I'd never signed those adoption papers," he muttered to himself.

Sam's insides felt hollow, like the emptiness would swallow her whole. Maybe she could run away and find her mom somehow.

"Do you know where she went?" she asked.

His eyes flickered, his face turning mottled red. He turned and took a step.

He did know where she'd gone to—she could see it in the set of his mouth. Sam imagined herself packing up and taking the ferry to the mainland. Landon could get some money from his parents if he had to. She could take a taxi or something and find her. Her mom wouldn't turn her away if she showed up. A seed of hope sprang up in her for the first time since she'd seen the ripples in the water.

"Where'd she go?" Sam asked again.

His foot connected with a chair, and it scuttled across the kitchen floor, smashing into the cabinets. He turned back to her.

"I don't know where she is! Even if I did, you think she wants you with her? If she wanted you, she would've taken you."

Sam shook her head, fear crawling into her middle and pitching a tent. He still hadn't answered her question. He knew where she was; he just wasn't telling. Sam hated him then more than she ever had. Her eyes stung, but she blinked hard.

"She'll come back." The words were dead before they came out.

"Shut up." His voice was thunder.

Sam choked back the rock in her throat. She had to find her mom. She couldn't stay here. "Where'd she go?"

"I said shut up!" He grabbed her arm and hauled her off the couch.

His fingers cut into her flesh. "Stop it!"

"Don't tell me what to do." He dragged her into her room.

Sam's feet worked to keep up with him.

He opened the closet door and shoved her inside against the tangle of hanging clothes. The door shut, and she reached for the handle, but his weight was against the door.

The darkness closed in and pressed against her body. It swelled, filling the closet with a presence all its own.

"It's real simple, Sam." He spat the words. "You don't move, you don't talk, you don't so much as breathe, you hear me? You do, and you'll be as gone as your momma."

Sam clutched a handful of clothing and squeezed tight. A moment later, the floorboards squeaked, and she knew he was leaving her room. Her legs gave way, and she sank to the floor.

Sam slept like that, a shoe cutting into her back, her head against a stack of jeans she'd outgrown. She didn't come out until morning, and by then, Emmett was gone. Later, he put a lock on the closet door.

Now, she wrapped her arms around her stomach and closed her eyes. Outside, a peal of thunder shattered the air. She clenched her trembling fingers into tight fists and tried to still the storm inside her.

Fifteen

"Come on, Max." Landon exited the clinic and patted his leg. Max came running, stopping short of plowing him down. His black coat was slick with rain. "Ready to go home?"

Max barked, his tail waving high. When they reached the Jeep, Landon opened the door, and Max hopped in the passenger seat, his muddy paws leaving marks.

He turned the key in the ignition and started the wipers. Strange how things had changed since Sam came back to the island. Instead of being driven by his work, he was driven by the clock. The days went slow, and he wished he could fast-forward to the time he could see Sam again.

Traffic in town was getting heavy with summer people descending on the island. They darted through puddles, carrying bright umbrellas. He tapped his fingers on the steering wheel, waiting for the light to turn green. When he got home, he'd change into work clothes and help Sam paint.

The irony struck him that his help would speed her departure. But how else was he to spend time with her? Their friendship seemed to have recovered from the double date, and he sensed Sam relaxing the day before. At times he wanted to brush her hair off her cheek or rub a splotch of paint from the tip of her nose. But he knew their relationship was precarious.

His feelings for Sam ran so deeply, he wondered if he'd ever be able to uproot them if she left. Even Caden had gained a spot in his heart. The thought of losing them tied a knot in his gut, tightening painfully.

Landon shook his head sharply. He wasn't going there. He'd lost Sam once, and he wasn't going to let it happen again. There was too much between them; surely she could see that.

By the time he pulled into the drive, his mood had mellowed, the fear of losing Sam hovering in his mind like an unwelcome houseguest.

"Let's go, buddy." He went inside to change, letting Max traipse around the wet grass. While he rummaged through his drawers for an old T-shirt, his thoughts went back to Scott's words.

Knowing Sam had gone to the tavern and knowing how she'd behaved there were two different things. Had anyone else asked her out besides Tully? Scott said she flirted with Phil Henderson, and the thought sprouted a seed of jealousy. Like Tully, Phil was known for his philandering, a pernicious habit aided by his dark good looks.

Why did Sam flirt with a married man? Why did she flirt with any of them, when they probably had one thing on their dirty minds? Why was she willing to settle for so little?

Landon shoved his feet into his old tennis shoes and exited the house. Max came bounding around back, his tongue flopping out of his mouth.

Landon had forgotten to set out fresh water. Even though Max had probably already helped himself to a puddle, Landon walked back to the spigot and ran water into his pet's dish. Max lapped it up noisily.

Landon straightened and looked toward Sam's cottage, suddenly feeling less than eager to go. Sam had flirted with half the men in the bar and tortured him with a double date, and still, he pined for her.

"I must be a glutton for punishment, huh?"

Max lifted his head, his eyes bright, a drop of water clinging to his tongue.

A bolt of lightning pierced the gray sky, and the rain picked up. The darkness made it look three hours later than it was. "Let's go see Sam."

Max darted ahead, and Landon jogged behind. Did Sam look forward to seeing him at the end of the day? Or was he just a means to an end? Maybe she just endured his company to get the job done quickly and get back to Boston.

She'd been quiet about previous relationships when he asked. Maybe Sam didn't want to tie herself down to anyone. Maybe she wanted to be free to go out with anyone and everyone.

He ran his fingers through his damp hair as he slowed to a walk past the two bikes and up the steps onto the covered porch. He rapped twice and waited. Max sat at his side, panting, his black head cocked.

After a minute, he knocked again. Maybe she'd gone for more supplies. But her bike was outside, and it was pouring rain. He turned the doorknob, finding it unlocked, and stuck his head through the door.

"Sam?" He turned his head and listened.

No answer.

Strange. Maybe she was at Miss Biddle's. No. It was their neighbor's night out with her lady friends. He stepped into the house, inhaling the paint fumes.

"Sam? Caden?"

He scanned the room and saw the drop cloth in the kitchen. In the middle of the floor sat an open paint can. The clean brush still lay on the sink, and a glance at the dry walls told him she hadn't painted anything.

He stooped by the can, dabbing a finger on the surface. A skin of dried paint coated it. He frowned. Sam was too frugal to leave paint out like that.

His mind turned and twisted places he didn't want to go. What if she was hurt? What if Caden was hurt and they'd called an ambulance?

He looked through all the rooms and saw Sam's purse sitting by the front door. Something was wrong. He was ready to pick up the phone and dial the hospital when he heard Max's bark.

Landon exited the house and saw Max with his nose to the ground by the shed. Thunder crashed overhead, and cold rain soaked him. The door to the shed was shut, and the stone that propped the door open was missing. He ran to the structure.

Over the rush of rain, he heard Sam's voice. "Landon!"

As he neared, she pounded on the door.

"It's okay, Sam, I'm here." He wiggled the knob and found it locked. "Where's the key?"

She called something he couldn't hear over the storm. He pressed his ear to the door.

"What?"

"On the kitchen counter!"

"I'll be right back."

He ran, his legs working as fast as they could. Where was Caden? He hoped she hadn't gone after help. But why would she when the key was right here? He snatched the key from the counter and returned to the shed. How long did it take for paint to form a skin? She must have been in there for hours.

The key slid easily into the lock, and he twisted the knob. Sam came through the door and into his arms. She clung to him, her fingers digging into his shoulders, her face buried in his chest.

Landon put his arms around her. "It's okay. It's okay now." He rubbed her back and wondered what had frightened her so much that she trembled against him. What he would give to crawl into her mind and know what she was thinking.

He wanted to ask her what happened, where Caden was, how long she'd been in there, but he didn't want to break the spell. He wanted to stay just a moment in a world where he could be her sanctuary.

He lay his head on hers, sheltering her from the rain. She smelled of honeysuckle shampoo and earth and gasoline. She felt warm and soft, and her vulnerability made him want to keep her in his arms forever.

Her lungs worked fast, her shoulders rising with each breath. "It's okay," he whispered against her hair.

She spoke into his shirt. "It was just like before."

He tried to siphon meaning from her words but couldn't. Before he could ask, she spoke again.

"Dark and hot." Her throat sounded scratchy, her voice raw. "Like the closet."

He moved his palm to cradle the side of her head, dread creeping into his heart. "What closet?"

She clutched at his shirt. "Mine. He used to lock me in."

Landon's eye sockets burned. He could feel her heart thumping against his, mimicking the same fright. "Emmett?"

She nodded, her head moving against his palm.

Rage swelled inside him. He'd known even as a child that Emmett was trouble. He'd feared for Sam, though she never talked about

Emmett. The way he treated her like a slave was enough to prove the man's cruelty.

He remembered his frustration with her only minutes ago and scolded himself. Who was he to judge her? Who knew what other demons she fought? She'd been wounded and still bled. He wanted to hold her until she knew she was safe. Until she knew *he* was safe.

Sixteen

Sam's legs trembled under her weight like a seedling in a storm as she entered the house. She ran a hand across her head, and it came away with cobwebs. The odor of dust and dampness clung to her clothes.

Landon shut the door. "Why don't you grab a shower? I'll fix something to eat; you must be starving."

She walked to the phone instead. "I have to call Melanie. Caden will be worried."

"I'll call. Where's the number?"

Did he seem eager to talk to Melanie? Sam wondered if they'd seen each other since the double date. But she was too tired to argue with him. She was weary, so weary of doing it all alone. "By the phone, on a scrap of blue paper."

Minutes later she stood under a stream of tepid water, letting the dirt and memories wash away simultaneously. She had avoided small spaces all her life, avoided the possibility of being trapped in the dark. The nightmare was a living thing, not forgotten, only pushed down deep. Today it had surged to the surface, and she wondered if she'd be able to bury it again.

She stayed under the flow of water until she stopped shaking.

When she got out, she wrapped up in her robe, the only clean clothing she had.

"You look better," Landon said when she entered the living room. A sandwich and bowl of soup sat on the freshly painted coffee table beside a glass of water. The kitchen, still covered in drop cloths, was off-limits.

The realization that she'd lost a whole afternoon's work sank in, and she sighed. She didn't want to think about the house and the work still to be done. She just wanted to rest and eat and forget.

Sam sat across from Landon in the recliner and picked up the water, drinking half the glass in one gulp. Next, she started on the soup, lifting the spoon to her lips. "Thanks for this."

He watched her eat, silence filling the room. She knew she should feel awkward after making herself so vulnerable, but she didn't. Outside, the sound of the rain pounding the roof was interrupted only by the rumble of thunder.

"Caden's on her way home," he said. "Melanie was concerned when she couldn't reach you. Apparently she came over, but of course, no one answered. I apologized and explained what happened."

"Thanks," she said again. The soup soothed her raw throat. She'd hollered for Miss Biddle off and on all afternoon whenever the noise of the storm died down. Time passed slowly without any way of keeping track, and she was surprised it was still daylight when Landon came. She remembered the feel of his arms around her and relaxed a little. She'd never been so glad to see anyone.

Sam realized she hadn't thanked Landon for rescuing her. The bowl of soup finished, she set it down but left the sandwich on the plate. "I don't know what I would have done if you hadn't come."

The corners of his lips turned up a fraction of an inch. "I'm just sorry I didn't come sooner."

"I was in a hurry. I went out to get the paint pan and roller, and I kicked the rock out of place. The wind blew the door shut." Sam could feel the panic of the moment, and her heart stuttered.

"You never told me what Emmett did." His eyes fastened on hers.

Lamplight from the end table illuminated one side of his face. His jaw tightened, and a shadow tumbled across his cheek.

She wet her lips. "There was nothing you could have done."

"I could've told my parents. He wasn't fit to raise you."

She shrugged. Truth was, she had been ashamed. Emmett told her she deserved the things he did, and after a while, she believed him.

"What else did he do?" Landon's lips tightened, but his eyes . . . his eyes were like the gentlest of touches.

She knew what he was thinking. "Not that." The thought of Emmett's hands on her were enough to turn her stomach. Thank God he never touched her that way.

"He was a cruel man."

Sam picked up her sandwich and held it, her mouth dry. "Never did see what Mom saw in him."

"I wish he were still alive."

Sam looked at him. Light glimmered on the surface of his eyes. Was he crying for her?

"If he were, I'd kill him." His fist squeezed the armrest.

Something seeped into her. A kind of comfort she didn't remember feeling before. It seeped into the deep place where she hurt, but it would take a million gallons to fill the void. Even then, she had a leak. There wasn't enough comfort in the world to fill her up.

Landon leaned forward, elbows on his knees. "I would have protected you."

"You were only a child, same as me." She clutched the forgotten sandwich. Landon would have done everything he could if he'd known. He was like a brother then, the big brother she never had. Even now, he'd move heaven and earth to protect her. She knew it as sure as she knew the tide would come in later.

The front door flew open, startling her. Caden entered, ducking in out of the rain. She turned and lifted her hand, then shut the door. The sound of the car's engine had been lost in the storm.

"Hi," Sam said. "Did you have fun?"

She whirled around. Her daughter's eyes were red-rimmed.

"What's wrong?" She glanced at Landon, thinking Melanie might have mentioned something on the phone, but he shook his head.

"Amber's neighbor came over, and they left me out." She blinked rapidly. "I wanted to come home a long time ago."

Sam set the sandwich down. "I'm sorry, honey—"

"Miss Walker tried to bring me home, but you weren't here." She flung the accusation like a stone. "I had to go back there for the whole afternoon."

Caden seemed to notice Landon for the first time, but before she said anything, she looked back at Sam. Her gaze flittered over Sam's robe.

Sam clutched the collar.

"It wasn't her fault," Landon said.

Caden's lips clamped together, and Sam knew her daughter was remembering their conversation from the night before. Fear bubbled up inside Sam like the contents of a hot cauldron. How stupid she'd been to tell her daughter about Bailey. She should have known Caden wasn't mature enough to keep this kind of secret.

"It's never her fault." Caden rushed to her room and slammed the door.

Sam slumped in relief.

Seventeen

Friday afternoon, Sam reattached the flower boxes below the windows and planted purple phlox in them. Caden had done a nice job of ignoring her since their argument a few days before. Melanie told Caden she'd been locked in the shed, but Caden still blamed Sam, and she carried her grudge like a steel shield.

Sam was hooking up the water hose when Landon pulled into his drive.

He waved. "Be right over." Max bounded out of the Jeep and across Miss Biddle's yard, straight to the backyard and Caden. Maybe the dog could draw her daughter out of this sulky mood.

By the time Landon came, Sam had uncoiled the garden hose and was watering the newly planted flowers.

"You been rolling in the mud today?" His tone teased.

She glanced down at her dirty shorts and mud-splattered knees and arms. Globs of mud clung to her tennis shoes. The storm had left a soggy yard, and she hadn't put mulch down in the beds yet.

She stepped to the next flower box and let water run into the dirt. Landon's shirt and shorts were streaked with dried gray paint. "Yeah, well, you don't look so hot yourself," she teased back.

"I never said you didn't look hot, just dirty."

Sam smiled for the first time that day, her spirits rising. Feeling playful, she turned and aimed the hose at Landon.

He jumped back. "Hey!"

Laughter bubbled up in her. She ran toward him, laughing aloud when he bolted. She was nearly out of hose when he suddenly turned and snatched it from her fingers.

He aimed the nozzle at her, ready to fire.

Sam gasped, backing away, not losing eye contact. "Don't do it." It was her firm-mom voice. It worked on Caden, but she realized it might not have any effect on Landon.

Landon smirked, matching her steps. "Not so fun now, is it?"

She held her hands up, palms out. A drop of water clung to his nose, and his hair stood up on end at the crown of his head. A giggle slipped. "Landon, stop it."

"Are you laughing at me?"

She shook her head, her lips betraying her. Sam's body shook with suppressed laughter.

A shot of icy water hit her in the belly. A squeal tore through her throat. The spray ended as soon as it began. "I can't believe you did that."

"You have a count of three."

"Come on, now." She gestured at the house. "We have work to do."

"One."

Behind her somewhere was a bucket that had filled with rainwater. She backed in its general direction, nearly tripping over the empty flower containers. "We have to get mulch tonight."

"Two." He cocked an eyebrow.

She glanced around, now a yard away from the bucket.

"Three."

She grabbed the bucket at the same time the water hit her. Keeping her back to him, she pitched the water over her shoulder, hitting him square in the face. Laughter escaped her lips.

"You've had it, lady!"

Sam ran, her feet slipping in the wet grass. When she'd outrun the length of the hose, she turned.

Landon was right behind her. Before she could escape, he picked her up, tossing her over his shoulder like weightless baggage.

The world turned upside down. "Put me down, you cretin." It was hard to laugh with his shoulder pushing into her stomach.

"Flattery will get you nowhere." He rounded the corner of the house, nearing the spot where he'd dropped the hose.

Sam swatted him on the backside and tried to kick her feet, but he grasped her legs firmly.

"Am I interrupting something?" Sam didn't recognize the male voice.

She tried to crane her neck but couldn't turn far enough.

Landon bent his knees until her feet touched the ground. She righted herself, swinging her now-loose hair over her head. Then she smacked him in the gut for good measure. His stomach was as hard as a plank of wood.

"Hey, Scott."

The man walking across her yard was a grown-up version of Landon's friend. His buckskin-brown hair was longer, parted in the middle and tucked behind his ears. He stood a few inches shorter than Landon, and he was still trim, except for a little paunch under his tucked-in shirt. Scott was the first guy she'd dated, the first guy she'd kissed. The first guy whose heart she broke. She felt the smile sliding from her face.

"Sam." Scott nodded his head upward. He'd ignored her ever

since the night of the homecoming game. Not that she could blame him.

Sam's belly hurt, more from laughing than anything. She caught her breath. "Hi, Scott." She pulled the wet material of her shirt away from her body.

He tore his gaze from her. "I brought that segment on pets and poisons I taped for you," he said, holding it out to Landon.

Landon took it, stepping slightly in front of her as if to guard her. "Thanks."

Sam looked from one man to the other, feeling an awkward silence fall into place. Water dripped from her hair down the center of her back.

Caden tore around the corner, gathering their attention. "What's going on?" She looked between them, no doubt noticing their wet clothing and hair. Sam realized she'd heard them playing.

"Scott, this is Sam's daughter, Caden." Landon looked at Caden. "This is my friend Scott."

৶   ৶   ৶

"She's got a kid?" Scott asked, disbelief in the angle of his eyebrows.

Landon watched Sam disappear through the front door. Caden had trotted away with Max, pitching a stick for him to fetch.

Landon rubbed his neck. "You didn't have to be so rude."

"I wasn't."

He cared about Scott. He did. But he cared about Sam too, and he was tired of being caught in the middle. "We aren't in high school anymore, Scott. It was a long time ago."

His friend shoved his hands into the pockets of his Dockers. "You were looking awful cozy."

He wanted to tell Scott to take a flying leap. So Sam had hurt him. How long would it take the man to recover?

Then again, he still hadn't recovered from losing Sam. What was it about her that bewitched them?

Scott watched Caden walk around the side of the house.

"Must not have taken her long to get over you."

Landon clenched his teeth and felt heat bleeding through his veins. Scott had known about Landon's feelings for Sam back then and warned him against telling Sam how he felt. Though Scott's words stabbed him, they only echoed his own thoughts. How could Sam have been with someone else so soon after he told her he loved her? Had she met the guy at a bar? Had it been a one-night stand? A long-term relationship? He imagined another man's hands on her smooth skin and felt sweat break out on the back of his neck.

"Don't do this to yourself, man."

Landon looked at the front door of the cottage. Scott didn't understand Sam. He only knew the pain he clung to from Sam's betrayal. And Landon could hardly blame him for that.

Landon looked at his friend. "I can't help it. I love her."

༅   ༅   ༅

Sam grabbed a dry tank top and pair of shorts from the stack on top of the dryer. After changing into them, she peeked through the front curtain and saw Scott hadn't left. Having no desire to face the silent one-man firing squad, she sank onto the sofa.

All teenagers did dumb things, things they weren't proud of—especially when observed through the eyes of their grown-up selves. She was no exception.

Scott had been her first boyfriend. He was quite the stud back then, with a different girl turning his head every few days. Landon reminded her of that after Scott kissed her, and she got so angry at him they didn't speak for a week.

They'd been going out for three months—a record for Scott— when it happened. The Whalers were three quarters into whipping the Vineyarders, and Scott and Sam sat side by side in the home section of the bleachers.

The cheerleaders chanted below them, flipping their hair across their shoulders with each snap of the head. Scott's attention darted to Elizabeth Wittington, a pretty blonde with slender legs and major cleavage.

She smiled at Scott, and Sam's stomach knotted. He had an eye for pretty girls, but when she was alone with him, he acted like she was the only girl in the world. She'd wondered the night before as she lay in bed if she was falling in love with him.

Now the notion frightened her.

The Whalers scored another touchdown, and the bleachers shook as fans shot to their feet. The band blared out their fight song.

Two rows down, Aaron Stevenson, the varsity baseball pitcher, turned and aimed a crooked smiled at Sam. Funny how popular she'd become with the boys since she started dating Scott—as if all the guys suddenly wanted to find out what was so special about her.

Scott high-fived his buddies, then they sat down. He tucked the stadium blanket around her and smiled. "Warm enough?"

"Sure." With all the bodies crammed around her, she was sheltered from the cold fall breeze.

The cheerleaders started another chant, and she watched Scott's eyes slide down to Elizabeth again. The girl swung her hips in time with the words, and he watched every move. Sam's stomach took a dive.

She hated the ache that sprang up inside. She wished she'd never started dating Scott. What if he broke up with her? The ache inside her grew, and she wrapped her arms around her stomach. Why hadn't she listened to Landon? She'd let herself care for Scott, let herself need him, and she knew better than anyone how dangerous that was.

Sam jumped up from her seat, and Scott looked up at her, startled. "I'm—uh—I'm going to get something to eat."

"Want me to go?"

She tried for a casual smile. "That's okay." The blanket fell back onto the bleacher.

Sam squeezed down the row, stepping over feet and nearly tripping over a handbag. When she reached the aisle, she jogged down the steps and onto the grass, walking the short distance to the concession stand.

She remembered the way she felt the night before, when Scott kissed her good night. His lips left a warm path running all the way to the pit of her stomach. When he touched her, she felt it everywhere. He'd cradled her cheek like she was precious.

Now he was gawking at Elizabeth.

She crossed her arms, hugging herself against the coolness of the night. Her feelings for him were real, and they left her raw and vulnerable. She wondered how smart it was to hold her heart out to him so he could throw it down and stomp on it.

Fear sucked the moisture from her mouth, and her breathing became shallow. She tore away from the line, wanting to hide until this panic passed. People were everywhere, classmates talking and laughing like they hadn't a care in the world.

She spied a gap between the concession stand and the tall chain-link fence and darted around the corner into the shadows. The wood was hard and stable against her back. She caught her breath, closing her eyes against the night. What was wrong with her? What was she going to do?

"You okay?"

Sam gasped, her eyes popping open. Aaron Stevenson stood three feet away.

"Sorry, didn't mean to scare you."

She straightened and tried to erase the emotions that must've been on her face. "It's okay."

He put his hand on the chain-link fence, wrapping his fingers around the wires. "I saw you run back here. You okay?" he asked again.

Aaron had only spoken to her once, in the seventh grade to borrow a pencil. He was quiet for a jock but didn't want for girlfriends. Looking at him now, she noticed he had the longest black eyelashes she'd ever seen on a boy. A contrast to his tall, masculine frame.

"I'm fine."

He leaned against the fence, hooking his thumbs through his belt loops. "Scott's a jerk, you know."

She looked at him, wondering why he'd say that. Everyone liked Scott.

"For staring at other girls." He nudged her foot with his. "You deserve better."

His words massaged her ache, releasing its knotted fist. Scott, and her feelings for him, seemed far away, and with the detachment came relief.

"You're twice the girl Elizabeth Wittington is." He leaned in toward her. "If you were my girl, I wouldn't need to look anywhere else."

His fingers ran down her cheek, leaving a warm trail. His eyes looked almost black in the shadows. He planted his other hand against the building, just above her shoulder. She wondered how he'd gotten so close.

Instead of feeling threatened, she felt liberated. *See, Sam, Scott doesn't have your heart. You don't need him. You don't need anyone.*

His warm breath fanned her face. His lips closed over hers. She felt the softness of his lips on hers, the warmth of his hand on her neck. But his touch didn't reach into the core of her, and she relished that fact. *This is how it should be, Sam. Don't let them get too close. You'll only get hurt.*

Her hand settled on his waist, thoughts of Scott far away. Sam pulled him closer, confident and empowered. Aaron Stevenson wanted her. She could handle that. She could handle him.

He leaned fully against her. His hand slipped inside her jacket and up her side, his palm brushing the side of her breast.

A curse split the shadows.

Aaron jumped back, banging into the fence with a clatter.

Scott reached into the space and grabbed Aaron by the sleeve of his coat, dragging him out. Before he could take a swing, Aaron pushed him away. Scott's fists tightened, his upper body leaning forward. He was no fool. Aaron was a head taller and a lot bulkier.

Scott turned to her then, his nostrils flaring. But she saw through the anger. She clasped her elbows and looked away. A whistle pierced the night, and the band struck up the fight song.

It seemed like an eternity before she saw Scott, in her peripheral vision, walk away. She didn't have the nerve to go back up into the stands. Later, Landon returned her purse. Scott didn't speak to her after that, and Aaron and the rest of the popular kids went back to ignoring her.

Now, Sam shifted on the sofa, letting her head lay against the cushion. She knew Scott had told Landon everything, but Landon never asked why she did such a foolish thing. Which was good, because she had no rational explanation for her behavior.

Sam peeked out the curtain and watched them. Scott stood with his arms crossed, and Landon looked away from him. Scott was probably warning him away from her, telling him he was too good for her. Well, as far as Sam was concerned, he could save his breath. Because no one knew that better than she did.

Eighteen

"Sorry about Scott yesterday." Landon finished screwing the new strike plate into the shed's doorjamb. He shut the door, and the new doorknob latched perfectly.

"You don't have to apologize." Sam picked up the rock they'd used to prop open the door and tossed it down to the edge of the water.

Amber was visiting today, having made up with Caden. She sat on the pier, her corn-silk copper hair whipping in the wind, but Caden had waded out beyond the end of the pier, chin deep. Only her head, covered in her fluorescent orange swim cap, was visible. Sam had warned her about undertows. "Caden, come back this way," she called.

Landon took the key from the lock and handed it to her. "He's my friend, and he was a jerk. I feel responsible."

Sam sighed, remembering the way she cheated on Scott. "I was the jerk, remember?"

Landon picked up the empty doorknob container and instruction sheet, wadding it up. "Still. There must be a statute of limitations on that kind of thing." He grinned.

She shrugged, still focused on the bay. Caden hadn't moved an inch. "That girl." She opened her mouth to call again, but Landon set his hand on her arm.

"Caden." He waited until she turned toward him, then gestured for her to come in.

Without hesitation, her daughter broke into a breaststroke. Sam was grateful and annoyed at the same time.

Miss Biddle crossed the lawn, holding two glasses of lemonade. "Anyone thirsty?"

They thanked her for the drinks, speaking loudly so she could hear.

"I remember the way you two were always stopping in for my lemonade and just couldn't help myself. Samantha, the cottage is looking spiffy."

"Thanks." She stared at the house with a fresh eye. "It should fetch a good price."

Miss Biddle wiped her plump hands on the tails of her bright floral shirt. "I wish you'd reconsider and stay, dear."

Landon's eyes met Sam's as if to say, *See, I'm not the only one who thinks so.*

"It would be nice to have a child in the backyard again. Just like old times." Miss Biddle fingered the large silver pendant on her necklace.

Caden had swum in, and she hoisted herself onto the pier beside Amber. Max ran down the length of it and lay beside them.

Sam took a sip of her lemonade, letting the sweet and sour blend on her tongue. The sale of the house was the ticket to Caden's future. Sam had no other way to pay for her college, and she was going to give her daughter a better start in life than she'd had. Caden wouldn't scrub toilets and floors for a living. If she wanted to be an anthropologist or attorney, Sam wanted to give her that opportunity.

Landon made conversation with Miss Biddle. When Sam drained

the rest of her lemonade, she handed over the glass and thanked her neighbor.

"Well, I'm off to a croquet tournament. See you kids later."

Sam hadn't been called a kid in years and hadn't felt like one since she was five.

ⁿ ⁿ ⁿ

"The house looks very charming, Sam," Melanie said when she arrived to take Amber and Caden for a sleepover at her house. "When do you think it'll be ready to list?"

"About a week, I think." Sam glanced at Landon, but he looked away.

Caden and Amber squeezed past Melanie and out the front door, loaded down with Caden's overnight bag and Amber's case of sidewalk chalk.

"Caden," Sam called.

She stopped and looked back.

"I was thinking I'd take the day off tomorrow, okay? We can go to the beach or something."

"Cool." Caden trotted down the porch steps.

"Have fun," Sam called.

When they left, Sam decided it was time to tackle Emmett's room. She shut the door that first day and hadn't gone back in except to close the window. His was the only room not needing a coat of paint. Now that she'd sorted through the rest of the house, it was the only room left.

She opened the door and flipped on the light switch, bracing herself for the smell of cigarettes and Old Spice. Holding her breath like a silly child, she strode to the window and opened it. The

evening air was warm and still. When she turned, Landon stood in
the doorway watching her.

"Are you okay?"

When had she become so transparent? "I'm fine." She brushed
her hands and looked around. Where should she start? Melanie had
advised her to leave the furniture until the house sold, so the bed-
ding needed to stay. Hopefully the house would sell furnished, and
she wouldn't have to worry about the contents.

In Emmett's room, only drawers and the closet needed to be
cleaned out. She looked at the white five-panel door, then turned
away.

"Let's start with the drawers." They could shove the clothes into
bags and give them to charity. *It'll be done and over with before I
know it.*

She pulled a bag from the cardboard container and snapped it
open. The first drawer contained long white socks. She shoved them
into the bag, suppressing the shudder that rose in her. Just touching
his things made her long for a shower. He'd worn those white socks
with everything: shorts, jeans, dress pants. White socks and those
brown leather boat shoes. She hadn't seen those lying around, but
then, he'd probably been buried in them.

A drawer on the chest squawked as Landon pulled it open. She
opened the next drawer and grabbed the stack of clothes, dumping
them into the sack. Something in the pile caught on her fingers.
She lifted her hands and saw a dainty gold chain dangling from her
fingers. At the end was a locket. Her mom's.

Her dad had given it to her one Christmas. It became like an
extra limb, tucked inside her mom's winter sweater, swinging from
her neck as she leaned over the garden, lying cockeyed on her pillow first thing in the morning.

Sam never knew she hadn't taken it with her. The oval pendant's gold plating was faded on the side she'd worn against her skin. On the front, tiny swirls were etched into the brushed gold. Sam remembered running her little fingers over the designs when her mom held her as a child. She'd open the locket and show Sam the pictures. Sam had forgotten that until now.

She slid her stubby thumbnail into the groove and pried it open. On the left side was a picture of her around the age of eight. Her mom had updated it at some point. Sam had never seen the photo before and didn't remember the occasion.

On the right side, where her dad's photo used to be, a picture of Emmett stared back, mocking her. She didn't know why she expected her dad's picture to be there still, but the fact that it wasn't angered her.

Her mom left the locket behind, just like she'd left Sam. Had it been so easy for her to discard them from her life?

"What'd you find?" Landon set the garbage bag on the bed and looked over her shoulder.

Sam snapped the locket shut, opened the bag, and tossed it in. "Nothing." *I can throw things away too, Mom.* Her mouth felt like sandpaper, and where was the stinking breeze? It was like breathing in an ashtray around here.

She hauled open the next drawer and shoved clothes in the bag as fast as she could. She wasn't stopping to look at anything else. She didn't care anymore. It was all going out the door.

When she filled the bag, she grabbed another and continued. There were cards and junk in the bottom of some of the drawers. She gathered and tossed them without looking.

When they finished the chest, Landon carried the full bags out to the front room to give them space to work in the confined quarters.

She slid the last empty drawer of the dresser shut and moved on to the nightstand on her mom's old side of the bed. With any luck, it would be empty.

Landon knelt on the other side of the bed and opened the nightstand drawer. "There's a lot of junk in here. Do you want to go through it?"

Sam opened the top drawer and sighed. Emmett hadn't bothered to get rid of her mom's things. On top of the pile was an old copy of *Ladies' Home Journal* with Nancy Reagan on the cover. "Just pitch everything."

She snatched a fresh bag and started grabbing things. The magazine, an old Harlequin novel, its pages yellowed by time. *Don't look, Sam; just throw it all away.*

A tube of hand lotion went in the bag, followed by a tea light and a lighter. She scooped up the rest of the contents and dumped them in the bag, shutting the drawer.

"Sam?"

The second drawer was as full as the first. She reached in. "What?"

"I think you should see this."

"Just pitch it." There was nothing from her past she wanted to see. Not pictures, not memorabilia, not anything. She just wanted to trash everything and get out of this room. Out of this cottage. Off this island.

"It's a letter." Landon held up an envelope.

"I don't care." She was tired of being pulled down nightmare lane. She refused to go any farther. Her past was bad enough the first time around; she had no desire to repeat it.

"It's from your mom, Sam."

All the more reason to get rid of it. "Throw it away." Her tone was sharp, but she didn't care at the moment. Why should she pore over an old letter? It was probably one her mom had written Emmett when they were dating. He'd lived on the mainland then.

"When did your mom leave?"

Sam leveled a look at him. Why couldn't he just drop it? "The summer after fifth grade. You know that."

He looked at the envelope.

A strange knot started in her throat and worked downward like a braid, twisting tightly.

"It was written after she left."

An earthquake rumbled inside, shaking her to the core. Sam stared at the letter but saw nothing. Her mom had written Emmett after she left? How come he hadn't told her? She scratched the last question. Why would he have done anything kind toward her?

"He never told you?" Landon asked.

"No," she whispered.

He stood and held it out to her.

Sam shook her head. She didn't want to read it. Not now.

Landon set it on top of the quilt. She wondered that it didn't burn a hole through the fabric. Her hands shook as she opened the last drawer of the nightstand. She grabbed the whole drawer and pulled it out, then upended it into the bag, banging the bottom so every last scrap of paper fell.

Why had her mom written after she left? Did she regret leaving? Did she ask about Sam? Did she want Sam to come and live with her? The questions haunted her like a merciless ghost. But she was afraid to know the answers.

She heard the floor squeak and wondered when Landon had come to be behind her. He squatted on the floor and leaned against the side of the bed. "You're upset."

"I'm fine." It was her mantra, and she saw no reason to ditch it now. She gathered the ends of the bag in her hands and started to rise to her feet.

Landon put a hand on her shoulder. "Let's talk."

"I don't want to talk." She wanted to leave, go outside and breathe fresh air again. "We need to clean out the closet." She stood, and his hand fell away.

Sam set the bag out of the way, then opened the closet door. Clothes and boxes and assorted junk filled the space from top to bottom. Her energy left her at the sight, drained away like someone pulled a plug on the ocean. And the smell. Musty Old Spice and sweat. The stench penetrated her nostrils, filled her lungs, and leaked into every cell of her body.

She shut the door and spun on her heels. The living room passed in a blur, then she was outside. She leaned against the screen and filled her lungs with the night air. The door clacked shut behind her.

She heard Landon's footsteps and closed her eyes. The wind whistled through the tree branches, swishing the leaves together. She listened to the sound of a wave colliding with the shore, waiting for the ocean's music to soothe her. Somewhere in the distance, a car's tires squealed.

Just another week. You're almost done. You can make it that long.

But she pictured that letter on the bed, waiting to be read. Part of her wanted to burn it. Another part—the insecure eleven-year-old with a hundred ever-present questions—begged to tear open the envelope and get her answers.

Landon's hands settled on her shoulders, squeezing gently.

"I don't want to talk," she said, just to clarify.

He kneaded her shoulders. "I know."

She relaxed a bit, letting him soothe muscles she hadn't known ached until he touched her. She remembered the day her mom had left and the way Landon was there. He didn't talk or make her talk. He was just there.

He was always there, comforting in a way no one else ever had. She leaned back against him, wanting to soak in his presence for just a little while. She was tired of being independent. So tired. What would it hurt to lean on him for a while? To fully surrender? If she couldn't trust Landon, who could she trust?

His arms came around her, wrapped around her middle, and his head rested on hers. His musky cologne filled her senses. Sweet peace enveloped her, and she imagined it was how a baby chick felt under her mother's wing. Safe. Sheltered. Loved.

"You don't have to be strong all the time. It's okay to feel," he whispered against her hair.

She knew it was true. But she'd lost the ability somehow. She was like a wick clipped too short to hold a flame.

He pressed a tender kiss to the top of her head, and she melted. *Why can't life be like this? Why can't I stay here forever and let him love me?* Only when he held her did she realize she was a starving beggar, and he was the bread she so desperately needed.

She clutched his arms, hoping he wouldn't let her go. Her fingers intertwined with his.

He pulled her into him, holding her tightly. His flesh was warm against the chill of the night, his breath moist against her temple.

"You deserve so much, Sam."

The knot inside her loosened. And a different kind of ache began. One that quickened her heart and stole her breath. It was better than the high of alcohol, more real, more . . . everything.

She turned into him, wrapping her arms around his waist. His heart thudded against her ear. He was warm and solid. Her hands moved against the ripples of his strong back.

His arms cradled her head, the same way he'd held her when he released her from the shed. He saved her then, like he'd saved her from childhood bullies, like he was saving her now. From loneliness. She was dying of it, but here he was, like always, giving her what she needed.

Sam leaned back and looked at him. She allowed herself to touch his jaw, feeling the rough stubble against the pads of her fingers. She explored the planes of his face, angles so familiar she saw them in her sleep.

The line of his upper lip was a sharp edge, and she let her finger trail down to the fullness of his lower lip, then to the tiny cleft in his chin.

Their eyes met and clung. His palm cupped her chin, and her heart forgot to beat. He leaned down, and she arched toward him, aching to feel his lips on hers. They touched her gently, no more than a whisper, testing the waters. But she felt it down to her toes. His lips moved over hers again, slowly, giving, not taking.

He was Landon, her trusted friend, but in that moment he was so much more. He was passion, he was affection, he was mercy. She wanted it all, and she wouldn't stop until she had it.

She leaned into him, her hands sliding around his back. He deepened the kiss, and her world was a kaleidoscope of color and light. All of it beautiful.

"Sam."

She felt her name on his lips and relished it. But she didn't want to talk. She wanted to feel. It had been so long since she was able to.

He pulled back a fraction of an inch, until only their noses touched. Their breath mingled in an intimate dance. His hands framed her face. "Sam," he said again. His lips brushed hers. "I love you." He kissed her again. "So much."

She let the words sink in. Soothe her. But instead of settling in a deep sea of pleasure, they begged an answer. Did she love him?

Before she could explore the thought, Emmett's words taunted her. "*Don't ever let yourself love, Sam. Just soon as you do, they leave you. Love never brings anything but pain.*"

The words caught in her mind. Her lips moved mechanically against Landon's.

Her stomach twisted. The pleasant sensations flowing through her battled with the bitter reality of life. When had love ever worked out for her? What good was love when it ended in pain? She didn't need Emmett's words to teach her. She was a capable student in the school of life.

Get away, Sam. Before it's too late.

Panic bubbled up inside until she thought she'd burst. She broke the kiss, stepping backward until she connected with the screen. Her chest heaved.

Landon's eyes narrowed. "What's wrong?"

Sam shook her head. This was wrong. The confusion on his face tugged at her, breaking her. *Be strong, Sam. Protect yourself. No one else will. Not even Landon.*

"What, Sam?" He reached out his hand.

Sam flinched away. She couldn't let him touch her again. She'd almost lost her head, and she wasn't sure she could trust herself. She needed to get away.

But she remembered the letter lying on the bed, the smell of Emmett's presence, the locket her mom had left behind.

She wanted to go someplace far away. She turned and opened the porch's screen door. "I have to go." Her feet scrambled down the steps and took her to her bike.

"Wait, Sam."

She hopped on the bike, straddling the seat.

Landon took her arm. "It's dark. I'll leave; you stay here."

"I have to go." She didn't know where, hadn't thought that far ahead. Her foot fumbled to find the kickstand.

"I can take you. It's late."

His presence, so reassuring and peaceful moments before, now felt like a heavy fur coat on a scorching August day.

Sam shook off his hand and glared at him. "Let me go." She steeled herself against the hurt in his eyes as his hand fell away.

Her feet found the pedals, and she pushed off. The driveway pebbles popped out from under the tires. She turned out on the road, the moonlight guiding her path. Her legs pumped hard, but the wind in her ears wasn't enough to blow away her thoughts.

What were you thinking, Sam? Where was the distance you've learned to keep? It's one thing to let a man in your bed, quite another to let him in your heart.

Stupid!

Now Landon knew how she felt. She didn't have to say the words to speak the truth loud and clear. How would she keep him away until she left? She didn't know if she had the strength.

Sam pedaled hard, not allowing herself to coast, punishing herself with the pain in her thighs. She took the corner onto the main road fast and headed toward town. Her lungs gulped fresh air. A sheen of sweat broke out on her stomach, but she kept going as if she could outrun her thoughts.

Landon's words washed over her, but she pushed them away. Her mom once claimed to love her too, but where was she now? Where had she been when Sam needed her?

Needing someone was the act of a fool, and she was done with that.

The road turned to cobblestone, and she slowed her pace. The gears ticked as she coasted behind a Mercedes. A breeze blew in from the ocean, cooling her skin. When she reached the tavern, she pulled into the lot and parked her bike under the bright lamp.

A loud eighties tune floated out the door of the building, beckoning her. Someone laughed inside, a wild, loose laugh induced by too much beer. She entered the dark haven, stepping through the crowd to a seat in the corner. She wasn't in the mood to socialize. She was in the mood to forget.

A server came over, a young kid with a Coppertone tan and a quick smile. "What'll it be?" he asked over the music and chatter.

She started to order a beer, but on second thought decided on something stronger. "A shot of whiskey."

"Sure thing."

Sam watched him skirt a patron and slip behind the bar. Tully slid a bottle toward a woman. The woman reached into her purse as she stood, pulling out a wad of cash.

Money! You left your purse at home. Sam's mood plunged even further. *Great, Sam, just great.*

The server approached with her shot and set it down on her table. "Thanks."

Sam looked at Tully and knew she'd have to ask the favor. She downed the shot, feeling the liquid burn its way down her throat, before she approached him. She smoothed her T-shirt and ran her hand through her wind-blown hair.

His face lit when he saw her, his eyes swinging down her snug shirt, then back up. "Hey, Sam. Good to see you."

"You too," she hollered over the music, taking a seat on the only empty stool. She leaned forward, and he came closer. "Listen, I have a little problem. I forgot my purse at home."

He backed away and waved his hand nonchalantly. "It's on the house tonight."

Finally, something was going her way. She smiled her gratitude. "Thanks a lot."

"Don't worry about it. What can I get you?"

The whiskey was beginning to warm her insides. "Shot of whiskey?" He flashed a grin before turning to pour the shot.

"How you doing?" The man on the stool beside her wore an expensive shirt and a contagious laugh. He eyed her appreciatively.

"Not bad." The truth was, she was feeling better already.

"You from around here?"

Sam shook her head as if she could make it true. "Boston."

"Nice city. I'm from Hartford. Name's Steven."

Tully set her whiskey down and went to make a mixed drink.

She introduced herself to Steven, and when she finished her drink, he signaled Tully to bring her another. After her third shot, his conversation amused her, and her limbs were like cooked noodles. Tully stopped and chatted when he was able. Landon was a distant thought, too far away to reach, and the thought made her giddy.

When Steven left, Tully leaned against the bar, staring. "You have the most gorgeous set of eyes. Deep brown, with those amber spokes. Like you've got a fire going inside."

Sam laughed, not sure why she found it funny. "And you have some really great green eyes." She leaned closer. "I mean blue. Very nice."

He reached up and touched her hair, tucking it behind her ear. That was funny too. Sam chuckled. She turned her head, and the room spun. She blinked. "Where'd everybody go?"

"Crowd always thins out around now." He leaned closer. "What do you say we get out of here?" He gave her his Brad Pitt smile. "I can get someone else to cover the bar."

She liked the idea. "Sure." She fumbled for her purse on the stool, then remembered she didn't have one.

"It's on me, remember?" Tully removed his apron and went to talk to a server.

When he came back, she slid off the stool but got her foot tangled in the footrest. Tully caught her with firm hands.

"Steady there."

She laughed and clung to his arm. His bicep was thick and hard. She squeezed playfully. "Not bad." She remembered his buff physique from their date. "Goes with your six-pack."

She kept hold of his arm as they left the tavern. The air was notably fresh after the smoke-filled bar, and she drew in a breath.

Tully led her around back, where he was parked. Sam worked hard to set one foot in front of the other, giggling when she tripped over a gap in the sidewalk.

She felt so good. She spun around in a Mary Tyler Moore move, laughing.

When she lost her balance, Tully caught her body against his. He was solid. His hair fell over his forehead, and his dark skin made his teeth look camera-perfect white. So handsome. "Hey, good-lookin'," she said.

"Hey, gorgeous." He held her to him. "I never did get a proper good night kiss."

"Oh yeah." She slid her arms up his chest and around his neck. "I suppose I owe you one, huh?" She felt bold and confident and good. In control.

He claimed her lips, and she kissed back. It was nice and easy.

When he pulled back, he took her arm and helped her into his car. Her head swam pleasantly, and she leaned it back against the leather headrest. He got in the driver's side.

"My place okay?"

Sam closed her eyes, enjoying the swirling sensation. "Sure."

Nineteen

Landon picked up the copy of the *Inquirer and Mirror* and scanned the headlines, his eyes unseeing. Where was Sam? He'd watched out the window for the last two hours, waiting for her to ride up on her bike, waiting for the living room light to shine through the curtains.

But nothing.

Maybe he should look for her. What if a driver didn't see her in the dark and hit her? He snapped the paper shut and tossed it onto the sofa beside him.

Max, his head resting on his front paws, gave a deep sigh.

His mind returned to the kiss for the hundredth time. Why had he moved so fast? He shouldn't have told Sam he loved her. Should have known it would scare her away.

Landon stood and paced the small living room. He'd take it all back if he could just know Sam was safe. He longed for the day when a flashlight in her window told him everything was all right. Her well-being was more complicated now. Instead of her stepfather tormenting her, she had ghosts. And how could he fight those? The steel cage she had built to protect her heart kept him from reaching her, and the letter stirred it all up again. He shouldn't have said anything. He should have tossed it like she asked.

He sank onto the couch where he could see her cottage. But tonight she'd let him hold her, let him comfort her. He'd do it the rest of her life if only she'd allow it. Why couldn't she see that he wanted the best for her, that he'd do anything for her, that he would never forsake her?

Instead, she ran, she pushed, she fought. It was enough to make a man crazy.

His one solace came with the memory of the kiss. Yes, he kissed her, but she returned the gesture with so much fervor his knees had shaken. He remembered the feel of her soft lips responding to him and wanted to capture the feeling and lock it away in his heart.

She might deny it with her words, but hers hadn't been the kiss of a friend. The way she looked at him, the way she touched him, told him more than words ever would.

Maybe that's what had frightened her off. Maybe it wasn't his confession of love, but the realization that she loved him too.

He breathed a laugh. A man could hope, couldn't he?

He glanced at his watch and saw it was half past eleven. *Where are you, Sam?*

The phone pealed then, and he rushed toward it. Maybe she needed help. Maybe she'd blown a tire and was stranded somewhere.

"Hello?"

"Hey." The sound of Scott's voice punctured Landon's hope. "Hope I didn't wake you."

Landon let out the pent-up breath. "No. Just sitting here."

"Listen, I was working late tonight, and guess who I saw when I was driving through town?"

Landon straightened. "Who?"

"Sam. And she looked pretty toasted too, stumbling all over the place."

"Where was she?" He would go get her. She couldn't ride home on her bike like that. What was she thinking?

"Tavern parking lot. But she wasn't alone, buddy."

His thoughts jammed, and dread snaked its way along his nerves. "Who was with her?"

Scott was silent for a moment, and Landon squeezed the phone as if he could wring an answer from it.

"Listen, Lan, I didn't call to rub it in. I just want you to see the truth before she breaks your heart, man."

Too late. "Who was she with?" It was all he could do to control his tone.

He heard Scott sigh. "Tully."

"I've got to go."

"Wait, Landon."

He walked across the room and shoved his feet in his tennis shoes. "What?"

"She was getting in his car, and she wasn't exactly fighting him off, if you know what I mean. She's a grown woman; she can do what she wants." He paused for effect. "And clearly, she wants."

"You said she was hammered."

"She's still a willing participant."

"I've got to go." Landon clicked the off button and tossed the phone onto the recliner. He flipped through the phone book and found Tully's listing. A friend from school had lived on Tully's street, and it was only a ten-minute drive. Five if he hurried. He grabbed his keys and jogged to the Jeep.

What was she thinking? At this hour Tully was undoubtedly taking her home, and Landon had no doubt what he intended to do to her there. The man had practically drooled over Sam in her bathing suit. He would take advantage of her drunken state and think nothing of it.

Landon's tires spun as he backed out of his drive. He should've asked Scott how long ago he'd seen her. What if he got there and it was too late? He imagined Tully running his beefy hands all over Sam, and anger tore through him. He pressed down on the accelerator, breaking the speed limit.

Moments ago he reveled in the fact that Sam had responded to him, but apparently she wasn't all that selective.

It made no sense. Why did she fight him so hard? Was loving him such an awful thing? Tully was nothing but a player out to use her, but she'd run from Landon's arms to his. Is that what she wanted? To be used up and tossed away like an old rag?

By the time he turned onto Tully's street, his fingers gripped the steering wheel hard. He drove through the residential neighborhood, slowing to read the street numbers. When he came to Tully's, he turned into the drive. The bartender's old Mustang sat next to the front porch, and a light burned inside.

Landon took the porch steps two at a time, then pounded on the wood door with the side of his fist. How long ago had they arrived? Were they in the bedroom now? He ground his teeth together and pounded again.

A muffled curse leaked through the door.

A fresh rush of adrenaline surged through his veins. *Keep it cool, Reed. Just get her out of there and go.*

Tully jerked open the door and cursed again. "What do you want?" His disheveled hair hung over his forehead, and his chest was bare.

Landon reined in the desire to slug his face. "I came for Sam. I'm taking her home."

Tully squinted. "What?"

"Where's Sam?" Landon pushed past Tully, his gaze sweeping the room. Not seeing her, he strode down the short hall.

"What's your problem?" Tully was on his heels.

Landon came to the first door and looked in. The lamplight revealed Sam sprawled on the bed. She wore only her bra and shorts, her hair splayed across the pillow.

She saw him and sat up. "Landon." Did he imagine the relief in her tone?

Landon started toward her, but Tully grabbed his shirt and jerked him back. "Listen, dude, you got no business here."

Landon whipped around and pushed him off. "No. You listen. I'm taking her home."

Tully pushed Landon hard. He staggered backward to keep his balance. "We were right in the middle of something, if you know what I mean. She doesn't want to go home." He tossed Sam a glance. "Do you, doll?"

Sam twirled a strand of hair in her fingers, watching it with fascination. She was like a little girl, vulnerable and innocent. When she turned her fawn-brown eyes on Landon, he wondered if they held a plea.

Landon glared at Tully. "She's in no shape to make a decision, and you know it."

"Get out." Tully planted his feet.

He wasn't going to get her out of there without a fight. So be it.

He charged Tully, landing a swing square on his jaw. Tully's head whipped to the side. Before he could right himself, Landon jabbed his fist hard in his gut, driving the air from Tully's lungs. It was like hitting a block of concrete, but Tully doubled over.

Landon turned to get Sam. He pulled her arm. "Come on, Sam."

She looked up at him. Almost in slow motion, a sultry smile curved her lips. "Landon."

He was going to have to carry her.

Tully charged him from the side. Landon flew into the night-stand, knocking the lamp to the floor. The room darkened. His head banged against the wall.

Tully jerked him upright and slugged him across the face. Pain exploded in his head. Before he could recover, Tully's fist hit his stomach, knocking him backward over something. He hit the floor hard.

"Hey . . . stop." Sam's voice cut through the darkness.

His head throbbed, and he struggled to fill his lungs again.

Tully came toward him, a shadow in the dark. Landon swung his foot across the floor, sweeping Tully's feet from under him. He fell with a thud.

Landon attacked, fists flying, hitting their mark. Tully fought back, but Landon planted a fist square in his face, and finally Tully stilled, groaning.

Landon stood and moved to the bed, wiping blood from his lip with the back of his hand. "Come on, Sam." He gathered her in his arms, breathing hard.

She curled against his neck, pointing back toward the bed as he walked away. "My shirt."

"Never mind." Landon stepped over Tully and carried her outside. He stood Sam on her feet and opened the car door. "Get in."

She sat down but didn't pull her legs in. She cocked her head and sighed leisurely as if she sat on the end of a pier.

He lifted her legs and tucked them inside the car, noting her bare feet. With a glance backward to make sure Tully wasn't on his feet again, he shut the door and got in the other side.

With the turn of the key, he started the engine and backed out of the drive, his tires churning up gravel. Only when they were on the road did he remember to breathe again.

Sam turned in her seat and ran her hand down his arm. "You're so strong."

He tried to ignore the effect of her touch. *Just drive, Reed. She's drunk as a skunk and doesn't know what she's doing. Probably thinks you're Tully.*

"Put on your seat belt, Sam."

Instead, she trailed her fingers down his arm and gathered his hand in hers. She lifted it to her mouth and pressed a kiss to his bruised knuckles.

He swallowed.

She kissed his wrist, then his forearm, leading a trail upward. He tightened his other hand on the steering wheel.

"Your seat belt, Sam." He braked for a stop sign and reached across, grabbing the strap. Her bare shoulders glowed under the moonlight.

"What am I thinking?" he muttered, dropping the buckle. He released his seat belt and tugged off his T-shirt.

It slid easily over her head. "Help me out here." With some assistance, she poked her hands clumsily through the sleeves, and he pulled the shirt down, covering her. Once he buckled them both in, he put the car in drive and took off.

Sam turned toward him, her knees poking the console, and ran her fingers across his bare stomach.

"That's more like it," she said. Her fingers trailed upward.

His muscles tightened. She probably thought she was still on Tully's bed. He grabbed her hand. "That's enough, Sam."

She laughed, a sultry sound he'd never heard from her. "What's the matter, baby?"

Landon tightened his hold on her hand, ignoring her question.

"Party pooper," she said, pouting. She leaned her head against his arm.

He relaxed, hoping she'd settle down now. His jaw smarted from Tully's last blow, and he could feel his pulse in his temples. At least Sam was safe. He wondered how much she'd remember in the morning. Enough to feel foolish, no doubt.

Why had she run off and gotten drunk? Didn't she know that never solved problems? It only created new ones.

He looked down where she rested her head against his shoulder. She turned and pressed a kiss against the flesh of his arm, setting a fire inside him.

Well, you wanted her to loosen up. I guess you got your way.

Little had he known she'd loosen up for someone else. He'd gotten to Tully's in time to stop the jerk from taking advantage of her, but clearly, they'd gotten far enough.

He gripped the steering wheel. *Stop it, Reed. No point torturing yourself.*

By the time he pulled into Sam's drive, she was dozing. He turned off the ignition and eased away. "Sam. Wake up." He wondered why he whispered.

She blinked in the darkness of the car, sitting up straight, looking like a lost little girl. Some of his anger drained.

"We're home. Let's get you inside." When she didn't move, he went to her side of the Jeep and took her in his arms, shutting the door with his hip. His T-shirt fell to her thighs, and her bare feet dangled toward the ground.

She buried her face in the curve of his neck. Her warm breath heated his skin, and her honeysuckle shampoo filled his senses. Part of him wanted to cradle her in his arms forever; the other part wanted to throttle her for being so careless. He didn't understand. If being with him was so scary, why would she run straight into Tully's arms? Into his bed, even? If he lived to be a hundred, he would never understand Sam completely.

He entered the house and strode through the darkened interior. In her room, he set her on her feet. She clung to him, sliding her arms around his back.

"Sam, let's get you in bed."

"Mmm." She snuggled against his bare chest, kissing his flesh. She ran her hands over his back.

His mouth went dry. *Get a grip. She probably did the same thing to Tully a few minutes ago.* He pulled her arms away and reached behind him to flip on the lamp. Soft light flooded the room. He walked to the bed and pulled back the quilt. "In you go." He took her hand, leading her to the bed.

The mattress sank as she sat, then she looked up at him slowly with a smile that fueled the fire under his skin. She tugged his hand, pulling him down beside her.

Her pupils were dilated, her eyelids half-closed. Her hair fell over one eye, and he brushed it back off her cheek.

She captured his hand against her face and turned, pressing a kiss into his palm, her eyes fastened on his.

Get out of here, Reed.

He made a move to stand, but she grabbed his shoulders. "Where you going?"

"Home."

She lifted one eyebrow. "What for?" She pivoted to face him, one of her long legs swinging off the floor and across his lap. She straddled him, her knees planted on both sides of his thighs.

She wrapped her arms around his shoulders. "Stay, please?"

Her eyes were like cruel pools of seduction, pulling at him relentlessly.

He felt her lips on his neck and swallowed. *Have mercy.* What was she doing to him?

"Sam." He rasped her name. His hands found her waist and pushed back. He stood, lifting her with him, then lay her on the bed, tucking her legs under the quilt. He had to get out of there. Quick. "That's enough, now," he said.

She lay back against the pillow and stuck out her lower lip. With her hair billowed around her face, she looked like an angel. A very tempting angel.

He pulled the covers up to her chin.

She snuggled into the pillow, sighed softly, then closed her eyes. "Have it your way," she mumbled.

She looked peaceful at last, lying there in her childhood bed under the same window she used to set her flashlight on. She was safe for tonight. He touched her flushed cheek with the backs of his fingers, drawing them downward. Her skin was like a dewy rose petal. So soft. So fragile. He would fight a hundred Tullys if necessary.

"Good night," he whispered. Turning, he flipped off the lamp with a click.

Sam's sleepy voice carried to him in the darkness. "I love you."

Twenty

A throbbing pain in Sam's temples snatched her from sleep. She turned on the pillow and groaned, laying her hand across her forehead as her mind slogged to wakefulness. Her eyes opened, then she swiftly shut them. She choked back a word she forbade Caden to say.

Sam turned her head, shielding her eyes against the morning light, and saw an empty space beside her. Where was Caden? Her watch read 9:47.

Her daughter had spent the night at Amber's. Right. The thought relieved her. She wouldn't have to get up and make breakfast.

Then she remembered the letter Landon found in Emmett's drawer. The memory of his kiss washed over her anew. He'd told her he loved her. She'd run then, gone to the tavern and gotten wasted. The headache. It all made sense now.

Tully.

She had a dreamlike memory of being at his house. He'd poured her a drink. His bed. She'd been in his bed. He'd pulled her T-shirt over her head and tossed it over his shoulder.

Oh no. She put her hands over her face. What happened next? She didn't remember taking off the rest of her clothes. She didn't remember sleeping with him.

You probably didn't do much sleeping at all, you idiot.

Sam groaned again and turned her head into her pillow. Did they even use birth control? *What have I done?*

She tried to remember what happened after Tully removed her shirt. *Think, Sam!* But she couldn't think at all with her brain beating against her skull. She dragged her feet from under the covers and sat up slowly, holding her head like it might fall off.

Her tongue was superglued to the roof of her mouth. How could she have been so stupid? She'd gone straight from Landon's arms to Tully's with only an alcohol binge in between.

You'd think you'd have learned this lesson a long time ago. Isn't Caden reminder enough?

Sam's shirt was wadded up around her waist, and she tugged it down, trying to gather the energy to go for painkillers.

She took another look at the blue T-shirt. It wasn't hers. Its sleeves hung to her elbows, and the crewneck fell low on her chest. There was a gray paint stain on the hem.

Landon.

A flash fired in her mind. He'd been at Tully's house. He'd—

Oh no. He and Tully had fought. She remembered Landon flying across the room and something crashing to the floor. What if Landon . . . What if he was hurt?

She jumped to her feet. Her head spun. *Slow down, Sam. What happened next? What happened after that?* She stood still, her balance precarious. She remembered being in Landon's arms. He'd carried her into the house.

Sam's breath released audibly. He couldn't have been hurt too badly if he brought her home. She didn't remember the drive, but that was okay. Landon was all right, and she hadn't slept with Tully. That's what mattered.

Thank God.

She took careful steps, exiting her room. Where was her purse? Had she left it at Tully's? The bar? She had to get something for this headache. She entered the living room and saw her bag lying by the front door as always. She remembered leaving it behind.

Sam fumbled for the bottle of Advil, then emptied three into her palm. After she washed them down with a glass of water, she went back to her room and lay on top of the covers. It hit her fresh that Landon had come to her rescue.

How had he known where she was? Had she called? It was hard to say what happened when she could only remember snippets.

She closed her eyes and pulled the T-shirt down over her stomach, wrestling with the excess material.

Her eyes popped open. She suddenly remembered Landon pulling the shirt over her head. She'd been in her bra when he came to Tully's. Lying on the bed in her bra.

He'd seen her drunk and brainless. Half-naked. She cringed.

Maybe he'll know now. Maybe he'll realize what you are and leave you alone.

The thought brought little comfort. She was ashamed that she'd lost control. That she'd somehow dragged Landon into the middle of it. He'd gotten hurt trying to get her out of her foolish mess.

Like a flash of lightning, another memory struck. They were standing beside the bed. She was kissing his bare chest. Running her hands all over his back. He was pushing her away.

Oh no.

Sam remembered feeling bold and confident at the time, like she was Lolita or something. Now she just felt stupid.

What had happened next? She rubbed her temples, hoping for

clarity but finding none. He'd put her in the bed. He'd sat beside her. Or had she pulled him down?

Had they talked? What else had she done?

Her legs were hot, and she kicked the quilt from under them, searching for the coolness of the sheet. With the movement came another recollection. Landon had been sitting on the bed. She swung her leg over him like some kind of whore. She tried to kiss him, but he lifted her off him and put her back in the bed.

She couldn't remember what happened next. It was like a black hole. The harder she tried to remember, the quicker it slipped away. Humiliation filled her. She wanted to go to sleep and wake up in Boston. Far from this house, far from Landon, far from the disgrace of the night before.

Instead, she settled for the quick oblivion of sleep.

A knocking sound awakened Sam. She sprang up and felt the remnants of her hangover. The Advil had helped some, but not enough.

The knock sounded again. Someone was at the door. The clock read 10:56. Caden. Melanie was supposed to bring her home after breakfast. She ran her hand through her snarled hair, hoping she didn't look as bad as she felt.

Her feet covered the distance to the door quickly as she wiped her bleary eyes and tried to look like she hadn't just rolled out of bed. She unlocked the door and pulled it open.

Landon stood on the porch with a mug of coffee. He hadn't shaved yet, and stubble lined his jaw. She met his gaze, the night before too fresh in her mind. What did he think of her now? She could feel her cheeks heating at the memory.

"Brought you some coffee." He held out the mug.

Sam took it and stared at the brew. Steam swirled upward, carrying the robust aroma to her nose. Her stomach lurched. "Thanks." She set it down on the end table. Her hand was unsteady, and a bit of it sloshed over the side onto the fresh white surface.

He stuffed his hands in his pockets. "How are you feeling?"

She licked her parched lips. "Fine." She had a new memory of them in his Jeep. Sam had been kissing his arm from his hand to his bicep. She closed her eyes, wishing he'd somehow disappear from her porch.

"I thought we could get mulch today. We could finish the beds."

The word didn't make her think of flowers, but of what she'd done the night before. She'd come close to repeating the same mistake she made the night of Landon's going-away party. Only that night, she'd run from Landon to Bailey.

And Bailey had never come home.

Her head throbbed. "I'm not up to working today, okay?" She made a move to close the door. "Thanks for the coffee."

He stopped the door with his hand. "What about the house?"

There was still work to be done, and her need to escape the island was greater now than ever. But she needed to finish alone. Landon's presence did things to her. Things she couldn't understand, much less explain. And she shouldn't have to explain. Why couldn't he just stay away? Stay out of her life and stop torturing her? No one else drove her to distraction like he did. If he hadn't been here the night before, none of this would have happened.

"It's my house, Landon. My problem."

"I want to help."

Sam looked him square in the eye. "I don't want your help," she said sharply. "I can finish on my own just fine."

The corners of his mouth fell, and she noticed a cut on his lower lip. It occurred to her that she should thank him for rescuing her. But she was tired of him coming to her rescue. It was him she needed saving from, couldn't he see that?

The light in his eyes dimmed. She ignored the prickle of guilt.

"Have it your way, Sam." He let go of the door. "But at some point, we need to talk about last night."

Just when she thought he was going to let it drop, there it was. He set it at her feet like a dog with a dead rabbit. Embarrassment and anger waged war. So she'd done something stupid. Did he have to rub her face in it? Was he going to shame her for getting drunk and going home with Tully? She was an adult. She wouldn't let Landon shame her.

Sam remembered the moves she'd made on Landon and felt her limbs go hot. Okay, so she'd shamed herself. She crossed her arms, hugging herself.

"I was drunk," she said. "I didn't know what I was doing."

He looked at her so incisively, she was afraid he could see everything she hid from him.

"That's not the part we need to talk about," he said softly.

The compassion on his face alerted her. She realized he was talking about everything that had come before. Before her shameless behavior, before Tully, before the whiskey. He was talking about the reason she'd fled from him to begin with. But she couldn't talk to him about that. Didn't even want to think about it. She wanted to get in a boat and go far away. Just like her mom had done all those years ago.

The thought smacked her with the force of a two-by-four, stealing her breath, and she wondered if she wasn't so different from her mom after all.

Twenty-one

The warm water washed over Sam's head and ran down her bare back. She wished all her troubles could flow so freely off her. She imagined her mom's letter lying on Emmett's bed the way it had the night before, just waiting to be opened. She didn't know if she had the courage to do it. What if it showed she really never cared about Sam at all? It was one thing to suppose it, another to have it confirmed. She couldn't deal with that right now.

She had known coming back here would be hard for all the obvious reasons. Stirring up her dad's death, her mom's abandonment, and Emmett's ghost was bound to be painful. But she hadn't banked on the even greater distress of facing Landon.

You're almost done, Sam. Just hang in there another week and you can go back to Boston and forget all about this place.

But she wondered if she would be able to forget Landon. She hadn't forgotten him before. Not really. And he'd dug more deeply into her heart since she'd come back.

Sam finished her shower, and by the time she dried off and dressed, Caden was home and watching TV.

"Did you have fun?" Sam asked, hoping they were on speaking terms now.

"Yeah."

Sam sat beside her on the sofa. "What did you do?"

Caden shrugged. "Fixed each other's hair, ate breakfast."

"I like your braid," she said. They were talking like friends for the first time in a long while. Sam wondered how long it would last.

"Mrs. Walker did it. She made pancakes and took us to the park."

Sam smiled even as a pang of jealousy twisted inside. How did Melanie find so much time to spend with her daughter? She was a single mom too.

The phone rang. Sam waited, wondering if she should get it. Maybe it was Landon. Or Tully. What would she say to him? To either of them?

You're a grown-up, Sam; you'll come up with something. She got up and grabbed the handset off the end table. She'd forgotten about the coffee Landon had brought. Her stomach was feeling better; maybe she'd reheat it. She answered the phone.

"Sam? Hi, it's Patty. How are you?"

Sam hadn't talked to her boss since leaving Boston. "Hi, Patty. I'm doing good. How are things there?"

"Exceptionally well. We got the Merrek building back."

"I thought Murphy's Maids got that contract." Her boss was concerned after they'd lost the job. She'd been about to open an office in a new location, but the loss of the Merrek building meant less income for the company, and they couldn't afford the new space.

"They did, but the owners were unhappy with their work."

"That's great." She set her coffee in the microwave and punched the buttons. "Maybe you can get that office space now."

"That's what I'm hoping. I just wanted to make sure you were on track to be back a week from Monday. That's when we're scheduled to start at the Merrek building. I'll need you."

Sam looked around the cottage at the walls needing a second coat of paint. The ceilings, which she hadn't planned on doing, now looked dingy against the white walls. They would need a coat of paint. The wood floor still needed to be polished and the cupboards painted. She'd have to work her tail off to get it done alone. "Don't worry about a thing," she said. "I'll be home on time."

"Oh, good." Relief coated her words. "I know how home repairs can go. Everything seems to take more time than you bargain for."

Wasn't it the truth? If Landon hadn't helped, she'd be way behind schedule. "No need to worry. I'll be there a week from tomorrow, bright and early."

After she got off the phone, she drained the coffee, then changed into her painting clothes. Her headache was a dull throb now.

Sam walked toward the door. "I'll be back in a few, Caden. I need to get some stuff from the shed."

Caden glanced up from the TV. "What time are we going to the beach? Can we go to the surf side?"

Sam stopped on the threshold. She'd forgotten about promising Caden she'd take a day off. She had so much to do and no help. She couldn't ask Landon. And now she definitely had to be back in Boston on time.

Sam turned, her hand grasping the doorknob. "I'm really sorry, Caden, but we can't do it today. I have to paint. My boss just called and—"

"But you said you'd take the day off." Her whine was like fingernails on Sam's spinal cord.

"I know what I said, but that was before Patty called and—"

"You never do anything fun!"

Did Caden think she wanted to work today? That she didn't want to go hang out at the beach like she hadn't a worry in the world? She was always caught between her daughter and work. She was tired of having to choose.

Sam took a steadying breath. "Let me get the work done. Maybe I'll finish early, and we can go next Saturday." She didn't know if she could get done by then, but at this point, she was willing to offer hope. "If you help me, I'll get done quicker."

A pool of tears rose to Caden's lash line. "You could get it done in time if you wanted."

That might be true if Landon were helping, but she knew she'd be pressed to finish on her own. "I've got all this work to do and no help. I'm not sure it'll get done on time as it is."

"Landon's helping."

Sam shook her head. "Not anymore."

"Why not?" Caden glared at her.

Sam opened her mouth to explain, then closed it again. What could she say that an eleven-year-old would understand? "It's just the way it is. I'm sorry."

"Maybe he could take me to the beach." Hope lit her face. "I could play with Max in the water. Please, Mom?" Those brown eyes, so like her own, begged.

Sam wanted Landon farther away from them, not closer. Asking him to spend time with her daughter was foolish. And what if Caden slipped and called him Uncle Landon or something? She could just imagine how Landon would hate her if he knew. As much as she needed him to keep his distance, she couldn't bear it if he hated her. She couldn't risk letting Caden go with him.

Sam shook her head. "I'm sorry, Caden."

Her daughter looked ready for a fight, her face all flushed, her mouth pursed.

Sam was beginning to feel a little heated herself. Everything she did was for Caden. Even the sale of this house was for her future, for college. They could go to the beach in Boston anytime, and it wasn't like she hadn't taken her since they'd been on the island. When would Caden learn life wasn't all about her?

Sam bit her tongue and turned to go.

"You're so unfair!"

Sam slammed the door and leaned against it, staring at Caden. Hadn't she just let Caden have an overnighter at a friend's house? Now she wanted something else. Sam's head was beginning to pound again. Caden had no idea how good she had it.

Her daughter blinked, and her tears overflowed. "All you care about is work, work, work!" She dragged her fist across her face, wiping the tears. "You're always leaving."

Sam's fist squeezed the doorknob, and she narrowed her eyes. "I'm leaving for a few minutes, Caden. When my mom left, she left forever."

The air seemed to still, as if waiting for Caden's response.

Fear spread slowly across Caden's face, starting in her eyes and working its way down to her mouth.

Sam studied her, wondering what was going through her head. Did Caden think she might leave her? She remembered what it was like to be a child at the mercy of an adult's whims. Caden probably felt she was at Sam's mercy. Her daughter was dependent upon her. Sam wasn't much, but she was all she had.

She took a step toward Caden, her hand reaching out.

Caden snapped her head toward the TV, an old *SpongeBob* episode Sam knew she was no longer interested in. She was only eleven, and a much younger eleven than Sam had been. Sam had to keep reminding herself of that.

There was anger in the set of her daughter's shoulders, even in the tears that trailed down her face. Sam had to say something, undo what she'd done. But how? Sam never knew what to say anymore. How was she going to handle the teen years if she couldn't deal with Caden now? But maybe all the attitude had nothing to do with adolescence and everything to do with Sam.

The thought was like swallowing a cold stone. "Caden . . ." Sam drew a breath and let it out. "Why don't we paint together today? It might be fun. Then we can go to the beach on Saturday."

Sam would paint all night if she had to. What was a little sleep other than a chance for her past to haunt her?

Caden crossed her arms. "I don't want to go with you." Her words wobbled like fury on stilts.

Sam sighed. So much for trying to accommodate. She felt her own ire rising. "Well, I'm all you've got, kiddo."

Caden looked at Sam, her chin raised in defiance. "I'm going to ask Landon to take me." Her freckles disappeared on her flushed cheeks.

Heat gathered in Sam's temples, where a sledgehammer began to pound rhythmically. "No, you're not."

"Yes, I am! You can't stop me."

Sam had to get a handle on her. She took a breath and forced a calm tone. "You're grounded from TV."

Caden sprang to her feet. "I don't care! I'm telling Landon he's my uncle!"

Sam sucked in a dry breath. It settled heavily in her lungs. "Caden Elaine Owens." She stared at her daughter in shock. Caden sassed her and gave her attitude, but she'd never been this defiant. The girl's face twisted in an expression Sam hadn't seen before, and Sam didn't doubt she meant what she said. "No, you won't." Sam's voice was firm, covering the fear Caden had planted in her.

"You can't stop me." Caden turned and ran to the bedroom, slamming the door.

Even as the sound echoed in her head, Sam realized what Caden said was true.

Twenty-two

Working alone, the painting went slow. Trimming out the house took most of the afternoon, and by the time the sun was sinking in the sky, Sam was glad for an early supper. She and Caden ate in silence on the porch, away from the paint fumes, her daughter ignoring her attempts at conversation.

After Caden put her plate in the sink, she came back out and trotted down the steps. "I'm going for a ride."

Her earlier threat played in Sam's mind. What would stop her from riding down to Landon's house and dumping her secret on his front porch? If he found out about Bailey, it would only be a matter of time before he found out about her part in Bailey's death. The thought jerked Sam from her apathy.

"No, Caden. Stay in the yard."

Caden whipped around, glaring, her hands poised on the handlebars, her foot ready to swing over the seat. "Why?"

"Because I said so." It would have to be enough, because Sam wasn't giving her a better explanation.

Caden pressed her lips together, and Sam wondered if she was going to defy her. Instead, Caden dropped the bike, letting it thump onto the ground. "Fine." She gave Sam one last glare, then

strode through the long grass and toward the shoreline, arms swinging stiffly by her side, her tawny hair blowing behind her. When she
reached the water's edge, she stepped up onto the pier and walked
down its length. At the end, she sat, her back toward Sam, her feet
dangling over the edge.

Sam needed to go back in and paint, but she wondered if she
should leave Caden on the pier without supervision. Sam had done
nothing but say no all day, and the thought of another fight made her
tired. Besides, it was only waist deep there, and if Caden fell in, she
was a good swimmer. Anyway, her daughter wouldn't get in without
her swim cap, and Sam could keep an eye through the window.

She retrieved a new rolling pan and roller from the shed, casting
a look in the direction of Landon's house. She hadn't seen him since
that morning, when she told him to stay away. She wondered if he'd
listen. The thought of not seeing him the next seven days brought
an ache to her middle. When she and Caden left the island, they
may never see him again. The hollow spot inside of her seemed to
stretch out, growing, enveloping more of her.

That's the way you want it, right? She gathered the supplies and
left the shed, remembering Landon holding her outside the shed,
the rain pouring down on them. She remembered how safe she felt
in his arms. He was a refuge in the storm.

*All the more reason to keep away from him, Sam. You don't need
that kind of false security.*

Back in the house, she poured paint in the pan and ran the roller
through it. *Stay focused on the task, Sam, and forget everything else.*
When had worrying done any good?

Sam peeked out at Caden periodically. Her daughter didn't
move from her spot on the end of the pier. How many hours had
Sam spent in that same spot? Often with Landon at her side,

splashing her legs with his foot. Caden would be okay once they got back to Boston. Sam wished she could fast-forward through the week and be on the ferry back to the mainland now. She imagined the freedom she would feel as the island grew small on the horizon.

Suddenly Landon appeared in her daydream, waving good-bye from the shore. *Stop it, Sam.* She shook her head as if to dislodge the picture, then climbed on the ladder to reach the ceiling. The white paint went on smoothly, covering years of dirt and grime, obliterating evidence of Emmett's smoking habit.

A few minutes later, she checked on Caden, reloaded the roller, and climbed the ladder, bracing her thighs against the top. The breeze had died down, leaving the air inside hot and still. She wiped the back of her hand across her forehead. A trickle of sweat ran down her back. Outside, a mower roared to life, and the scent of cut grass drifted through the window.

She extended the roller upward, and it hit the corner of the bedroom door, falling from her hand. Instinctively, she reached out, hoping to catch it before it hit the floor. Her hand grabbed at air. The movement unbalanced her. She clutched at the ladder, but it was too late.

Sam untangled her feet from the ladder, and they hit the floor first. But one foot landed on the roller handle and turned outward.

She heard a snap. A jolt of pain shot up her ankle. She smothered a groan. Sinking to the floor, she pulled her knee to her chest and rocked, squeezing her eyes shut. Sam focused on breathing. *In and out. In and out.* Her breath caught every few seconds as if her body had forgotten how to breathe.

Sam eased her foot to the floor, wondering if she'd broken her ankle. At the very least, she'd snapped a ligament or tendon. She

peeled off her sock inch by inch, shuddering at the pain the movement caused.

The flesh had begun to swell. She needed to get ice on it, quick.
She couldn't afford a trip to the doctor, but if it was only a tendon
or ligament, she could handle it herself.

Sam's ankle throbbed angrily. The kitchen seemed a mile away.
How would she get all the way to the refrigerator? She lay back
against the rug and moaned. The thought of moving her foot an
inch was enough to make her cringe.

She needed Caden. After catching her breath, she propped herself
up and sucked in air, releasing it with her daughter's name as loudly
as she could. She stilled, listening. All she heard was the mower that
had started up awhile ago. With the noise of that, Caden wouldn't
hear her calling.

The phone. A quick scan of the living room told her it was only
a couple of yards away, on the coffee table. She could get to that.
She propped her weight on her palms and used her good foot to
propel her backward. Her right foot dragging, she moved like an
injured crab.

Sam clamped her teeth against the pain. She had broken one
bone—her big toe, when she caught it in Landon's bike tire—but
this was worse. Her joint throbbed so hard, she could feel the injury
in her head.

When she neared the table, she stopped and reached for the phone.
She had two options, and one of them held no appeal. She punched
in Miss Biddle's number, then propped her foot on the coffee table
to elevate it while the phone rang. She grimaced as her calf connected
with the edge of the table.

The ankle had swollen to the size of a softball, and the flesh had
deepened to a shade of purple. She thought she remembered hearing

someone at Caden's gym saying that swelling was good. Maybe she hadn't broken it after all.

Sam realized the phone had rung at least a dozen times. Miss Biddle wasn't home, apparently. She jabbed the off button. The mower hummed in the distance. Even so, she drew a breath and called Caden's name again. Maybe she was near enough to hear now.

After calling three more times, Sam gave up. Elevating her foot had eased the pain to a bearable degree. Sam laid her head back against the sofa and caught her breath. She could call Melanie. She was sure Melanie wouldn't mind coming over. Though it would take longer, it was better than having to call Landon to rescue her again.

Then she realized it was Sunday. Open-house day for Realtors. She punched in Melanie's number anyway and let it ring. *Please, please pick up.* She wet her dry lips and stared at the refrigerator across the house and wished she could beam over the ice tray. Even once she got the ice on, then what? Would she be able to walk? Given the way her foot ached now, she couldn't imagine it bearing her weight.

When Melanie's machine clicked on, Sam hung up. There was no getting around it now. She turned the phone on and dialed Landon's number.

"Hello?"

Sam paused, gathering her courage. "It's me."

"Sam." His tone was so hopeful, she hated having to tell him the reason for her call.

"I need your help. I'm hurt." Her foot slid downward an inch, and the edge of the table cut into her ankle. She sucked in her breath.

"I'll be right there." A click sounded in her ear.

She punched the off button and used her hands to reposition her ankle. *Please don't let it be broken.* How would she finish the house if it was? Even if it wasn't broken, how would she manage? And her job. Would she be back on her feet in seven days? She couldn't afford more time off. Her credit card was nearly maxed, and her savings was gone.

Sam laid her head against the couch and closed her eyes, trying to block out the pain. Ten seconds later, Landon barreled through the door.

"What happened?" He was at her side before she could blink.

"My ankle. I fell off the ladder." She felt stupid once the words rolled off her tongue. Who falls off an indoor ladder? There were only five steps on the thing, and it wasn't like she was doing a high-wire act.

He looked at her foot, taking care not to touch the injury. What an idiot she was. Last night she got drunk, and Landon rescued her. Today she fell off a ladder, and Landon rescued her. It was a disturbing pattern.

Her independent streak rebelled. She didn't want to be rescued. She wanted to take care of herself. She didn't want to need him or anyone else.

You can't even get to the fridge, Sam.

"Be right back."

Sam watched him stride to the kitchen and open the freezer door. He wore a sleeveless shirt that showed off his V-shaped torso and muscular arms. Was it only last night that she'd planted kisses on his arm and snuggled against his neck?

She tore her gaze away from him and studied her ankle. It didn't look like an ankle anymore. It looked like a bloated purple balloon. And it ached like the dickens.

He returned with a bag of frozen peas wrapped in a paper towel.

Sam gritted her teeth when he set it on her ankle.

"We need to take you to the ER."

She shook her head. Regardless of what her insurance might cover, her deductible was high and hadn't been met. "It'll be fine. The ice will help."

He lifted the cold pack. "Look at it, Sam. It needs an X-ray."

She tried to sit up, leaving her leg at a ninety-degree angle. She regretted the movement. "I think it's just a ligament or tendon. I heard something snap."

"What if it was a bone?" He adjusted the placement of the pack, wrapping it around the outside.

"Can't you tell if it's broken?"

"I'm a vet, not a doctor. It needs an X-ray."

Sam huffed. "So examine it. I'll bark twice if it hurts." Okay, so the pain was affecting her attitude. Why didn't he ever listen to her?

He stood and walked to the door. "I'll get my Jeep."

"I never said I'd go," she called as he left. The screen door slapping in place was her only answer.

Sam wanted to get up and lock the door. She was sure it wasn't broken. She could just prop it up and rest, pop a couple of Advil, and it would be fine by morning. But she couldn't get up. Even the thought of getting to his Jeep made her groan.

She knew there would be no deterring Landon at this point, and she was hardly in a position to fight. Sam was going to the ER whether she wanted to or not. She would have to charge her co-pay and worry about the rest of the deductible later. Maybe the house would sell quickly.

When he returned, she realized Caden would have to go with them. "Caden's out on the pier—or she was. Could you get her?"

A moment later, she heard him calling Caden, then the soft rumble of his voice as he talked with her. While Sam waited, she took off the cold pack and lifted herself onto the couch. Her ankle,

now level with her hips, pulsated with pain. She was about to elevate it on the couch's arm when Caden and Landon entered.

"Mom?" Caden looked at Sam's discolored, bloated ankle.

Sam tried to smile. "It's fine, honey. It's just a sprain." She narrowed her eyes at Landon. "But Mr. Reed seems to think I need a
doctor."

Landon hung back in the kitchen while Caden sat by her on the
couch. Sam placed the bag of peas back on her ankle. The swelling
had gotten worse, if anything.

Landon returned with a glass of water and three Advil. Despite
Sam's ire, she wanted to hug him. She gulped the pills and set the
glass on the table.

Caden watched silently while Landon slid his hands under Sam
and eased her off the couch. She held her foot as steady as possible,
but there was no stopping the agony. She settled her arms around
his neck as he turned toward the door.

ঙ   ঙ   ঙ

The Advil had put a small dent in the pain, and now that it was elevated on the gurney, the ache eased. The doctor examined it and
took X-rays. Now they waited for a verdict.

"How you feeling?" Landon asked from his chair beside her bed.
The soggy bag of peas lay across his thigh.

"Better." Sam looked at Caden next to Landon. Her daughter
did her best to fake nonchalance, but Sam knew she was worried.
She gestured toward the peas. "Guess you got out of eating those,
huh?"

Caden's mouth turned up a bit.

The doctor entered the room with an X-ray film, which he put on a board on the wall. The light flicked on. He studied the picture, tilting his head back to look through his tiny glasses.

Seconds later he flipped off the light and turned to Sam. "No break, young lady. Looks like you've torn a ligament, though."

Sam exhaled in relief. "Just as I thought." After sending Landon an I-told-you-so look, she asked the next question bearing down on her. "How long will it take to heal?" She had to finish painting and apply polyurethane to the floors. Those things were absolutely necessary.

"I'll send a nurse in with an instruction sheet, but you need to stay off your feet for forty-eight hours. After that, you can gradually ease your weight back on it. I suggest using a crutch at first. You tore it pretty badly."

Forty-eight hours? "I can't stay off it for two days." She would barely get finished as it was.

"You will if you want it to heal correctly. I can give you a doctor's excuse for work if you need one."

That was a whole other concern. "How long will it take to get back to work?"

"Acute ankle sprains heal in two to six weeks."

Sam's jaw dropped. Hers had better heal in one week, or Patty was going to have a fit.

"I'll send the nurse in. Take care, now." The doctor left the room, pulling the door shut behind him.

"Not what you wanted to hear," Landon said. "But at least it's not broken."

Sam swallowed. "You don't understand. I have to be back at work next Monday. I don't have six weeks. I don't even have two."

"I think he meant it takes that long for it to heal completely. Maybe if you rest it over the next seven days, you'll be able to work, even if you have to limp a little. You can wrap the ankle in order to stabilize it."

Rest it the next week? Landon knew she couldn't do that. The cottage had to be finished. She wouldn't be able to get away from work even for a weekend to come back and work on it. Not with all the time she'd taken off already. Not to mention the travel expense of going back and forth.

Frustration lumped in her throat. "I have to finish the cottage." Couldn't he see how important this was? She'd worked so hard to get it done. For Caden's future.

The nurse came to give her take-home instructions. Rest. No pressure on it at all. Ice. Compression. Elevation. For forty-eight hours. After delivering the directions, she left to retrieve a wheelchair.

"I can help, Mom." Caden's small voice begged her attention. Her mask of indifference had lifted, and Sam caught a glimpse of the old Caden.

"With what?"

"The painting and stuff. I can do it."

Caden couldn't possibly do all the work. Sam was proud she'd offered. She smiled at her daughter. "I appreciate that, hon." The ache in her ankle made her want to check out for a while. "We'll figure it out later, all right?"

There was really nothing to figure out. Sam would have to do the work. She could load up on painkillers and paint on one leg, right? She'd wrap her ankle during the day and elevate and ice it at night. She could hop around to keep her weight off it. She imagined the jarring it would cause and cringed. Maybe she could borrow a crutch from someone.

Landon came to her bedside and rested his hands on the metal rails. "I see that look in your eyes."

"What?" she asked innocently.

"You need to do what the doc said. Otherwise, you won't be able to work come next Monday. Or worse yet, your ankle won't heal right."

Sam lowered her voice so Caden wouldn't hear. "You know I can't do that. There's too much work for a kid. The floors will be a challenge even for me."

"Then just leave it. Does it really matter if they're done? The house will sell as is."

How could he understand how much every dollar counted to her? He was a successful veterinarian, and she was a struggling single mother. "You wouldn't understand."

A house in tiptop shape could fetch thousands more than a house that still needed work. Stopping now was like throwing thousands of dollars into the sea. She'd worked too hard to be so wasteful.

"I can see by the stubborn set of your jaw that I'm wasting my breath."

Good. Maybe he would stop pestering her about it.

He sighed. "Fine. I'll take off work this week and—"

"No," she said firmly. She wasn't putting him out again. He was always helping her.

"—move my appointments to next week. I can just work extra hours . . . when you're gone." Something deadened in his eyes when he said the last part. He looked down as his fists tightened around the bed rail.

"No," she said again. "This is my problem, and I'll handle it."

"I've got vacation time coming, no big deal." He shrugged one shoulder.

"Some vacation. You'll work on my house all week, then work extra hours when you get back."

"We're friends. Friends are there for each other, right?" His green eyes warmed again. For just a moment she wanted to get lost in them.

He made it sound like nothing. Sure, friends were supposed to be there for each other, but why was it always him being there for her? It made her feel needy. She wasn't needy.

The nurse entered with a wheelchair, her wide hips swaying. "All right, Miss Owens, let's get you on your way."

Sam sat up, giving Landon one last look. "This conversation isn't over," she said quietly.

He smiled, a little too cocky for her liking. "It is. You just don't know it yet."

Twenty-three

From Sam's vantage on the couch, she watched Landon and Caden roll on paint. Pillows propped up her foot on the coffee table, and Ace bandages encompassed her swollen ankle.

The pain was better today but had awakened her at least a dozen times in the night, forcing her to hobble from the couch through the house for the Advil.

Since this morning, though, Caden hadn't let her get up once. Landon came early and set to work. Caden dutifully brought out the bag of peas every three hours and set the timer on the stove for twenty minutes.

Sam measured time by her ice pack. The TV was off by her own choice; there was nothing worthwhile to watch. Caden tuned the radio to an oldies station, and as Sam watched Landon pour paint into the pan, she tapped her fingers to the upbeat tune.

"Hungry yet?" he asked.

She was tempted to say yes just to relieve the boredom. "No."

"Need more Advil?"

"It's not time yet," Caden answered. "The bottle says every four to six hours."

"Okay, then, Nurse Owens." Landon tossed Caden a smile.

Sam was surprised at her daughter's response to the injury. She'd never seen this mother hen side, and she realized Caden would make a great big sister. After their argument the day before, she was relieved her daughter's anger had been curbed, even though it had taken an injury to do so.

Still, Sam felt better about staying within earshot of Caden and Landon. One slip was all it would take to unload her secret and change everything.

Awhile later, Landon prepared a simple lunch and carried it to the backyard, then he lifted Sam off the sofa as if she weighed nothing.

Sam rested her arm on his shoulder. "This is ridiculous. I feel so helpless."

"You're not helpless, just injured. Let someone lend a hand for a change."

She tried to relax her body in his arms. He was always helping her, for heaven's sake. *And you're always pushing him away.*

Caden was diving into her sandwich when Landon settled Sam into a chair and pulled up another one to elevate her foot.

Above the whooshing sound of the waves rushing the shoreline, Sam heard the crunch of gravel in the driveway.

"I'll be right back." Landon trotted down the porch steps and around the house.

"Wonder who that is." Sam dug into the bologna sandwich and chips, gulping down the ice water. The throbbing in her ankle intensified, and she realized it was time for medication.

Caden offered to get it, and while she was in the house, Landon returned, holding two crutches.

She grinned wryly. "Where did those come from?"

"Scott. Hopefully they're the right height." He leaned them against the wall at her side, then seated himself across from her.

Sam was surprised Scott was letting her borrow them. She'd always figured him for the sort whose kindergarten report card read "Does not share with others." Besides, it was obvious the man wanted her gone yesterday, and that he disapproved of her friendship with Landon. Little did he know she didn't want Landon here any more than he did.

Sam set her glass back on the table. "Getting tired of carrying me around?"

"Yep." He smiled around the bite of food.

When they were finished eating, she hobbled back into the house on the crutches. By the time she made it to the couch, she was glad to elevate her ankle again. The jarring steps had aggravated it, and it seemed all the blood had rushed down, resuming the staccato throb.

Landon and Caden finished the kitchen and moved into the living room. The furniture was squished into the center of the room to allow access to the walls. "Bridge Over Troubled Water" played in the background. Not her favorite song. She laid her head against the sofa back and listened to the sucking sound of the rollers working against the walls. The window behind her was open, and fresh air trickled in, alleviating the heavy smell of paint fumes.

Landon balanced on the ladder, rolling paint onto the ceiling. His denim shorts hugged his hips, and Sam followed the long line of his sturdy legs to his tennis shoes. He rose up on his toes, and his calf muscles bunched in hard knots. She looked away.

She must be bored if she was checking out Landon. Wasn't there a book or magazine anywhere in this stinking house? Sam tapped her good foot and drummed her fingers on the end table. She wanted up! She wanted out of here. She wanted to do the work herself, not sit here watching others do it. Stupid ankle.

Aretha Franklin's voice crooned about respect from the radio. Caden turned it up, then resumed rolling the wall beside Landon's ladder. He began singing, working in time with the beat.

Seconds later, Caden joined him. She swayed with the rhythm, waggling her head as she sang the words.

Caden and Landon traded a smile, singing in unison. Sam's mouth curved into a grin. Caden was a good dancer. She was doing more dancing than painting as her roller went over and over the same spot.

Landon wasn't doing much better. When Aretha started on the chorus, he turned toward Caden, holding the roller like a mike, and belted it out.

Caden's laugh was more melodic than the music. She turned her roller up and sang with him. They faced each other, cranking out the lyrics at the top of their lungs. Caden shimmied her shoulders, and Landon wiggled his hips like a defective backup singer.

A laugh caught in Sam's throat.

Landon finished the chorus on an odd pitch. "Take it, Sam." He pointed to her.

Sam said rather than sang the words. "Sock it to me." No one wanted to hear her sing.

Caden called over the music, still bopping to the song. "You can do better than that, Mom."

Next time the line came, Sam sang it. She couldn't be any worse than Landon.

Landon whooped, then stepped down from the ladder and took the main part while Caden did the backup.

Sam watched, knowing a silly grin had spread across her face, but she couldn't look half as silly as the two of them bebopping around the living room with rollers in their hands. They weren't getting much done, but they were having a blast.

Watching her daughter interact with a man triggered something in her. The music's volume seemed to decrease as she watched them together, behaving like father and daughter. How many days like this had Caden missed? She was nearly a teenager, and her formative years were quickly fading. How would the lack of a dad affect her future? How would she learn how to relate to a man when she'd had no role model?

Landon set down his roller and took Caden's, setting it in the pan. He took her hand and twirled her toward him, then back out. Landon still had two left feet, despite his claim that he'd outgrown them. His jerky moves made Caden look all the more graceful.

Caden laughed as she spun. "Is this the way they did it in the olden days?"

"Hey," he said. "Watch it."

"This is how they dance now." Caden did a move with her feet, then wiggled her hips as Aretha crooned.

"Not bad. You must have gotten your rhythm from your mom." Landon did a move that reminded her of a lame turkey, bobbing his chin in and out.

Sam and Caden laughed.

"Ha!" Caden shouted over the music. "Mom can't dance."

He raised his eyebrows at Sam. "Too bad about your bum ankle, or you'd have to show her your stuff."

"Yeah, too bad," Sam said sarcastically.

When the song wound down and the next one started, Caden turned the volume down. Landon gave Caden a high five, then handed back her roller.

Sam watched them paint side by side, wishing things were

different for Caden. What if Bailey had lived? Would he have married her? How would Landon have reacted? Sam wasn't sure she could have gone through with it. Either way, she'd cheated Caden out of a father. The thought stabbed her hard.

Sam shook the thought away. She didn't want to go back to that dark night. Hard as it was to live in the present, it beat living in the past.

Caden finished a portion of the wall and moved the paint pan to the other side of the ladder, then loaded her roller.

Landon whistled to the tune on the radio while he rolled over a water leak on the ceiling. When he needed more paint, he descended the ladder.

"How about if we grill burgers tonight?" He addressed Sam. "I can grab some at the grocery."

She was about to agree when she noticed his foot descending straight toward the paint pan. "Watch ou—"

His tennis shoe landed square in the middle of the pan. Paint sloshed out over the metal edges.

He looked down, going still, his mouth going slack.

Sam sucked in her breath.

"What?" Caden asked, then peeked around the ladder. Her mouth dropped. "Oh."

Landon lifted his foot and watched the paint run off his shoe, trickling back into the pan.

A laugh bubbled up inside, and Sam pressed her lips together.

"How"—he paused, shaking his leg to get the paint off—"did the pan get over here?" He slowly turned toward Caden, a funny scowl on his face.

Sam could tell her daughter was torn between horror and humor. "I"—her mouth worked—"I had to move it."

"You had to move it," Landon repeated.

"It was in the way." Her eyes were as wide as silver dollars. "I'm sorry." A giggle sneaked out, contradicting the apology.

"You look real sorry." He shook his foot again.

It reminded her of the way Max's leg shook when his belly was rubbed.

Another laugh sneaked out of Caden's mouth.

"That's it." Landon broke out toward Caden, his wet foot sliding on the plastic.

Caden squealed and took off toward the door. Landon followed, leaving white footprints behind on the drop cloth. Sam wished she could follow, especially when she heard a belly laugh from Caden that she hadn't heard since she used to blow on Caden's toddler belly.

When the phone rang, she reached for it and punched it on, realizing her jaws ached from smiling.

꒰ꛋ꒱   ꒰ꛋ꒱   ꒰ꛋ꒱

By the time Landon finished chasing and tickling Caden, they were out of breath. He'd forgotten how much fun kids were. He realized Caden was probably starved for male attention. She was eating it up.

He took off his shoe and ran it under the outdoor spigot, rubbing the paint away with his fingers.

Caden plopped down on the grass nearby, breathing hard and still smiling. "I'm tired."

When he was finished cleaning his shoe, he took the other one off and helped Caden up. "Piggyback ride?" He turned and offered his back.

"I'm too old for that." Her eyes said something different.

"Says who? Hop on." It was all the encouragement she needed. He squatted, and she wrapped her little arms around his neck.

"Hang on," Landon said as he stood, hooking his elbows around her knees. She laughed as he rose to his feet. The sound was the sheer delight of a child. If she was struggling with an adolescent attitude as Sam said, all traces of it were gone now.

He jogged up the porch steps, bouncing Caden as much as possible. She tightened her arms around his neck.

He gasped. "You're choking me."

He turned and let Caden open the screen door of the porch. After she let go, he stopped and let it swing into her backside.

"Hey!"

"Sorry." He snickered.

"Yeah, you sound real sorry." She tightened her arms around his neck in a chokehold.

He was laughing when he entered the house. "Your daughter—" He stopped when he saw Sam was on the phone.

She glanced at him, then quickly looked away.

He eased Caden off his back and went to retrieve his roller. Then he saw the wet paint he'd trailed across the plastic and went for the roll of paper towels. When he returned, he wiped up the mess. Sam's quiet voice carried across the room.

"Well, uh—I really can't. I fell off a ladder and twisted my ankle yesterday." She explained the situation.

Landon wiped harder at the mess than necessary. He could tell it was Tully on the phone. Landon supposed the guy wasn't going to give up until he got what he wanted.

Over his dead body.

"No, that's okay," Sam said into the phone. "I've got it covered."

She was talking about the work on the house. *She* had it covered?

He nailed her with a look, which she missed entirely because she was looking the other way.

"Sure. Sure. Okay."

Was he asking her out? Sam couldn't even walk across the room, much less go on a date with that idiot.

"All right. See you." She punched the phone off, and it clunked as she set it on the end table.

The mood in the room shifted. Even Caden seemed to sense it and went back to work quietly. He moved the pan away and climbed the ladder. Was Sam going out with Tully again? Her ankle would only keep her off her feet so long, and then what? What if she wanted Tully?

The clock was ticking. Landon had six more days with Sam, and the reality of it hit him with new urgency. Six more days to make her see how much he loved her. Six more days to make her see she had nothing to fear. But would six days be enough, or would she and Caden go back to Boston and leave him forever?

Twenty-four

Rain came later in the afternoon, changing their plans from a back-yard barbeque to hot dogs under the broiler. Tully's phone call had somehow deflated the fun. Landon brooded, and Caden looked between the adults with speculative glances.

Later that night, Caden took her bath, then Sam sent her to bed. She must have been tired, because she didn't complain. Landon insisted on finishing the ceiling before he called it a night.

Sam sat on the couch, the pack of peas on her ankle growing soggy. Outside, rain still pattered against the leaves. The damp carried through the screen, alleviating the smell of paint.

The afternoon had been filled with taut silences, and Sam never felt like more of a burden. She wished she could pay someone to finish the house, but she had eighty-two dollars left, hardly enough to get them through the week. A loan would take too long, even if she could get one, and she didn't think she could.

Landon was giving up his vacation to help her out. As much as her helplessness rankled, she couldn't forget that. "I'm sorry you have to do this."

He was near the doorway of Emmett's room, the ladder angling toward the wall. "I don't mind." His words were clipped.

Sam wanted to tell him to go. She wanted to get up and finish the work herself, but her pounding ankle stopped her. She still couldn't set it on the ground without pain. There was no way it could bear her weight.

"It's obvious you don't want to be here. You've hardly said a word all afternoon."

"I don't mind being here as long as I don't have to overhear conversations with your boyfriend."

Heat flooded Sam's face, and she looked away. "He's not my boyfriend."

"Could have fooled me." The bristles of the brush jabbed at the corner of the ceiling.

Maybe he was remembering the way he carried her half-naked from Tully's house. Sure, she almost slept with him, but she was drunk. That didn't make Tully her boyfriend. She'd allowed herself to get wasted and made a foolish decision.

Hadn't Landon ever done something foolish? She watched him painting, his lips pressed together. No, Landon was too prudent for that. But surely there had been other women. Girlfriends.

Sam watched his arm move the brush up and down in short strokes. His shirt revealed tanned skin and well-defined muscles. No man who looked like him had trouble attracting women. Especially when the inside matched the outside. She couldn't say that about many people. So why was he still unattached?

"What about you?" she dared. "Have you had any serious relationships?" She was suddenly unsure she wanted to hear the answer. She wondered if anything was becoming of him and Melanie. "How are things going with—"

"If you so much as whisper Melanie's name, I'm out of here."

She held up her right hand, palm out. "I thought she liked you."

He studied her, and his face softened, the corners of his mouth relaxing. "She only agreed to the double date to help me, Sam. She and I are friends, and we'll never be anything more."

"Oh."

He descended the ladder. "As far as girlfriends, there have been a couple. Not very serious, though." He leaned back, half sitting, and propped his foot on the lowest rung.

Sam waited for him to go on, curious about the women who'd captured his attention. "Anyone I know?"

He shook his head. "Don't think so." He crossed the room and lifted the bag of peas from her ankle. "Better get this back in the freezer."

"Wait." She touched his arm. When he looked at her, she withdrew her hand and returned it to her lap. "Tell me about them." She tried for nonchalance. "Have pity on a bored, injured woman."

"Are you implying my love life is boring?"

"On the contrary. I'm curious to know how the great Landon Reed has avoided the holy bonds of matrimony."

"I could ask you the same thing."

"You first." She said it like a dare.

He heaved a sigh. "Fine." The other end of the sofa sank with his weight. "What do you want to know?"

Sam wanted to know everything. Had he been in love? Why had they broken up? Had they broken his heart? "Whatever you want to tell."

He leaned over, setting the brush in the pan, then sat back. "I've had two serious relationships. Tracie was first. We dated about six months."

When he didn't go on, she prodded him. "What was she like?"

"Tracie?" He shifted toward Sam. "Outgoing, vivacious."

"Cheerleader type?" She had been right on target with Melanie.

"Exactly."

No one could be more opposite Sam's personality, and something in that bothered her.

"Drove me nuts." He grinned at Sam.

She found herself smiling back. "Why?"

As his grin slipped away, a frown creased his brow. "There was never any quiet. It was all go-go-go, like life was a party and she didn't want to miss a moment of it."

"What's wrong with that?"

"It was exhausting. She was exhausting."

"So that's why you broke up?" The thought brought her relief for some strange reason.

"That, and Max didn't like her."

Sam laughed. She couldn't imagine Max disliking anyone. He was a big black teddy bear. "What about the other one?"

"Max liked her."

She elbowed him. "That's not what I meant."

He spread his paint-stained hands across his thighs. "Jennifer. We dated for almost a year."

She saw his expression change. His eyes grew more thoughtful, and he looked down at his hands, scratching dried paint from his thumbnail. Jennifer had meant something to him. "Recently?"

"Fairly. Broke up a couple of months ago." He propped his knee on the couch beside her, almost touching her thigh.

"What was she like?"

"She was quieter—thank God." He shared a smile with her. "Sweet lady. The kind who wouldn't say a bad word about anyone." He breathed a laugh. "She used to say I was the last honorable man on earth. She was a volunteer with me on the Marine Mammal Stranding Team."

"You seem fond of her. What happened?" Sam wondered for a moment if she'd died. His talk of her held sadness.

"Nothing really happened. I just—" He puckered his eyebrows and shook his head. "There wasn't a spark for me, you know? I cared for her a lot. I respected her. I enjoyed her company."

"How did she feel?" Sam leaned her head against the sofa back and watched him.

"She said she loved me, and as much as I cared for her, as much as I wanted to fall in love with her, I just didn't return those feelings."

"So you broke up with her?"

"It was hard. She didn't deserve to be hurt, but it wasn't fair to stay in a relationship that wasn't going anywhere."

"Have you seen her since?"

"A few weeks ago on a Stranding Team project." He nudged her leg. "Enough about me. Tell me about the men in your life."

They didn't have time to talk about all the men who'd passed through her life. Most of them meant nothing. Some of them were only faces in her mind. "There's only one that was serious." Now that it was her turn, she felt under a microscope.

"Go on."

Sam didn't want to talk about herself, but Landon had opened up. It was only fair. "His name was Jeremy. He was a CPA in a big firm back in Boston." What did she want to share about Jeremy? He'd been as close to a boyfriend as she ever had. They went every-where together for over a year. After a while, he complained that she didn't let him in, that she pulled away when he hugged her.

"What happened?"

He asked me to marry him. Caden was eight, and he was great with her. Sam had thought they were headed for marriage, but once he got down on his knee on the manicured lawn of Boston Common, fear rocketed through Sam. Her heart felt like it would burst from her chest, and she couldn't breathe fast enough to keep up with her pulse.

Even now, her mouth grew dry just thinking about it.

She shrugged. "It didn't work out."

"Come on. I spilled my guts."

Landon's big hand rested on his thigh. It was inches from her own, his long fingers tapering down to blunt fingernails. Hands that could tighten into fists and fend off an enemy. Hands that could open to caress and soothe.

"I don't know what happened. He asked me to marry him."

His eyebrows hiked upward. "He did?"

She scowled. "You don't have to look so surprised."

"It's not that. It's just—that's pretty serious." He studied her. "You said no?"

She remembered the way Jeremy's face fell. Like gravity pulled everything downward in one slow, agonizing move. She had known they were moving in that direction; she just didn't how she felt until he asked.

"It didn't feel right." *You were afraid.* There was no denying the fear she experienced when he pulled out the pink velvet jewelry box and opened it. She didn't stop to question her decision at the time. She just knew she couldn't do it.

Sam didn't want to talk about Jeremy anymore. "So you've never proposed to anyone?" she asked.

"Nope." He brushed her hair behind her shoulder, sending shivers along her scalp. The earlier tension had faded, but a new kind of tension filled the air, mingling with the smell of damp earth.

"Why?" It came out as a whisper.

His gaze swept across her face like a gentle caress. He was Landon, the boy who protected her from bullies, the man who was still her savior. His love for her shone through his eyes. Though she didn't deserve it, she soaked it up.

He ran the backs of his fingers across her cheek. "Ah, Sam. You already know the answer."

Her belly tightened, and the pain in her ankle was forgotten.

His eyes locked with hers, then lowered to her lips. He leaned toward her, and she could feel a desperate anticipation building inside.

"Mom?"

Sam drew back quickly at the sound of her daughter's voice.

Landon's head fell forward, his chin nearly touching his shirt.

She looked around him at Caden, who stared at them as if she'd forgotten what she was about to say. Sam realized her daughter was grown up enough to know she'd interrupted something. "What is it, honey?" She sounded out of breath.

"I was just—um—wondering if we could invite Amber over tomorrow." Her sentence was a decrescendo, as if the importance of it had faded in light of this new discovery.

"We'll see. Go on back to bed now."

"Okay. Good night."

"'Night," she called.

Caden padded back through the bedroom doorway and pulled the door shut. Sam leaned her head back. The mood had been broken, and now she only felt awkward. She wondered what Caden was thinking.

"Your daughter has rotten timing."

The corner of Landon's mouth was tucked in. She couldn't help but smile at his pitiful look.

"It's late anyway," he said. "You need your rest." He stood and stretched, then retrieved three Advil and a glass of water from the kitchen. When he returned, he handed her the pillow and helped her shift on the sofa so that her foot was propped on the couch's arm. Once she was settled, he draped the faded quilt over her and set the phone nearby.

He sat on the edge of the sofa beside her. "Want anything else before I go?"

She wanted the moment back. She wanted to feel his lips on hers. She wanted him to stay. "No," she said instead.

"All right, then. I'll lock the door on my way out."

"Okay."

He pulled the quilt up to her chin and tucked the blanket around her. Then he leaned down and placed a kiss on her forehead. "Good night." The movement was soft but quick and left her wanting so much more.

As he walked away, turning the lock and shutting the door behind him, she felt like a petulant child.

Twenty-five

After Landon left, Sam couldn't sleep. Keeping her foot elevated was a necessity, but sleeping on her back was a drag. From her spot on the couch, she could see straight into Emmett's room. She could almost see his brawny frame coming through the door, the Winston clamped between his lips.

Sam threw off the quilt and gathered her crutches, pulling herself upright. The living room lamp turned on with a click, and she navigated the maze of furniture. When she made it to the doorway, she saw the letter from her mom lying on the bed. She stopped, balancing on one foot and the crutches.

She should have been told about the letter long ago. Yet again Emmett's cruel hand reached from the grave. She remembered all the nights she lay in bed, listening to the water rushing the shoreline, wondering if the tide would bring her mom back to her the way it had carried her away. She waited and hoped and begged God to bring her home the same way she'd begged for her dad after he died.

And all that time, her mom's final letter lay in the next room. Maybe it would have closed the door on Sam's dream of her return. A closed door was better than a false one. She had learned that lesson well.

Sam wondered if Landon thought she was a coward for not reading it. The thought chafed. *Maybe you are a coward, Sam. It's only
an old letter, words on paper. How can it hurt you now?*

She was many things, but a coward was not one of them. She
crossed the space in one clumsy movement and snatched the letter
from the quilt. Tucking it under her arm, she pulled the door shut
and returned to the couch.

Her foot ached from all the motion, so she propped it on the
wooden coffee table and leaned back. The envelope was well worn,
like it had been opened and read a hundred times. She couldn't
imagine Emmett lingering over it like a lovesick fool.

Before she could stop herself, she pulled up the flap and slid out
the sheet of notebook paper. Her mom's neat script slanted across
the page. Sam's eyes devoured the words.

Emmett,

I'm sorry I left you the way I did. I knew if I told you how I felt
you would sweet-talk me into staying, and I'm not strong enough
to say no to you. There is a restlessness in me—it has always been
there inside me. I was suffocating there on the island where so many
bad memories lay waiting for me.

When we married I thought I would be able to pick up and move
on after John died. I have tried my best, but I now know that marry-
ing you wasn't fair to either of us. I signed the house over to you. It's
all I have to give you. I will file for divorce as soon as I have the money.

I'm sorry.

Ellen

Sam scanned the words again. She looked for her name or some
mention of her but didn't find it. The hollow place inside of her

swelled and swallowed her whole. Her mom never mentioned her. Not once.

Emmett hadn't kept her mom's last words from her. None existed.

The letter was only about her mom. Her thoughts. Her feelings. Her life. *Well, what about me, Mom? What about the child you abandoned so you could follow your own selfish dreams? What about the kid who sat at the end of the pier, watching for your boat for weeks after you left? What about the girl who cried alone in the darkness of her closet?*

Sam's hands shook with anger. She folded the letter and ripped it in half, then ripped it again and again for good measure, until all that was left was bits of paper. Some landed on her lap; other pieces fell to the floor between the sofa and table.

Many nights she'd lain in bed wondering if her mom was out there somewhere aching for the daughter she left. Sam imagined her guilt and regret. She imagined her showing up on her doorstep someday, full of apologies.

Now the truth smacked Sam in the face. In one quick gesture, she swept the pieces of paper off her lap. She felt rejected all over again. She'd thought her mom didn't have the power to hurt her anymore. That she'd already done all the damage one mom could do.

She was wrong.

ॐ   ॐ   ॐ

Sam awoke to a knock on the door. Her eyes were heavy, and the sun shining through the curtains stung them. She lifted her foot down and realized the Advil had worn off sometime after she fell asleep.

"Caden," she called. "The door."

"Take your time," Landon called from the porch. "It's just me."

By the time Caden padded through the living room, she'd rubbed the sleep from her eyes and ran her hand through her tangled hair. A yawn threatened, but she stifled it.

Caden unlocked and swung open the door.

"Breakfast is served," said Landon. He balanced a white box on his palm like a server with a tray.

"Donuts!" Caden clapped her hands together, bouncing on the balls of her bare feet.

"Good morning, ladies." He set the box on the coffee table.

Landon's presence warmed Sam from the inside out. "'Morning." She knew she was a mess. She hadn't fallen asleep until way after midnight.

"Caden, can you get the paper plates and napkins?" Landon asked.

"Sure." She watched her daughter run to do his bidding, wishing Caden were so compliant for her.

Her ankle hurting, she set her foot on the table and reached for the bottle of Advil.

After dining on donuts, Sam showered as best she could on one leg while Caden and Landon piled the living room furniture into the kitchen. By the time she was dressed, Landon was sweeping the wood floor in preparation for the polyurethane finish, and she remembered her mom's letter. Sam looked at the center of the living room, now bare. The bits of paper were gone, and she wondered what Landon had thought when he saw them. *It doesn't really matter, does it? I have a right to my anger.*

Determined not to let her mom ruin the day, Sam decided to put the letter behind her. With fresh perspective, she surveyed the room. Now that the rugs and furniture were gone, she could see stains. Her heart sank.

"Don't worry," Landon said. "I refinished the floors when I moved into my mom and dad's, so I know how to get those out. They look like surface stains. Are you sure you don't want me to refinish the floor? If I run out of time, I could always finish it after you leave."

"While you're working extra hours to make up for this so-called vacation? I don't think so."

Landon retrieved his dad's old drum sander and insisted she sit in the sun while he worked. "It's going to get hot and dusty in here," he explained. "Anyway, you could use some fresh air."

He brought her a fresh bandage and the bag of frozen peas, and she rewrapped her ankle and set the bag on it. The Advil had kicked in, and for the first time since the injury, her ankle didn't hurt.

Since Caden couldn't help with the floor, Sam let her invite Amber over. They drew pictures on the pier boards with sidewalk chalk until the sun grew hot, then they waded into the cool water, squatting until their slender shoulders skimmed the surface. Their laughter floated on the breeze, mingling with the leaves that danced overhead, shading her from the hot sun.

After dinner, Melanie called. "I was getting ready to come get Amber and wondered if Caden would like to spend the night again."

The girls responded with loud squeals, especially when Melanie promised to take them to the beach the next day.

By the time they left, twilight had settled over the yard, bringing out the night sounds she remembered so well. Sam leaned back on the porch chair, listening to the orchestra through the screen, her hand resting on Max's head.

"The dust has settled if you want to go back inside." The door squeaked as Landon stepped through it. He handed her a glass of soda, and the ice tinkled in the glass as she took it.

"Nah. It smells better out here." The smell of paint fumes had faded, but all the sanding left a sawdust smell.

Max walked to the screen door and pushed, letting himself out.

Landon sank into the chair beside her. "It's all cleaned up and ready for a coat of varnish. Sorry the stains took so long. I'd hoped to start varnishing this afternoon."

"You hardly owe me an apology. Anyway, I think I'll be able to help tomorrow, so we'll get back on track."

Sam could feel his gaze on her. "You don't want to rush it."

"It hardly even hurts now. And I can put my weight on it."

He stared at her. "Sam."

She stopped herself from rolling her eyes. "I'll take breaks." She pinned him with a look until she was sure he understood that she wasn't backing down.

"You're the most stubborn woman I've ever known."

She cocked an eyebrow. "I prefer to call it *determined*."

"Most stubborn people do. And don't forget, I taught you to drive."

Sam humphed. "What's that got to do with anything?" She lifted the soda to her lips and let the fizzy liquid glide down her throat.

"Do the words *stick shift* and *'Sconset* ring a bell?"

She hadn't thought about that in years. A smile threatened. Emmett wouldn't let her use his car, so Mrs. Reed let Landon teach Sam to drive in her old beat-up Citation. It had taken them two hours to reach 'Sconset, normally a fifteen-minute drive.

"So it took me a while to get there." She cocked her head like Max. "With a little determination, I managed."

"And then insisted on driving back."

"So what?"

"In the dark."

"Are you afraid of boogeymen?"

"Three hours and forty-five minutes to 'Sconset and back. My knuckles were white for a week."

"But I learned to drive a stick shift."

"Stubborn."

"Determined."

Sam relaxed into her chair, listening to the oscillating buzz of insects and the ever-present whoosh of waves lapping the shoreline. Darkness had swallowed up the heat of the day, and the breeze that slipped through the screen refreshed her.

"Listen to that," Landon said. "It's so peaceful."

She closed her eyes and let her ears do all the work. To her, the sound was comforting. It had lulled her to sleep many a night when everything else was so frightening. "You love it here, don't you?"

A loon called out from somewhere near the shoreline.

"I really do," he said.

She remembered loving this place before her dad died. But then things happened that tainted the island, coloring it a gloomy shade of gray. She had to admit the shadows had lifted a bit recently.

"The winters stink," she said. Especially along the shoreline, where cold winds whipped across the ocean. It was almost impossible to keep a house warm. Not to mention expensive.

"True. But the summers are worth it." The cushion on his chair crinkled as he shifted. "Besides, I have good memories here."

The irony struck her that although they had grown up two doors apart during the same time period, their childhoods were polar opposites. She laughed wryly.

"Come on, they weren't all bad." She could tell he'd turned toward her by the sound of his voice. "Remember the time capsule we buried? It took you five weeks to decide what should be in it. If it had been up to me, I would have taken five minutes."

Sam opened her eyes and turned toward him. She hadn't realized the chairs were so close together. "I remember." They'd dug it up the summer they graduated and laughed at the items she'd selected: An unopened pack of Hubba Bubba bubble gum, two ticket stubs to *Home Alone*, a cassette tape of *The Joshua Tree* by U2, and a beaded bracelet Landon had made for her. She wondered what they'd done with those things.

The light from the living room window lit Landon's face, and a shadow settled into the cleft of his chin. "And the time you found that dead bird and insisted we have a memorial service."

That was before her dad died, before all the good had been sucked from her life. She found the starling under a bush in Miss Biddle's yard. Her tender heart had broken. "That's not a good memory."

His lips twitched. "You sang Simon and Garfunkel's 'Sparrow' and buried the thing in a Pop-Tarts box."

Sam remembered Landon digging the shallow hole in his mom's flower garden and waiting patiently for her to finish. "Okay, I see the humor."

"And then there was the time—"

"Okay, okay, I get your point. There were good memories too." It was just that the bad outweighed them by a sandy beach mile. She studied Landon's face. He was at the center of every good memory since her dad's passing. His presence brought her joy and peace. Maybe that's why her life had been so empty since she left the island. Maybe Landon was the healing water that would quench her loneliness. She let the thought wash over her the way Landon's gaze washed over her now. In the depth of his eyes was a fathom-less pool of emotion. In the strength of his arms was stability. In the heart of his soul was a steadiness she longed for.

His eyes flickered down to her lips. "Sam," he whispered.

The sound of her name on his lips ignited a yearning in her. A yearning for comfort. For joy. For love. A need to surrender to this aching desire.

Caden wasn't here.

The bow in his lip begged to be touched. She leaned toward him, wanting to feel his mouth on hers. His fingers cupped her chin as they closed the gap. His breath was the softest whisper on her skin. As her eyes fluttered closed, she felt the warmth of his lips. Her palm closed around the roughness of his jawline.

He deepened the kiss, and she arched closer, cursing the arm of the chair that dug into her ribs, separating them. It was the way a kiss should be, stopping time, stealing breath.

He drew back, and a whimper left her throat. But he was on his knees in front of her before she could say a word. He grasped her waist and pulled her into him. He framed her face with his gentle hands and kissed her again. Her hands slid around his back.

His mouth was patient on hers. "Sam," he whispered against her lips.

Sam clutched at his shoulders, wanting to be closer, wanting to climb inside him. She wasn't sure even then she would be close enough.

His fingers worked into her hair, sending shivers down her spine. "Sam." He paused, his lips a breath away. "I love you so much."

His lips were on hers again, and she let his words sink in and fill the hole inside her. *I love you too, Landon.* For the first time she knew with certainty it was true. She not only loved him now; she had loved him long before she ever left. It was why she'd hated him for leaving. Why she'd told herself she didn't care if he left. Why she'd felt the need to prove it by sleeping with his brother. It was apparent in the way she responded to him, in the way she compared every man to him, in the way she'd carried him with her for the past eleven years. She wondered that she hadn't seen it until now.

Sam clung to him, feeling his love in the gentle passion of his kiss. She hadn't said the words to him. She'd never said them to any man. They worked their way up, ready to roll off her tongue, but her throat closed up, tightening around her voice like a boa constrictor around its prey.

Why couldn't she say it?

Because you'd be a fool to tell him, Sam.

The thought was an unwelcome intruder. She wanted to push the door closed on it, but it came from deep inside.

No. He loves me.

So did your dad. And he left you.

No! He died. He didn't leave me.

Same difference, isn't it?

It wasn't the same. He hadn't wanted to leave her. Sam's lips moved against Landon's, and she struggled to draw in air.

And what about your mom? She said she loved you too.

She loved me in her own way.

She didn't even mention you in her letter. You can't trust love, Sam. Haven't you learned that yet? You're a fool.

Her emotions tugged her back and forth in a familiar battle she wanted to win this time. She could trust Landon. She could. She leaned into him and grasped his shirt, knotting it up in her fist.

He already left you once.

It was only for college. He was going to come back. He did come back. He loved me. He still loves me. This is right, I know it is.

If it's so right, why are you afraid?

The voice held enough truth to shake her. Tully didn't make her feel afraid. Neither did the other men she went out with. They made her feel empowered, strong, capable. With Landon she felt weak and afraid. Helpless.

And protected.

Who will protect you when he leaves?

Landon withdrew his lips from hers, searching her face. "What's wrong?"

Her dad had made her feel protected too. Even her mom, to a degree. She realized it the moment her mom left her at Emmett's mercy. Sam had depended on them, and their abandonment pulled the proverbial rug from under her. The shock never left her. It was burned into every cell of her body. Needing someone was a bad thing. Why had she forgotten?

Sam placed her hands on Landon's shoulders and pushed, giving herself space to breathe. Her heart threatened to break through her ribs. She felt like she was in the dark closet, trapped and afraid.

"Sam?" His eyes burned into hers, a cocktail of emotion. Confusion, hurt, fear.

She looked away, gripping the chair's arms with trembling fingers. Her breath came in quick gasps. She pressed her back to the chair.

Stupid! You're so weak. Why do you keep following your treacherous heart?

"Sam, talk to me." He placed his hands over hers.

She wondered how she could hurt him. *Just say it.* She shook her head slowly. "I can't." *I can't lose my heart to you. I can't take the chance.*

He touched her cheek with his fingertips. "Just say it. Whatever it is."

She gripped the wooden arm, feeling the rough edges dig into her palm. "I mean I can't do this." Her eyes begged for mercy. "I just can't."

He looked into her. "What are you so afraid of?" It was like he could see into her soul. He could. And yet he still loved her.

You don't deserve it. No one knew it better than she. Landon would know it too, if he knew what she'd done.

Then tell him.

No. She couldn't bear the thought of him knowing she'd betrayed him with his own brother. Or that she'd caused Bailey's death.

Panic welled inside her like an expanding bubble. She feared it would burst any moment. "I need to go in now." She jerked her hands from under his, and, startled, he leaned back against his heels. It was all the room she needed to stand and squeeze past him.

Sam didn't stop to grab her crutches from the wall. Instead, she limped toward the door.

"Wait, Sam."

She pulled open the door, wanting to slip inside and turn the lock. She longed to fall into bed and pull the quilt over her head. She wanted to go to sleep and find oblivion. She wanted to seal up the leaks in her heart that had allowed Landon to gain entrance.

Her sore ankle slowed her. Landon reached her as she grasped the doorknob. He laid his palm flat against the door, preventing it from opening.

She jerked the knob, but the door didn't budge. Her desperation mounted. "Let go!" He placed his other hand against the door, over her shoulder.

"Not this time."

She could feel the heat of his body against her back. Trapped again. She whipped around. "Just leave me alone." She shoved at his chest futilely.

"Why do you push me away?" His tone was gruff.

Because loving you is too scary. Why can't you understand that? She planted her palms on his chest and pushed. He was like a fortress, solid and immovable.

"Talk to me."

"No!" Even if she would have before, she was too angry now. Why did he force himself on her this way? She was tired of being at the mercy of other people. Her temples pounded.

She ducked under his arm, but he caught her shoulders.

"Let me go."

"Never," he said firmly.

She stopped fighting and leaned into the door, looking at him, her chest rising with each labored breath.

There was a determination in his eyes she'd never seen before. She always talked him into doing things her way, from riding on his handlebars to playing Scrabble. But the look on his face told her he wasn't giving in this time.

Well, that's too bad, because I'm not either. She crossed her arms over her chest and glared at him.

"Are you worried about the future? About your life being in Boston and mine here?"

She refused to answer.

"We can work it out, Sam. It's only logistics."

Location was the least of her worries. She felt like a cornered rat. The arms that held her in place were like shackles. She was twelve years old and locked in a dark closet, her lungs tight and constricted.

"My ankle hurts," she lied.

"Let's go inside and sit down."

Sam dragged her fingers through the hair at her temples and closed her aching eyes. *Go away. Please. Go away.*

"I'm not leaving."

Could he read her stinking mind now? She opened her eyes and narrowed them. *Jerk.*

Read that.

"Are you ready to sit and talk, or do you want to stand here all night?"

Mentally, she called him every name she could think of. What right did he have to interrogate her? Wasn't she entitled to her own private feelings? Just because he was stronger than her didn't give him the right to bully her.

His fingers tightened on her shoulders. "Stop pushing me away." His face softened.

Another gaping hole through which he would enter.

He tucked her hair behind her ear, and she stiffened at his touch.

"I just want to love you," he whispered.

Look away. Close your heart. Don't listen. A lump formed in her throat, where her own declaration had stuck earlier. How close she'd come to crossing that line! Even without having said it, she feared he knew.

"I've loved you for so long." His low voice rumbled through the still air. "Remember when I kissed you that night on the pier? You were thinking of Scott, but you stole my heart then. I loved you long before that last summer when I finally told you."

Sam fought the effects of his soothing voice by closing her eyes, shutting him out.

"And you know what, Sam? I think you loved me then too."

"No," she grated.

He touched a strand of hair, following it down to the ends. "You hide your heart from everyone else, but I can see inside you."

"You don't know anything." If he did, he wouldn't be standing here now.

He wouldn't be standing here now. The thought smacked her like a palm across her cheek. Maybe he needed to know the truth. Maybe then he would see who she was. That she was ugly inside, not worthy of his love.

"I love you. Nothing's going to change that."

He'll never forgive you.

Maybe that's what it's going to take to make him leave you alone.

Still, the notion of telling him made the words freeze on her tongue.

You said you wanted him to leave you alone. Did you mean it?

But how would he feel when he knew Caden was his brother's child? What would he think of her if he knew she'd caused Bailey's death and hid it from his family?

He'll hate you, that's what.

Isn't that better than this? Better than him loving you? Better than this fear?

Landon's finger grazed her lips, tracing the edges, and her knees trembled.

"Let me love you."

She felt the warmth of his breath, then the softness of his lips. A touch as gentle as a butterfly's wings that shook her to the core of her being.

She drove her palms into his shoulder and pushed him away. He called her stubborn, but Sam knew he wouldn't let her go this time. Not unless she made him.

"I never told you who Caden's father is." The words were a metal brush grating across brick. The panic that had built in her settled in a cloud of numbness that anesthetized her soul.

"What?" His arms were at his sides, now. His lips still swollen from hers.

Sam closed the door of her heart up tight, locking it securely. "The night of your party, I left with Bailey. We went out in your dad's boat." Her mind glazed over, the details of the night whirling through her head in vivid Technicolor. The earthy smell of rain in the air. The sound of laughter and music leaking through the yacht club's open patio doors. The sharp, tangy wind rolling off the ocean and tangling her hair.

"Bailey brought alcohol from the party. He knew I was upset, even if you didn't. He had a crush on me."

"I know."

The dread in Landon's voice wasn't enough to tear her from the nightmare. "We drank a lot. And talked. And drank some more." Bailey grew more somber with each bottle. She grew more boisterous. She was determined to prove to herself that Landon's leaving didn't bother her, that she wasn't in love with him. When Bailey kissed her, she eagerly kissed him back. Within moments, they were lying on the deck of the boat.

"One thing led to another." Sam's hollow voice filled the space between them.

She was vaguely aware of Landon stiffening, but she continued. The details were blurry at this point. She didn't remember getting dressed or when the rain started.

The next thing she remembered was reaching the dock at the marina.

Bailey shut off the motor and squeezed her hand. *"Are you going back to the party?"* he asked. She didn't want to see Landon again. Anyway, she was too drunk to face anyone, and suddenly she wasn't feeling so hot.

"No, I'm going home." She had come with Landon's family, but she decided to take a taxi back.

Landon's voice drew her back to the present. "You and Bailey?" She heard the shock and hurt in the softly spoken words, but the numbness deadened her to its effects. Even the shame the memory always conjured was absent.

Instead, the past curled its fingers around her arm and drew her back to that night.

Bailey had lain back in the captain's chair, letting the drizzle slap him in the face. His suit was getting soaked, but he was too drunk to care. *"I'd better wait here awhile, sleep this off,"* he said. She knew his parents would have a fit if they saw him like that.

"Sure," she said.

"Tie me off, okay?" He closed his eyes.

Sam grabbed her purse and pulled her flapping jacket tight around her body. Her long legs spanned the gap between the boat and the dock, but she wobbled on the boards, catching her balance. Just then, her stomach heaved. She ran to the other side of the pier and let her stomach empty into the water.

The wind must have covered the sound of her retching, because when she finished, she looked back at the boat. Bailey's mouth hung open in sleep. Her legs were shaky as they carried her up the boardwalk toward town, where she could hail a cab. It wasn't until much later that she realized she'd never tied off the boat.

Twenty-six

Landon stared into Sam's deadened eyes, pressure building in his chest. Sam had slept with Bailey?

Bailey was Caden's father? The betrayal knifed him. His own brother's betrayal. Sam's betrayal. His eyes stung. Bailey had a crush on Sam for months, but it was nothing more than that. Bailey had always been a sucker for the girls who played hard to get. Only Sam hadn't been playing. No one knew it better than Landon.

And Sam. He only told her he loved her three days before that night. It took him all summer to work up the courage to say the words he'd never said to any woman. Had it meant so little to her? So little that she had drunken sex with his younger brother three days later?

"He asked me to tie off the boat," she said.

The faraway look in her eyes frightened him, but the ache in his heart fogged his thinking. "What?"

"The boat." Her monotone voice droned. "He asked me to tie it off."

Sam was with Bailey the night he died. Dread slithered up his spine and coiled up tightly at the base of his skull. It had begun raining sometime during his party. He noticed Sam's absence, but he was busy talking with friends. He didn't notice Bailey's absence until most of the guests had left.

He shook his thoughts and focused on Sam. She stared blankly at the spot on his chest where she'd nestled moments before. He started to ask what she meant, then decided he didn't want to know.

"I got sick on the pier. From all the alcohol. When I was finished, I looked back at him." Her brow furrowed as she remembered. "He was lying back in the chair, already asleep." Her vacant eyes filled with water, and her mouth worked silently as if priming for the words. "I forgot to tie off the boat."

Landon forgot to breathe. Forgot everything except what Sam was saying. He didn't want to believe it. Bailey had been out on the water by himself. He got disoriented in a storm that rolled in so quickly. He was unable to get ashore before the small boat took in water. It capsized, and Bailey, always the heedless, impetuous one, had never put on a life vest. It's what the authorities said. What he and his parents believed all these years.

Now Sam looked at him, her face full of horror. "I forgot," she said as if she couldn't quite believe it.

He didn't want to believe it either. But everything made sense now. The way she shook at Bailey's funeral. The way she withdrew. The way she left the island soon after he went away to college.

It all made sense in its own terrible way. He remembered every detail of the night vividly. He remembered seeing his dad's empty slip and feeling the pit of his stomach harden. While his dad called for help, he'd borrowed Scott's boat.

The storm gave rise to brutal waves, and he never would have seen the capsized boat in the darkness if it had been farther out to sea. But the lights from shore cast a dim glow over the raging water.

Sam's voice cut through his thoughts. "It was all my fault," she whispered. "My fault he died."

Landon hadn't found Bailey that night. He jumped in the water and screamed Bailey's name until his throat was raw. It wasn't until he was back at the yacht club, wrapped in a blanket, that he began to worry about Sam. He hadn't seen her since the beginning of the party. What if she was on the water with Bailey? What if . . . ? When her machine picked up his call, he drove straight to her house.

Sam was safe and sound, but his brother's body washed to shore two days later.

Her voice jerked him from the past. "I'm sorry," she said.

Sam's face blurred. The weight of what she'd done settled like a leaden anchor inside him. Sam betrayed him. Bailey betrayed him. Caden was his brother's child. Sam caused his brother's death. She hid the truth all these years.

He shook with the burden. His eyes ached and his throat constricted. He stepped away from her. His love for her conflicted with simmering anger.

He couldn't string two coherent thoughts together.

Sam spoke, her quiet voice parting the sea of confusion. "That's what's inside my heart, Landon."

He remembered his own words. *"You hide your heart from everyone else, but I can see inside you."* Had it only been a few minutes ago he was so sure of himself? Now his thoughts were as unstable as quicksand.

෴   ෴   ෴

Sam guarded herself from Landon's pain. The confusion that creased his brow was the beginning of the end of his love for her.

He was seeing who she really was. What awful things she was capable of.

Before she could stop herself, she drove the last nail in the coffin. "Go home, Landon." The steadiness of her tone belied the quaking inside her. "Just go."

I don't deserve you, and I never will.

He took another step away, his gaze fixed on her. She felt his withdrawal, and her soul cried out, contradicting her words.

Love me anyway. Don't leave me.

Don't be a fool, Sam. It's not a matter of if, only when.

He stilled, not reaching for the screen door. His eyes impaled her, and she knew this moment would haunt her forever.

How could you do this to him? Look at his face, Sam. He doesn't deserve it.

He deserves better than you.

"Go home," she said firmly. "Just stay away from me." She was doing what was best for both of them. Someday the ache would go away. Wouldn't it?

His jaw tightened. "You don't mean that."

How could he know what she meant? What she thought? Hadn't she just proven he didn't know her at all? "I do," she said past the lump in her throat.

Say it like you mean it, Sam, or all this will be for nothing.

Sam listened to the voice. It had kept her safe so far. "I don't want you to come back, hear? Just leave us alone."

She saw regret and compassion mingle on his face, but she turned and opened the door before she lost her courage.

He didn't stop her this time.

Once Sam hobbled over the threshold, she closed the door and leaned against it. Her good leg was as unstable as a rickety table. Her hands trembled. She slid down the door, letting her legs fold, ignoring the pain in her ankle. It was no match for the pain in her heart.

With her head against the door, she heard the slap of the screen door. She heard the heaviness of Landon's feet on the steps. She had dropped her secret, and it had exploded like a bomb in his face.

He wouldn't be back. She had what she wanted.

But in the quietness of the room, she couldn't help but wonder why she only felt empty.

Twenty-seven

The call of an eastern phoebe jarred Sam from a restless sleep. Her mind had turned all night, like the constant tide, not allowing her past the fringes of light sleep.

She turned and squinted at the clock. It read 7:18. Her thoughts went back to the night before. The kiss. She allowed her mind to entertain the feelings Landon had invoked, let them linger for just a moment before she chased them away.

It was over now. He knew everything.

The glare of the sun through her curtains annoyed her. How dare the day be sunny and bright? It should be raining. The sky should be heavy and dark with angry clouds.

Stop wallowing, Sam, and get off your behind. You've got work to do.

The sooner she got done, the sooner she could leave. That thought alone roused her from the comfort of the bed. She couldn't begin to forget Landon until she was away from him.

Sam showered and checked her ankle. The swelling had gone down considerably. It hurt only when she put weight on it. She rewrapped it and popped two Advil. She didn't feel like eating but had two slices of toast anyway, then she set a few things on the front porch for lunch, since the floor would be off-limits until it dried.

Landon had already taped off the woodwork, so she hobbled on her crutches to the porch, where he'd put the supplies. It shouldn't be too hard to roll on the polyurethane, even with her bum ankle.

She opened the windows before she started. The curtains lay still against the warm morning, and she realized it was going to stink to high heaven quickly. She wondered for the first time if they'd be able to sleep there with the fumes. She turned on the bathroom fan and hoped for the best.

Saving the worry for later, she poured the liquid into the clean pan and set to work. The liquid spread easily, but her good leg fatigued from supporting her weight. The small kitchen took longer than she anticipated, but when she was done, she set the roller in the pan and stood back.

See, this won't be so bad. You can do it on your own.

Next she began moving the living room furniture into the bedrooms. It was a tedious process using only the strength of one leg. She set each piece on a rug and pushed so as not to scrape the floor. The sofa and chair barely fit through the doorway, and by the time the room was empty, her ankle throbbed.

When she finished moving the furniture, she checked her ankle. It was swollen again, and she knew being on her feet all day wasn't good, but she didn't really have a choice.

Sam began in the corner, leaving a path from the front door to their bedroom and bathroom. She'd have to wait until tomorrow to move the bedroom furniture into the living room. Caden would be here to help, but even so, the beds would have to be taken apart and reassembled. Why hadn't she thought about that?

Sam hoped the work would keep her mind off Landon and the loneliness that hit her the moment he left.

It'll be better when you're in Boston. You'll forget the island. You'll forget Landon.

She wasn't sure she believed the voice this time. She hadn't forgotten Landon before, not really. What made her think she would forget him now after he'd seeped so deeply into her heart?

The look in his eyes after she told him about Bailey flashed in her mind. The look of betrayal had been bad enough, but when she told him she was responsible for his brother's death, she killed something inside him. She killed his love for her.

It shouldn't hurt so much. Had she not accomplished what she'd set out to do?

Sam knew what he was thinking when that look passed over his face. He might have forgiven the betrayal. Maybe even the mistake that caused Bailey's death. But she had kept the truth from him when he was desperate for answers. A decent person would have told him the truth immediately.

He'd come to her in the middle of the night, after she took a cab home. She was sound asleep and awoke to a firm tapping sound.

Sam opened her eyes and looked around, trying to place the sound. The only thing she heard was the patter of rain on the roof. Her mouth felt like it was stuffed with dryer lint, and her head pounded.

The memory of what she'd done with Bailey came down on her like a hammer. She went out with him on the boat. She slept with him.

What have I done?

A tap on her window startled her. She saw the shadow of a person behind the gauzy curtains and started.

As the adrenaline faded, she came to her senses. Maybe it was Bailey. Maybe he'd come to his senses too.

What was she going to do now? *Why did you do such a foolish thing, Sam?*

The tap came again, louder, and she knew she'd better open the window before Emmett woke.

Sam pulled back the curtain. It was Landon's face, not Bailey's, that stared back at her. His widened eyes struck her with fear.

She jerked up the window, fighting the old wooden sash.

"Sam. Thank God." He laid his forehead against the screen.

A thread of anxiety rippled through her.

His breaths came hard, as if he'd run all the way over. His wet hair clung to his head. Even in the darkness, she could see his white dress shirt was soaked through.

"What's wrong?" She whispered so Emmett wouldn't wake.

He lifted his head and looked at her. "It's Bailey. We think he took Dad's boat out."

Thunder rumbled, and a few seconds later, lightning flashed across the night sky.

"Dad's boat is gone, and Bailey is missing."

Bailey was missing? In the storm? "I'll get dressed."

"No, wait."

His eyes were black shadows. "We've already found the boat. It capsized. There's no sign of Bailey."

Sam's breath caught. Her hand covered her mouth. "I have to help." She made a move to stand.

"There's nothing you can do." Landon's eyes grazed her face like a caress. Water trickled down his face. She wondered if tears mixed with the rain. "Sam, I . . . I thought . . . I was afraid you were on that boat too."

Her heart seized. Why would he think that? Had someone seen them together?

"I haven't seen you since you were talking to Miss Biddle by the refreshment table. I was so afraid I'd lost you." Landon reached out as if to touch her, but his fingers connected with the screen instead.

It had been right after she left Miss Biddle that Bailey approached and asked if she wanted to get some fresh air. It was his idea to take the boat out. He fished bottles of beer from the ice-filled containers behind the bar and slipped outside.

With sudden clarity, she remembered her last sight of Bailey sleeping in the captain's chair, the boat rocking gently He couldn't be dead. He'd just been sitting there. He'd looked so peaceful.

"Tie me off, will you?"

The words struck her heart like an arrow. She tied off the boat, didn't she?

But she couldn't remember doing it. *No!*

Think, Sam. You must have done it. You had so much to drink. Maybe you just don't remember.

But she remembered what happened after she got out of the boat. Her stomach had turned. She'd run to the edge of the pier and vomited over the side.

What next? She remembered looking back at Bailey, seeing he was asleep. She'd turned and walked away. She'd left him there in the boat.

Landon pulled away. "I have to get back to my parents. They're waiting at the club." He wiped the rain from his face. "We're hoping the boat just came loose from the dock. Maybe he'll just walk in the door and say, 'Hey, what's up?' you know?"

But she knew better. Bailey had been in that boat when it drifted off, and it was her fault. *Tell him, Sam.*

"I'll call as soon as they hear anything."

Say it! "Okay." She knew she should at least go with him. He needed her now. He would need her if Bailey never came home. But fear and guilt held her captive.

He called Sam the next morning and told her they hadn't found Bailey yet. In her heart, she knew they would never see Bailey alive again. Landon and his parents agonized over Bailey's disappearance, but she was too afraid to tell them what she'd done. When his body washed ashore the day after that, she was relieved the wait was over.

Now, the darkness of those days filled her again. She should have told them. Why hadn't she just been honest? How Landon must hate her now.

Sam filled her roller and swiped it across the floor, trying to shake the nightmare. Instead, the mindless task was like a playground for her wandering thoughts.

A knock on the front door startled her. What if it was Landon? What would she say? *Get a reality check, Sam. Why would Landon come back after what you told him? You're the last person he wants to see.*

She set the roller down and limped to the door. The lock turned easily, and she pulled open the door. Caden stood on the porch with her bag, wrapped in a beach towel, her hair hanging in damp straggles along her face.

"Hi, honey." She stepped aside to let her in and waved at Melanie as she backed out of the drive. "Watch the floor; it's wet over there."

Sam pushed the door shut. "Did you thank Mrs. Walker?"

"Yeah." Caden wrinkled up her nose. "Shooweee! It stinks in here."

"I have the windows open, but it's not doing much good."

She waved her hand under her nose. "I'm going outside."

"Change first," Sam said.

Caden disappeared into the bedroom, climbing over the sofa to get to the dresser.

A few minutes later she appeared in the doorway wearing her khaki shorts and Red Sox T-shirt. The sun had added a few new freckles on her nose, and her skin had darkened a shade. Like Sam, she'd never been one to burn.

"Did you have fun?" Sam asked.

"Yep. The surf side is sweet." She yawned. "I'm tired all of a sudden."

"It's the sun." Sam remembered the times Landon's mom took them to the other side of the island. The waves weren't huge, but to a kid with a Boogie Board, it was like a liquid amusement park. When she'd come home, she'd always been beat.

"I guess watching TV is out of the question." Caden stared at the TV pushed into the corner of their room.

"For now." Sam set the roller down. "When this dries, I'll need your help moving the bedroom furniture so I can do those floors." Even with the two of them, they'd have to take the drawers from the dresser and chest to lift them.

Caden plopped on her bed and stretched out. "We can't move this heavy stuff."

"Sure we can. You're a strong gymnast, right?"

"What about your ankle?"

"It hasn't stopped me so far." Sam gestured to the furniture she'd moved into the bedroom. Caden needn't know it took her over an hour to do it.

"Just have Landon do it." Caden clasped her hands behind her head and closed her eyes.

Sam knew she had to tell Caden something. Landon had been around constantly, and she would notice his absence sooner or later. She leaned against the door frame. "Listen, honey, Landon is busy. I don't think he'll be coming over anymore."

Caden turned her head toward Sam. "Why not?"

How much should she say? *As little as possible, if you're smart.* "He has a job, honey. We can't just expect him to drop his life and come to our rescue. Besides, we can do this. The two of us, what do you say?" She injected some enthusiasm as if it were some wild adventure and not boring house maintenance.

Sam knew Caden wasn't buying it when she sat up slowly and dangled her feet over the edge of the bed. "Landon said he was on vacation. He said he'd be here all week."

Sam hadn't counted on that. She guessed Landon and Caden had talked plenty while they worked together. "Things changed. His plans changed, so now it's just us. Don't worry—we can do it."

Caden cocked her head. "Something happened while I was gone, didn't it?"

The girl was far too perceptive for an eleven-year-old. Sam should have known. But this was grown-up stuff—and none of her business. Sam crossed her arms and spoke firmly. "We'll be finishing up the house alone, Caden. That's all you need to know." She turned to go.

"What did you do?" Her daughter's voice was accusing.

Sam turned. "This is none of your business, missy, and I'll thank you not to use that tone with me."

"You chased him away, didn't you?" Tears welled up in her eyes. "Why? He's the nicest man ever!"

Sam stared at Caden, her thoughts whirling. When had her daughter grown so attached to Landon? Was it because he was her uncle? Having a relative was a novelty for Caden. A male relative. Had Caden begun to think of him as a father figure? Sam remembered the way they danced together a couple of days ago and realized Landon had slipped into her daughter's affections the same way he'd slipped into hers. Sam's heart bottomed out.

"Amber's dad calls her princess." Caden swiped at the corners of her eyes. "I want a dad who calls me princess too."

If only it were so simple. "Amber's parents are divorced. Her dad doesn't even live with her." And sometimes it was better having no dad at all than a bad one. She wanted to tell Caden what Emmett had called her. Princess didn't come close.

"Well, at least she *has* a dad. I don't have anybody."

The words struck their target. "You have me." Sam was her mom, and she was committed to Caden. It was more than she had as a girl.

If Sam had hoped for an apology, she was disappointed. Instead, Caden glared at her.

Sam's head pounded, and she rubbed her temples. It was going to be a long four days.

Twenty-eight

Landon walked along the cobblestone sidewalks down Main Street, pulling back on Max's leash. Summer people and tourists meandered down the walk, pointing in windows and crowding into shops. They smiled and laughed, seemingly at peace. Meanwhile, his own thoughts spun like a whirlpool.

He'd gone back to work the past three days, trying to stay busy, keep his mind off Sam. He ran errands in the evenings, arriving home late and tired. Now, as the sun sank low on the horizon, he was out of reasons not to go home.

Sam.

He could almost feel his blood pressure building at the thought of her. He'd lain awake each night thinking about what she'd said. There was so much to take in, starting with Caden. Bailey's daughter. His niece.

His dad had a granddaughter he didn't know about, and his mom—would things have been different if she'd known? Would knowledge of Bailey's daughter have been enough to live for?

Her health declined rapidly after his brother's death. Bailey had been so much like his father, and his mother doted on him. Landon knew she loved him too, but there was a special connection between his mother and Bailey. When he died, something in his mother died as well. Bailey's death ushered in the end of their family as he'd known it.

And Sam was responsible.

The thought hit him fresh, and his heart squeezed as if a muzzle had clamped tightly around it. Why hadn't she told him all those years ago? She let them wonder for two days. Two unbearable days.

Hearing the truth had been hard enough without realizing why Sam told him to begin with. It didn't escape him that Sam had done it to push him away. She'd done everything in her power to deny her feelings, and when that failed, she broke his heart. First with her betrayal with Bailey, then with the truth about his death.

He hoped she was happy now. Alone and happy.

Max barked, and he rushed forward, pulling the leash taut.

Landon followed Max's line of vision. Scott stood beside his tour van, talking to a middle-aged woman dressed in clothes better suited to a teenager. He slowed his steps, wishing he could sneak away, but Max was already at Scott's side.

Max nuzzled Scott's hand, and he looked down. "Hey, Max." He petted the dog and looked at Landon. "Hey, Max's owner." He answered the tourist's question, then turned to Landon when she walked away.

"How's it going?" Landon asked.

"Great. Business is booming." Scott set his brochures inside the van. "I thought you were helping Sam this week."

He didn't want to talk about Sam, especially not with Scott. Maybe the guy had been right about Sam all along. Maybe Landon was just a fool. He shrugged. "Not anymore. I went back to work. It's busy right now with the summer people and their pets."

Scott glanced at Landon before rubbing Max behind the ears.

"Listen, I have an hour before my next tour. Want to grab dinner at the Even Keel?"

Landon looked away. He'd been hoping to let his friendship with Scott die. They'd grown too far apart. "Not tonight. I've got to get home. The yard needs mowing."

"Come on. It can wait 'til tomorrow. I'm not taking no for an answer."

Did he really want to go home where he might see Sam or Caden in the yard?

"All right," Landon said. *Just keep the conversation neutral, Reed. Work. Weather. Women.*

No, not women.

They walked down the sidewalk and crossed the street at the café. Landon tied up Max at the bike stand several feet from a young golden retriever on a pink leash. He petted both dogs before entering the restaurant.

The café, a tourist and islander favorite, was crowded and noisy. He and Scott followed the hostess, squeezing through the closely spaced tables to a spot in the corner. The smell of grilled steak and seafood mingled in the air, making Landon's stomach rumble. He realized he'd skipped lunch.

They ordered without need of the menu, then settled back in their chairs and talked for a while. When the conversation wound down, Landon watched a toddler at a table across the room throw her cup on the floor. Her mom bent to retrieve it, then the toddler threw it again.

He thought about Caden and how much he'd missed of her life. She was eleven now, and Landon's dad had never met her at all. Why hadn't Sam told them about the pregnancy?

He'd lain awake for three nights wondering about so many

things. When had she discovered the pregnancy? Is that why she left the island? How had she supported herself and Caden at eighteen with no education and no support? Why hadn't she told him and his parents? Didn't she know they would have helped her?

All these years, and he still couldn't get into Sam's head and figure out what made her tick. He'd thought he knew her, but he was wrong.

"Are you going to spill it or just sit there staring into space?" Scott asked over the music and rumble of chatter.

Landon pulled his gaze to Scott's. His friend had known him too long to be fooled. "I don't want to talk about it, okay?" He wouldn't have even come if Scott wasn't so adamant.

The server brought their food, and Landon was relieved to have a distraction. He ate quietly, hardly tasting his steak. When he finished, he set his napkin in his plate and finished his soda.

"Sam's giving you fits, isn't she?"

Landon pushed his drink back and gave him a hard look. "I said I don't want to talk about it."

Scott shrugged. "All right, all right." He adjusted his sunglasses on top of his head. "I was going to say if you want to talk about her, I'll try my best to be impartial." He held up his right hand as if swearing an oath.

Yeah, right. Scott had long since lost his objectivity regarding Sam.

"I'm serious." Scott leaned his elbows on the table. "Who else are you going to talk to?"

Truth be told, Landon did feel like a bottle of soda that had been shaken vigorously. He was afraid his top might pop off if he didn't do something soon. "I have friends."

"Not friends who know your history."

He was right, though Landon hated to admit it. It was impossible to describe what he and Sam had together, what they'd always had. Scott had been around for all of it, and he knew everything—except how bad her childhood was. She'd never told anyone at school when her mom left or how Emmett treated her. She seemed almost ashamed, and he knew, even as a kid, she would have throttled him if he told anyone.

But he wasn't in the mood to hear Scott cut Sam down. Especially when he felt like cutting her down himself. He'd never been so angry at her.

"I don't think so," Landon said. Some things had to be worked out alone. Even if it meant going home and exploding.

Scott shrugged. "Well, she's leaving soon anyway. This weekend, right?"

Landon glared at him.

"What? My point is, whatever she's done, she'll be gone soon. Then you can start getting your life back to normal."

Would things ever be normal again? As angry as he was, love didn't just disintegrate. Besides, he had a niece, and his dad had a granddaughter. Was he just supposed to pretend he didn't know? "You don't understand."

"That's because you won't talk to me." Scott looked at him with his intense blue eyes. "You're hurting, man. And mad. I saw it the minute I spotted you. And even though Sam isn't high on my list of favorite people, I want to help."

Landon thought he saw sincerity in Scott's expression. But this was a heavy load to drop. His own shock was still present and accounted for. Bailey had been Scott's friend too, though they weren't as close as he and Scott. How much more animosity would Scott have toward Sam if Landon told him?

Then again, with Sam leaving in a couple of days, what would it matter? Before Landon could change his mind, he spoke. "Sam told me something a few nights ago. Something that happened that summer before I left for college." He took a deep breath, stalling.

Scott waited patiently, studying Landon's face.

"Remember the night of my going-away party? At the yacht club?"

Scott's eyes shadowed. "The night Bailey . . ."

"Yeah." It wasn't a night any of them was likely to forget. "Well . . ." He struggled for the words. Maybe he shouldn't have said anything at all.

"Go on." Scott's calm words urged him on.

Landon cleared his throat. "Sam was upset with me. She'd been distant ever since I told her how I felt about her. She was upset about my leaving, though she never admitted it."

"I remember."

In fact, Landon and Scott had argued about Sam a few days before that. Scott dissuaded him from sharing his feelings with Sam, but it was something he had to do. He wondered now if Scott had been right.

Sam had been between them for a long time. He remembered all the times he'd stood up for her. Now he felt like a fool for having done so.

Just tell him, Reed. It's not going to get any easier. "That night, Sam and Bailey left the party together. I guess she was upset, and knowing Bailey, he wanted to talk."

"He had a thing for her."

Thanks for pointing that out. "I know." His brother had never admitted it outright. He knew Landon loved Sam, but Bailey's crush was obvious to everyone who knew him. Landon never dreamed Bailey would act on his feelings.

"Bailey took Sam out on the water. They got drunk."

Scott's eyes narrowed. "Sam was with him when the boat capsized?"

"Not exactly." Landon's mouth tightened. *Just say it, Reed.* "Sam and Bailey slept together." Landon looked away. He didn't want to see Scott's face. "They got drunk and had sex." The next part made his stomach knot. "Her daughter is Bailey's child."

"What?" Scott leaned forward, his face twisting in anger.

Landon choked back the knot in his throat. "It gets worse."

"Is that possible?" Scott's forehead creased as his brows pulled tight.

Landon gave a wry laugh. "Sadly, it is." He drew in a breath and let go of it, wishing the pain would leave with the oxygen. "Bailey took her back to the dock, but he stayed on the boat. I guess he wanted to sober up. He asked Sam to tie off the boat." Landon swallowed hard. "But she forgot."

Realization fluttered across Scott's face, and he swore. He ran a hand through his long hair, knocking his sunglasses askew, and leaned back in his chair. "How do you know she forgot?" Suspicion dripped from his words.

Landon gave him a stern look. "She was drunk, Scott."

His friend's jaw locked tight. Someone dropped some silverware, and Scott spoke over the clatter. "It's her fault, Landon."

So much for objectivity. Landon should have known he couldn't talk it out with Scott. Not when it came to Sam. "It was an accident. And Bailey was as much to blame as she was. He knew better than to drink like that, much less out on the water."

Scott stared at him. "I can't believe you're still defending her."

"I'm not defending her."

Scott cocked an eyebrow.

Okay, maybe I am defending her, but it's not like she did it on purpose. "You're not giving it a fair hearing," he said. "She was sick when she got out of the boat." *Scott has a right to be angry too. Bailey was his friend.*

"Listen," Landon said. "I'm angry too, but she didn't do it on purpose."

Scott stared somewhere over Landon's shoulder, his face taut. Landon wondered what was going on behind those eyes. Maybe he didn't want to know. Maybe he should have kept his mouth shut. He'd only stirred up more trouble.

"Even if it was an accident," Scott said, "she kept that from your family." He leaned on the table, his elbows spreading the width of it. "Have you forgotten what it was like? The waiting? Your mom practically had a nervous breakdown."

Those two days had seemed like a year. None of them slept, praying Bailey would miraculously appear, and they would all laugh about how crazy they'd been to think he drowned. And after his body was found, his parents fell apart, and Landon had nightmares about drowning for almost a year. He hadn't stepped foot in the ocean since.

"I remember." He wished he could forget.

"Sam knew all that time? She knew he was gone and she just— said nothing? She let your family wonder if Bailey was dead or alive?"

"She was an eighteen-year-old kid. She was afraid."

Scott brought his fist down on the table, and the salt-and-pepper caddy jumped. "Stop making excuses for her, Landon. I know you think you have some insight to her soul that the rest of the world doesn't have, but maybe it's time to consider that you're the one with the skewed vision of her."

Landon gritted his teeth. "You're the one who doesn't understand her. All you think of when her name comes up is what she did to you in high school. There are things you don't know." Landon looked away.

Scott stood quickly, his chair grating against the floor. "Well, I know this. You're not man enough to give her what she deserves." He tossed money on the table. "But I am."

Landon was on his feet before he could think. He grabbed the front of Scott's shirt in his fists and pulled him close. A glass on the table clattered over. "Stay away from Sam, or you'll deal with me." Landon locked eyes with Scott. He could feel his blood pounding in his temples. So help him, if Scott laid one finger on Sam, he'd rip him to shreds.

Scott's mouth slackened. He took on a look of nonchalance, an act Landon had seen him pull off before. "Maybe you're right, *buddy*." Scott pulled back, smoothed his shirt, and set his sunglasses in place. "Maybe the two of you are perfect for each other."

As if for the first time, Landon saw Scott for who he was. A jealous accuser who'd done nothing but heap guilt on other people. Landon lowered his fists to his sides, his shoulders back. "She's twice the person you'll ever be."

Twenty-nine

Sam woke to the low rumble of a mower's engine. She imagined Miss Biddle's nephew making stripes across the lawn and knew she had no business being in bed any longer. Beside her, Caden's form lay still, her mouth relaxed in sleep.

Her daughter had ignored her since their argument, and Sam wondered when Caden had come to dislike her so much. Anger seemed to be her daughter's reigning theme for the past couple of years. Now, Sam was forced to admit, Caden had cause to be mad. Sam hadn't realized Caden hoped she and Landon would get together, but her daughter was too naïve to know that was impossible.

Sam slipped out of bed and went to start the coffee, realizing halfway there that she could walk without much pain. At least her ankle wouldn't interfere with her job. She could show up for work Monday and start getting her life back to normal.

Is that what you want?

She shrugged off the thought. Normal might not be exciting, but it was safe.

She scooped coffee grinds into the filter, filled the tank with water, and plugged in the machine. She'd made a lot of headway with the house the last three days. The floor was completed, and the furniture was moved back into place. What remained was a list of small repairs: fixing the leaky kitchen sink, regrouting the bathroom tiles, defrosting the ancient freezer, and a host of other odds and ends. Few of which she had experience doing.

Sam knew how one small repair could end up taking half a day and hoped everything went smoothly. They would need to be on the ferry by early afternoon the next day to make the bus back to Boston in time for work Monday.

She poured a bowl of cereal, leaving enough milk for Caden, and sat down, waiting for the coffee to brew. The floor looked nice. It could use a couple more coats of polyurethane, but there was no time.

The sound of the mower's engine escalated, and she realized she would need to mow before she left. And pack. And call Melanie to let her know the house was done. Melanie had filed the paperwork for the listing the week before, and it would go on the market in three days.

Sam had visited Miss Biddle the day before and arranged for her nephew to keep up the yard after they left. It would cost Sam money she didn't have, but she knew it would pay off in the end.

Miss Biddle's words flashed in her mind. "Well, honey, I'm sure Landon would keep after it. He does mine sometimes when I'm in a bind."

"I don't want to be a bother," she'd said loudly enough for the woman to hear. "And you said your nephew was looking to make extra money."

"Sure, sure. He won't mind."

Sam thought she'd handled it very smoothly until Miss Biddle walked her to the door.

"You know, honey, I don't mean to butt in, but being old gives one the privilege of speaking one's mind, so I'm taking advantage of it."

She took Sam's hand in her warm, thick one. "A person would have to be blind not to see the way you push that boy away."

Sam opened her mouth in defense.

Miss Biddle raised her hand, palm out. "I'm not criticizing. Just making an observation." She squeezed Sam's hand. "Now, nobody knows better than I about pushing folks away. I've done it all my life, so I want you to listen up, okay?"

Sam nodded reluctantly.

"I've lived right here in this house most of my life, and you might have noticed that there was never a mister." Miss Biddle flattened her bronze-colored lips. "Not that I didn't have a chance, mind you. I was quite pretty back in my guitar-playing days."

Sam smiled, and the woman continued.

"But I was afraid. I had my reasons—we all do—and I scared away every last man I cared about." She gestured around the house. "And here I am, all these years later, heart intact.

"But lonely. I'd trade all the hurts I may have had for one true love at my side." Her eyes drooped at the corners, where creases spread like a fan. "I have no idea what's gone on between you and that boy, but the two of you have got something special, always have. So I'm going to tell you what I would do if I could turn the clock back thirty years." She leaned close and said with urgency, "Take the risk."

Now, the words came back to Sam, whispered in the same forceful tone Miss Biddle had used the day before. *Take the risk.*

It sounded so easy. Take the risk. She'd almost let the words settle on her heart like dew on fresh green grass. It was easy for Miss Biddle to say when she hadn't a clue what Sam had done.

The coffee finished perking, and she poured herself a cup. The smell of the strong brew cut through her daydream and brought her to her senses. Work was the order of the day if she was going to get done before she left.

Sam finished her coffee, then showered and dressed. Landon's tools were still on the front porch, so she retrieved them and set them on the kitchen floor. Later tonight, under cover of darkness, she would leave them on his porch.

Coward.

Maybe she was when it came to Landon, but he didn't want to see her either.

She pulled the pliers from the box and opened the cabinet under the sink. The leak had left a water stain in the cabinet board, but it felt solid enough. She turned on the water and waited to see exactly where the leak was coming from. Once she pinpointed the spot, she turned off the water and applied the pliers to the metal drainpipe.

Sam squeezed the rubber grip and twisted, but it didn't give. The old metal pipes were corroded. She worked at the fitting, straining and twisting, until sweat broke out on the back of her neck. Sam sat back on the rug, gritting her teeth. She wanted to bang the pipes with a sledgehammer, but she knew that wouldn't do anything but soothe her temper.

You can do it, Sam. Just take your time.

She blew out a breath and picked up the pliers, leaning inside the cabinet, and wrapped the jaws around the connector. Squeezing hard with both hands, she pulled the handles. Nothing.

Sam tried again, but it didn't budge. Her fingers ached by the time she sat up. It was hot in the house, and she already needed another shower. She walked to the window and jerked up the pane. The smell of freshly cut grass drifted through the screen.

Her gaze wandered out to the yard. Landon strode through her backyard, pushing his mower. His red baseball cap was pulled low, and his skin gleamed under the hot sun. He turned the mower and headed toward the house.

Sam pulled back from the window before he could see her. What was he doing mowing her yard? Helping her? The last time she'd seen him, his feelings were written clearly in his eyes.

But he was back. Warmth flowed through her at the slightest notion of hope.

Stop it, Sam! This isn't what you want. She closed her eyes, battling the feelings again, pushing them back to a place she could control them. *You just have this one last day. One day, Sam. You can do it. You can leave here with your heart intact if you just guard yourself today.*

The sound of the mower grew faint as he headed down toward the shoreline. Hadn't she told him to go away and not come back? Hadn't she given him every reason to stay away? Why did he keep coming around? How could he, now that he knew what she had done?

Maybe he would leave after he finished mowing. It didn't make sense, but then, his being here now didn't make sense either.

The bedroom door opened, and Caden stopped on the threshold, holding a bundle of clothes. Without a word, she headed to the bathroom, shutting the door behind her.

Sam wandered back to the kitchen and sank to the floor to give the pipe another try. Landon's presence captured her thoughts.

Without bidding, the memory of their kiss sprang to her mind and lingered there like the sweet fragrance of a rose. How was it he made her want more than other men did? Mere physical intimacy would never be enough for Landon. If she let it happen, he would fill her heart and soul until there was no border between them. They would intertwine like the threads of a heavy sailcloth, indivisible.

Nothing is ever indivisible, Sam. Things come apart, especially relationships. Even a sailcloth, if pulled and ripped hard enough, will come apart. *And imagine the damage when it does.* But she didn't have to imagine. She had been intertwined with her dad and mom. She knew what loss felt like.

⟋   ⟋   ⟋

Landon shifted the mower around a tree and continued on a straight path toward the water. After his conversation with Scott yesterday, he went home and paced. Then he went to bed and tossed, lying awake, his mind wandering two doors down.

He was still angry. What Sam had done was wrong; there was no defending her actions. But something else sank into his heart in the wee hours of the night. There was no denying his love for her. His father had always told Landon he loved him unconditionally. The fact gave Landon security. Sam had never been loved like that, and for the first time, he knew how his father felt.

Landon's love for Sam was deep and unswaying. It didn't matter what she did or if she hurt him. The roots of love went down to his very core. They could never be weeded out.

Once he realized that, panic set in. He had one day before she left the island. One full day to make Sam realize what she was giving up. He had wasted three days brooding about something that couldn't be changed.

He pushed down on the mower's handle, making a full turn and heading toward the house on his last strip of grass. A few feet away, Max plopped under the shade of a bush and rested his head on his paws.

He wondered if Sam knew he was there. Probably not. She would have tried to chase him away with a broomstick if she did. Well, he was going to be here for her whether she wanted him to or not. It was time she discovered what it was like to trust someone else.

When he reached the flower bed, he cut the mower's engine, took off his hat, and dragged his hand across his forehead. He looked up through the screened porch to the back door. She was surely awake by now. Even Caden was probably up and helping with the repairs. Sam was probably stressed over the work still undone. *Not stressed enough to welcome you, Reed.*

He drew in a breath and released a sigh. He'd fought uphill battles before, but none was more important than the one he'd fight today. Sam didn't have a corner on the obstinate market.

He set his hat back on his head and took the porch steps in one stride, sliding through the screen door. Without pausing, he lifted his hand and knocked on the freshly painted door. Then he waited.

Maybe he should've gone to her door before he smelled like gasoline and sweat. Too late now.

Thirty

A knock sounded on the door, and Sam jumped, knocking her head against the bottom of the sink. She smothered a curse and dropped the pliers. They clanked against the wood floor of the cabinet.

A glance out the kitchen window showed Landon's profile. Her heartbeat kicked up a notch. She wanted to crawl inside the cupboard and hide. Why did he have to come back? Why couldn't he just do as she asked for once and stay away?

Some treacherous part of her wanted to throw open the door and fall into his arms where she felt safe and loved. But Emmett's words still had hold of her mind. *"Don't ever let yourself love, Sam. Just soon as you do, they leave you."*

The knock persisted.

Fine. He wanted to talk? They'd talk. Sam threw the pliers inside the cabinet, rose to her feet, and strode the few feet to the front door. She yanked it open, the whoosh of hot air smacking her in the face.

"What?" she asked, not caring that her tone was rude. Not caring that he'd just mowed her lawn. Who'd asked him to?

His eyes widened slightly.

Before she could delight in catching him off guard, he straightened, forcing her to look up. "I came to help you finish."

"Eager to be rid of me?" she taunted.

"What can I do to help?"

"You can leave." She cocked a brow at him.

"Landon!" Caden's voice rang out behind Sam, and she watched Landon's face soften. He studied Caden as if he were seeing her for the first time, and Sam wondered if he was noticing the way her bone structure mirrored Bailey's or the way the tip of her nose turned up, just like Bailey's had. Two seconds later, Caden edged around her mom and embraced Landon.

Sam's gaze met Landon's over her head. Sam saw all the emotion swim across his face. He was hugging Bailey's daughter, his niece. Inside, a crater opened up. How selfish was she to keep Landon and Caden apart on their last day together?

"Can you stay?" Caden asked, pulling back.

Landon let the question hang, waiting for Sam to answer. Her pulse raced at the notion of Landon's company. All the more reason to say no. Then her daughter turned her brown eyes on Sam, and her heart melted.

"He's staying," Sam said reluctantly.

Heaven help me. She dropped the door handle and let him in. *You can let him in your house without letting him in your heart, Sam. Remember that. He's here to work, nothing more.*

"You can fix the leak under the sink. The pliers are in the cabinet." Let *him* struggle with the stinking fitting.

She retrieved the tube of caulk for the bathroom tile and left the room. The tile was wet from Caden's shower, so she dried it off and set to work.

Landon's presence in the house was like a morning fog, heavy and thick. She shut the door as if she could shut out his presence. The odor of the caulk filled the room, and she turned on the fan.

A few minutes later, a knock sounded. Maybe Caden needed to use the restroom.

"Yes?" She slid her finger down the caulk, smoothing the line.

"Sink's fixed." Landon's low voice rumbled through the door. "What can I do next?"

He'd fixed the leak in fifteen minutes? She'd spent that long trying to pry the pipe apart. She wanted to tell him to go home, but she knew he wouldn't listen. Besides, it wasn't worth the hassle Caden would give her.

"There's a list on the kitchen table," she said. "Take your pick."

Sam listened for an answer, sure he'd paused outside the door. Her heart thudded against her ribs. But moments later, she heard a noise coming from the bedroom.

She finished the bathroom and left the sanctuary with trepidation, but Landon was nowhere to be seen. She spied him later through the living room window, caulking the exterior window frames, Caden chattering at his side.

An hour later, she was reattaching the curtain brackets when Caden called through the windows. "Can I ride my bike, Mom?"

The thought of being alone with Landon scared Sam, but she was reluctant to ruin Caden's good spirits. Besides, the exercise would do her good. "Don't go past the end of the road."

"I know." She could almost see Caden rolling her eyes.

Not long after she left, Sam was standing on the couch, screwing in brackets for the curtain rod, when the front door opened. She didn't need to turn to know it was Landon, and she was relieved when he walked to the kitchen, presumably checking the list.

She ran the screw into the wall, tightening the bracket, and set the curtain rod in place. When she stepped down from the couch, Landon was watching her.

"How's your ankle?"

It was an ugly shade of yellow-green under the wrap and just a little sore. "Fine."

"The windows are caulked inside and out, and I fixed the gutter."

Bravo. Should she bow down and worship him? Didn't he know she didn't want him here? Sam knew she would've been in trouble if Landon hadn't shown up. She probably would've spent all morning on the leaky pipe, but she couldn't bring herself to thank him.

She picked up the next set of brackets and tried to think of one of the outside jobs he could do. If she couldn't make him leave, she could at least get him outside.

But with Landon staring at her, her mind went blank, and she wasn't about to shorten the distance between them by checking the list. She stepped up on the recliner, placed the bracket against the wall, and set the screw in place. When she applied the screwdriver, the bit slipped off the head and the screw fell to the floor, pinging against the wood.

"I'll get it," Landon said.

He retrieved the screw from behind the recliner and handed it to her.

"The floor looks good," he said.

Sam grunted as she set the screw in place, then drove it into the wall. She could feel him watching. Her skin prickled with awareness. Didn't he have something to do besides watch her?

"Listen, Sam, since Caden's gone, maybe this is a good time to talk."

Talk about how she slept with Bailey, how she caused his brother's death, how she kept it all a secret? No thanks. "I'm busy," she said, placing the other bracket against the wall.

He handed her the screw. "We'll finish in plenty of time."

Sam pressed the button on the screwdriver, sending the bit spinning, turning the screw into the wall. It whirled to a stop. "I don't want to talk."

She reached for the curtain rod in his hands, but he held it away from her. "Well, I do."

Who did he think he was, forcing his way into her house and telling her what he wanted? Had he let her finish the house in peace? No, he'd wormed his way back in here against her wishes, never mind that it was about to kill her.

"You can glare at me all you like," he said. "Fact is, I'm the one with cause to be angry, and we both know it."

If truth were a target, he'd hit a bull's-eye. But her anger didn't have to make sense. She never wanted to tell him about Bailey to begin with. If he hadn't pushed her—

"Come down so we can talk." He held out his hand.

The last thing she needed was his proximity. That's what got her in trouble before. She shrank away, leaning on the back of the recliner, her back against the wall.

He shoved his hands in his back pockets. "Fine." A muscle in his jaw jumped. "The things you said about Bailey the other night shook me. It's taken me a while to get my thoughts together."

At the mention of Bailey, his green eyes darkened. Maybe her position wasn't such a great idea. She didn't like the way it left her eye to eye with him, or the way the light from the window streamed over his face, highlighting the pain she'd caused. Sam looked down at her knees, where a swipe of white caulk slashed across her skin.

"I knew he liked you that summer. He never said anything, but I could tell."

She remembered catching Bailey's appraisal more than once. He'd kept his distance, though. She thought Bailey was upset with her at first, because Bailey had always been a flirt. It wasn't until that night that she learned the truth.

"I didn't know you had feelings for Bailey," Landon said.

"I didn't." The words were out before she could stop them.

He studied her like an artist who couldn't tell what was wrong with his painting. Confusion was etched in the crease of his brow and in the slant of his eyes. "Then why?"

"I—" *I was afraid. I was angry at you. I was drunk.* The words formed on her tongue, but common sense swallowed them whole. She clamped her lips shut.

"Help me understand, Sam. He was my brother."

The ultimate betrayal. He didn't have to say it. She knew full well what she'd done as soon as she sobered up. It was why she kept the secret. Sam never wanted to hurt Landon. But looking at him now, she realized she'd hurt him intentionally that time. Just to protect herself.

See, Sam, you don't deserve him and you never did. He could never understand why you did it. He's too good.

"You could have come to me when you found out you were pregnant."

Yeah, right. *I'm sorry, Landon, but I seem to be pregnant with your dead brother's child. Can I have some cash to tide me over?* "I had money saved up. Miss Biddle gave me—"

"I'm not talking about money, for crying out loud." He walked away, raking his hand through his hair.

Sam's insides quivered like the jittery heart of a caged squirrel. She clasped her hands tightly together, squeezing until her fingertips went white.

Landon came back toward her, and she pulled up straight, her back flattened against the wall.

He stopped shy of touching her. "I would've married you, Sam." The words sounded like they'd been dragged across his throat. "I loved you."

Sam warmed at the thought. Even knowing that Caden was Bailey's, he would have married her? What kind of love was that? A kind she'd never known.

Then his words replayed in her mind. He said *loved*. Past tense. Only one letter thrown onto the end of the word, but it said so much. Maybe at one time he felt that way, but now? She'd done what she set out to do. She'd killed the love he had for her. Why did it leave her feeling so empty?

"You just disappeared. You left without a trace." His eyes bored into hers, packing urgency. "I didn't know what had happened to you. I tried to find you, but it was like you fell off the face of the earth."

"I had to go."

"No, you didn't."

Did he think she'd enjoyed being eighteen, alone, and pregnant? "Emmett kicked me out." Sam remembered the fateful night vividly. She could still see jeans and shirts strewn across the lawn, her navy blue T-shirt hanging from an azalea bush, her toothbrush lying in the mulch. Her suitcases had been three plastic bags from Stop & Shop.

"Why?"

Because she wound up just like he said she would. Because he never wanted her to begin with. She shrugged. "He found out I was pregnant."

"I asked him where you were. I called him over and over asking if he'd heard from you."

"He didn't know where I was. And I never talked to him after I left." There was no reason to.

"But Miss Biddle knew?" His brows drew together, and his lips tightened.

It wasn't fair for him to be mad at her. "I swore her to secrecy. It's not her fault." Sam had decided to go to Boston only because Miss Biddle said a friend of hers might have a job for her. In the end, it hadn't worked out, but she'd survived.

"If only I'd known . . ."

Then what? Everything would have been peachy? He would have married her, knowing what she'd done, both with Bailey and to him? She would never believe it.

"Why do you look at me like that?"

"Like what?" *Like I don't believe you could've loved me after what I did? Like I'm unworthy of your love?*

"You're so jaded," he said. "Love isn't earned, Sam. It's a gift."

Well, dandy. Sam didn't know how to accept it. Was scared to death to unwrap it. She shook her head slowly. Couldn't he see he asked the impossible?

"What?" He took her hands, curling them up inside each one of his. "Tell me what you're thinking."

What could she say to make him see? How could she explain the hollow spot inside of her? The fear that paralyzed her? Even now, her breathing turned shallow at the thought of hope. Her gaze focused on some point on the wall behind him.

Sam swallowed past a dry throat. "Kids are like empty glasses when they're born. It's a parent's job to fill them up before they leave home." His large, warm hands cocooned hers. "It happened for you. But me?" She had to make him see how it was. "My cup's still empty. Sometimes you or your parents would start to fill it up, but then I'd go home, and it would get sucked dry." Her stomach tightened around its hollow core.

He squeezed her hands in his, his eyes pleading with her. "Let me fill it up," he whispered. His eyes turned glossy, shimmering sadness, reflecting his depth of sorrow.

Sorrow for her. For her desolate childhood, for the love she never had, for the child whose mother forsook her. The residual pain inside her was beyond tears. The pain had compacted, leaving room for a vacant spot where love was supposed to reside.

"Let me fill it up," he'd said. If only it worked that way. She was damaged goods, not fit for the likes of him. "You can't."

He leaned into her, the hardness of his stomach pressing into her knees. He was strong and virile. He deserved someone whole. Not someone like her.

"I can if you let me."

It would be so easy to believe. To let him take her in his arms and persuade her it was true. She would feel loved and full and secure.

For a while.

"Don't ever let yourself love, Sam. Just soon as you do, they leave you." All good things came to an end, especially love. And when it did, it left a shattered shell. What would become of her if she let herself love him?

It's too late for that. It was too late to stop the feelings, but she could stand guard from this point on. She would leave tomorrow and take her broken heart home to mend. It was the only choice she had.

"Marry me, Sam. Stay here and marry me."

Her heart tripped over itself, then raced ahead, leaving her lungs to catch up. She looked away.

"No." She pushed the words past her dry throat. Why couldn't he understand it could never be? She had to leave. Her survival depended on it. She pulled her hands from him, but her gaze swung back to his of their own accord.

He blinked back tears. "Sam . . . I—"

She steeled her heart against him. "You shouldn't have come back." It was his fault. If he'd just stayed away like she asked.

"How can I let you go again? I love you." Hurt glittered in his eyes. "Why do you have to be so stubborn?"

"If it's too much to handle, just leave." *Like Mom. Like Dad. Like everyone else.*

"You'd like that, wouldn't you? You keep pushing and pushing, and it would make it easier if I just left, wouldn't it?"

Yes, it would make it easier. "*Love never brings anything but pain. It's the one thing in life you can count on.*"

His eyes impaled hers, and his voice was heavy. "You don't see me leaving, do you? I'm standing right here. I'm not going anywhere."

It's only words, Sam. Don't buy in. He means them now, but he doesn't know the future. No one does.

His fingers touched her cheek, softly, as if tracing the delicate petal of a rose.

Sam flinched.

One corner of his lips twisted up in a wan smile. He let his hand fall. "The only thing I've done is love you, and you don't want me to do that. I wish I had the key to that heavy door you keep on your heart."

The back door opened, and Sam startled.

Caden saw them and came to an abrupt halt, her hands still on the doorknob. She looked between the two of them, and Sam imagined what she saw. Landon's strained face and glassy eyes. She could only guess at her own expression.

"What's wrong?"

There wasn't enough time in the day to answer that one.

Landon backed away from Sam and combed his fingers through his hair. "Nothing." He attempted a smile, but Sam could see right through it. No doubt, Caden could too. "Your mom and I were just talking. Let's go see what's next on our list. Maybe you can help me." He tousled her hair as he passed her, but the look she gave Sam told her everything she already knew. Caden knew they'd been arguing, and as usual, all the blame was at Sam's feet.

Thirty-one

Sam tossed her paper plate into the garbage can, listening to the sound of Landon's keys jangling in his hands as he left the house. He'd offered to run to the store with her list of last-minute items they needed for the house. With any luck, he'd be gone awhile. The tension between them through the afternoon had been nearly unbearable, and Caden's moodiness didn't help.

The work on the house was done, but there was no time to stand around and appreciate their efforts. She had to make some phone calls and pack their things. In the morning, she would clean the house, and they would be on the noon ferry.

Caden changed into her swimming suit for one last swim while Sam called Patty and left a message assuring her she'd be at work on Monday. When she hung up, she went to the bedroom and pulled out their suitcases.

Caden stood at the bureau mirror, tucking her blond hair into the orange swim cap.

"You'll have to wait until I finish packing to get in the water," Sam said.

Her daughter hadn't spoken to her all afternoon, and Sam wondered when she was going to unload. She always did eventually, and

Sam didn't have the strength to deal with another confrontation today. She should feel relieved that the house was done, that they were going home, but all she felt was a strange regret.

"Why do we have to go, Mom?" Caden asked, her lips turned down at the corners. With her hair in the cap, her brown eyes stood out. They looked sadder than Sam had ever seen them.

"You know I have to be at work Monday. Besides, gymnastics is on Tuesday, and you'll get to see Bridget and your other friends."

"But what about Landon and Max?"

Sam set a stack of shorts in the suitcase and straightened. "What about them?"

"Am I ever going to see them again?" Her voice rose. She crossed her arms and set her mouth in a straight line. "I don't want to go back."

Sam gave a wry smile. "You didn't want to come here, either."

"Well, I like it now. I want to stay."

Sam raised her voice. "And do what? My job is in Boston."

"You can get a job here."

Life from a child's perspective was always so simple. "You don't understand, Caden. It's expensive to live in Nantucket." Too costly, in more ways than one.

"We already have a house here."

Sam could see she needed to find another line of reasoning. "What about school? What about gymnastics? We have a whole life in Boston." *An empty life.* She pushed the thought away and sought to appease Caden. "Maybe we can come back and visit."

"I want to *live* here. With Landon and Max." Her eyes filled, tears trembling on her lower lashes.

Sam turned and gathered a bundle of socks. She knew what Caden was feeling. A part of her wished they could stay too. The negative memories from her childhood had begun to dissipate as they finished the house. The cottage didn't look or smell the same. She had begun to expect Caden's face instead of Emmett's when she woke in the morning.

But Landon was here, and she didn't have the courage or strength to see him every day.

Sam turned to Caden, softening as she watched her chin wobble. She drew in a deep breath and exhaled. "I'm sorry, honey. We have to go back home. I know you don't understand—"

"I do too! I understand that you don't care about anyone but yourself!"

She turned to go, but Sam caught her arm. "That's not true. Why do you think we came here, Caden? Do you think it was easy for me? The sale of this house will fund your future; that's the only reason I came back. You'll be able to go to any college you want, be anything you want to be. Do you know what that's worth? I didn't get that chance. Do you want to grow up and clean offices like me?"

Caden jerked her arm from Sam's grasp. "I don't want to be like you at all." Turning, she strode through the living room and out the door, slamming it.

Caden's words penetrated Sam's hard shell, exactly as intended. Sam walked to the living room window and watched her daughter march down the slope of the backyard toward the water, her slim shoulders squared. When she stepped onto the pier instead of getting in the water, Sam relaxed. At least she was obeying the rules.

Sam turned back to the chest and grabbed an armload of shorts, then dropped them into the suitcase. The house was still, and the emptiness of it felt heavy and oppressing. She had managed to chase away Landon and Caden yet again.

Miss Biddle's words invaded her mind like ants at a beach picnic.

"Here I am, all these years later, heart intact. But lonely. I'd trade all the hurts I may have had for one true love at my side." Sam wondered if she would grow into a lonely old spinster who dispensed advice to likenesses of her former self. *Stop it, Sam. Don't think; just survive.*

She shut the chest of drawers with her hip and pushed the last of her clothes into the bag, then pulled the zipper. She carried the heavy duffel to the living room and set it by the front door. She walked to the back window and peered out, checking on Caden. She'd gotten the beach ball from the shed and sat on the pier, holding it in her lap, her chin resting on its surface. Sam wondered what her daughter was thinking, then decided she didn't want to know.

The toiletries and remaining groceries needed to be packed away. She would see if Miss Biddle wanted what was left of the food.

Sam packed Caden's belongings, setting out her nightgown and clothes for the morning. Then she packed their toiletries, leaving out the things they still needed. When her thoughts turned to Landon, she told herself she'd deal with those later when she was far away. Still, the ache inside her refused to budge. Maybe she'd just shove it down deep where all the other hurt was.

She set Caden's bag by the dresser, leaving the toiletry case in the bathroom, and headed to the kitchen. The fridge was almost empty. She bagged the condiments and leftover lunch meat and set them back in the fridge until morning. She loaded dry goods into the cabinets, leaving out a box of cereal and utensils for breakfast.

Sam wanted to get a start on the cleaning, but the clock on the wall told her the sun would be setting soon, and she'd promised Caden one last swim. She slid on her flip-flops and left the house. When she looked toward the pier, she found it empty. She let the screen door slap into place and walked through the fresh-cut grass, her eyes roving the waterline through the trees from her backyard down to Landon's.

"Caden." She called her daughter's name over a gust of wind and the sound of water rushing the shoreline. When there was no answer, she wondered if Caden had gone off on her bike without asking. But when she turned back to the house, she saw it leaning cockeyed on its kickstand next to Sam's.

"Caden!" Sam raised her voice to encompass the nearby yards. Her daughter's last words echoed in Sam's mind, underscoring Caden's state of mind. Sam's legs carried her quickly down the slope of the shoreline and to the pier, her heart tripping in her chest. Her feet took the planks of the pier quickly, thudding along its length. She looked down toward Landon's pier, where Caden liked to swim because of the sandy bottom.

"Caden!" she called again, lifting her hand to block the light of the setting sun. Above the whoosh of the wind whipping around her ears, she heard a voice. She scanned the water, moving from the shore to farther out to sea.

Sam saw the beach ball first, a small dot on the surface of the water. Then she saw Caden's orange swim cap bobbing next to it. Her daughter waved frantically.

Sam's heart leaped up into her throat and stuck. She dove into the water, then kicked furiously to reach the surface. Her arms worked to propel her through the water. *Caden! Hang on, honey!* She was at least fifty yards out. A riptide must have caught her. Sam knew the strength of the undertow. She'd experienced the panic of being caught in one, but she was older than Caden then and knew what to do. Every summer it happened on the island. Some were lucky enough to be rescued; others were featured in the obituary column a few days later.

Sam pulled her head from the water and located Caden, then redoubled her efforts. *Please, God, let me get to her!* Her muscles worked hard, driving her as fast as they could through the cold water.

Sam gulped in air, then turned her head down, taking in salt water. She lifted her face, sputtering, then stopped long enough to find Caden. Sam saw the beach ball, floating farther to the east than Caden had been swimming, but where was her daughter?

There. She flailed several yards from the ball. How long could Caden stay afloat without it? Alarm rippled through Sam.

"Mommy!" Her plea was a watery gasp.

"I'm coming!" She kicked forward, panic pushing her faster than before. *Oh, God, let her be okay! Don't let her drown!* Periodically, Caden's cries penetrated the water in her ears, reassuring her.

Sam lifted her head and saw her daughter only a few yards away. She closed the distance and reached for Caden.

Her daughter's flailing arms seized onto hers. "Mommy!" She clutched at Sam, her weight sinking them both. Sam kicked to stay buoyant.

"Caden. It's okay, baby," she gasped. "It's okay."

Caden's skinny arms were around her, her head turned up to avoid the water. She clawed at Sam's shoulders.

"Calm down, Caden." Her own breathing was labored, her legs fatigued. She looked toward shore. It seemed a hundred miles away and growing farther by the minute. The ball bobbed away toward the horizon.

Caden's sobs pierced Sam's thoughts. The girl's fingers pressed down on Sam's shoulders, boosting her body out of the water. Sam kicked harder. "Honey, you have to calm down."

Her daughter's breaths were so rapid, Sam feared she would

hyperventilate. She took Caden's face in her hands and leaned back, forcing eye contact. Panic laced Caden's eyes, and fear shadowed her face.

"Caden, listen," Sam said firmly. "You have to calm down, or you're going to drown us both."

"Help, Mommy!"

"I am, but you have to—" A cold swell slapped Sam on the side of her face. She coughed, clearing her lungs. "You have to settle down, understand? It's going to be okay."

"I lost the ball . . ." she wailed.

"I'm here now; you're going to be okay." Caden's weight pushed her down, and Sam kicked again. Her ankle throbbed, but it was the least of her worries.

Water lapped up toward Caden's shoulders, and Sam watched a shiver of alarm run across her face. There was no chance of getting her to float on her back. And Sam wouldn't be able to support her daughter's weight on her body. She was too tired to stay afloat much longer. Why hadn't she grabbed a life preserver from the shed? But all she'd thought about was getting to Caden.

"Remember—" Sam gulped in a breath. "Remember what I told you about riptides? How they run along the shore?"

"I'm scared!"

Sam squeezed her face, her fingers making dimples in Caden's cheeks. "Listen to me, Caden! We need to swim along the shore to the end of the riptide." She sucked in a few breaths. "I'm going to get us to shore, but I need your help."

Caden's body shook, and tears poured down her face.

"I'm going to pull you along. You need to turn on your back and try to float. Kick your feet if you can."

Sam turned Caden and hooked her arm around her daughter's

chest. "Let's go." She tried to side swim, but Caden was fighting her, thrashing in the water. "Float, Caden! Kick your feet."

She kicked hard, her upper body stiff and straining against Sam's arm. They began to move. Her fingers dug into Sam's bicep. She heard Caden gasping for breath, heard her own labored breathing, and wondered how they would make it. *Please, God, I can't let her down!*

They made agonizingly slow progress. Sam prayed the riptide was short and would turn toward shore soon. "Come on, baby, kick!"

They might as well have been on a watery treadmill. For every stroke they made, the water undid their efforts. Sam's lungs burned with the need for oxygen. She needed to rest.

She let her legs sink under her. "Hang on," she gasped, holding Caden against her and kicking to stay afloat.

"I'm tired . . ." Caden cried, catching her breath, clutching at Sam.

"It's going to be okay," she assured her daughter. "We need to swim a little farther." She waited, taking in air. She held on to Caden tightly, trying to alleviate her panic, give her a sense of security. "Are you ready?"

Caden sucked in a wobbly breath and nodded. They started off again down the coast. Each inch of progress was laborious. "Kick, Caden!" They would never make it at this rate. Despair began to settle in, and she fought the same panic her daughter was feeling.

Keep going, Sam. Ignore the pain and keep going. For Caden. You've kept her safe all her life; you can't fail her now.

The thought of failing her was enough to give Sam a burst of energy. She used her free arm, making large strokes, and kicked harder. After a few minutes, she turned toward shore and pressed on.

Were they getting somewhere? Though her eyes were closed, her head down, she thought she could feel progress.

Sam continued until she had to stop for air. Her legs relaxed for the few seconds it took to get them under her. The rest felt like heaven, and she didn't want to kick again, but she had no choice. She pulled Caden close to her, both of them holding their chins up and dragging in air.

Sam looked toward the shore and gauged the distance. It was then she realized they were still being tugged away from shore. They hadn't swum past the riptide. And she didn't know if she had the energy to go on much longer. She thought of her daughter, who depended on her. Was she going to let Caden down when she needed Sam most? Sam couldn't bear the thought. She couldn't bear the thought of Caden dying.

If only someone were outside, but the shoreline was deserted. Caden's fingers slipped on her wet shoulder, and she clutched at Sam.

"Kick your feet," Sam said.

Caden turned her wide brown eyes up to Sam. A fresh batch of tears trembled on her lashes, and her teeth chattered. "I don't want to die, Mommy."

Sam pulled her close and held her tightly with one hand, using the other to stay buoyant. All her life Sam had done what was necessary to survive, and she'd done it on her own. She'd always managed to get them through, but now she wondered if she wasn't enough, if she wasn't strong enough to do this most important thing.

But this time, the cost of failure was death.

Thirty-two

Landon loaded two full bags into his Jeep, then started the vehicle and pulled out of the Stop & Shop parking lot.

He heard Max nosing through one of the bags. "No, Max." The dog sat on the backseat and looked out the window.

He couldn't believe Sam and Caden were leaving tomorrow. They'd stormed into his life and in a few short weeks changed everything. And yet tomorrow they'd leave, and life would return to the way it was. Except now his heart was broken beyond repair.

A taxi pulled out in front of him, and he slowed the Jeep. He fantasized about jumping on the ferry and going back to Boston with Sam. If she wouldn't stay here, he'd gladly go with her. Only one thing stopped him.

She had to want him. It had to be her decision.

He braked for a red light, watching a bicyclist lean into the turn, and drummed his fingers on the steering wheel. He could call her in Boston. He could write letters and send e-mail. He checked his thoughts. Once she left on that ferry, he knew his chance was gone. If he couldn't persuade her with his presence, what hope did he have in his absence?

He pulled onto his street, passing a neighbor walking his dog. He had to put Sam's departure from his mind and use the time wisely. *You have tonight and tomorrow, Reed. Make it count.* The sun was low in the sky now, and twilight would follow, signaling the end of the day. He wished he could reach out and halt the sun in the sky, stopping time. But in his gut he knew Sam didn't need more time. She needed a change of heart, and that was out of his control.

You wouldn't want it any other way. If she won't give you her love willingly, what would it mean, really? Some things had to be given freely or not at all.

He passed his own driveway, then Miss Biddle's, and turned into Sam's. Max stood as Landon turned the key, then the dog hopped over the seat and out his door. Landon grabbed the two bags and approached the house.

The front door opened easily. He entered the house and headed toward the kitchen. "I'm back," he called. No one answered, so he set the bags on the kitchen table and peeked in the bedrooms. "Sam? Caden?"

He thought Sam would be cleaning, and he'd intended to help. Where were they? Then he remembered a conversation from earlier in the day.

"*Can I go swimming one last time, Mom?*"

"*I'm not sure there'll be time. After we finish all this, I still have to clean.*"

"*Please? Just for a little while.*"

Landon had left the room at that point, but Sam must have agreed. He walked out the back door and across the porch. The pier was empty, and so was the shoreline. He stood with his hands on his hips, scanning the bay.

"Sam?"

His only answer was the ruffling of leaves as the wind tousled them. A second later, he heard the pounding of paws. Max rounded the corner of the house and came to lean against Landon's leg. Landon absently rubbed him behind the ears.

"Where are they, buddy?" He walked through the grass, across Miss Biddle's yard and toward his own pier. Maybe Caden was over there. Wherever she was swimming, Sam would be nearby. She didn't let Caden out of her sight when the girl was in the water.

But when he approached his pier, he found it empty. Strange. Remembering Sam getting locked in the shed, he considered checking it, but he'd fixed the doorknob. There was no way to get locked in now. They couldn't have gone anywhere, because their bikes were at the back of the house. Miss Biddle's car wasn't in her drive, so Sam wasn't there.

The wind died down, and now all he heard was the water lapping the shoreline. The silence was unnerving. A sudden thought caught in his mind. What if she'd left? Loaded their things on the ferry and headed back to the mainland? Would she leave without saying good-bye?

A sound caught his attention. A voice calling from far away. He turned his head, listening. It was coming from the water. He dashed down his yard, down the pier, his eyes searching.

Something floated on the surface, beyond his yard. A bright orange dot and another spot beside it. His stomach dropped to the bottom of his feet like an anchor.

Caden and Sam. They were out too far. The wind carried a voice that called for help. *Sam.* He didn't see the bright orange of a life vest.

He had to get to them. He started to dive off the pier, but reason pierced his fog of fear. He couldn't save both of them, especially if they were panicking. It took everything in him to turn and dash toward his shed. His feet pounded the deck boards, then the short grass. He threw open the shed door and grabbed a life vest and a preserver from the hooks on the wall.

Landon ran toward the water, throwing the vest over his head and tying a hasty knot as he went.

When he reached the end of the pier, he shed his shoes. "Stay, Max!" he ordered, then dove headfirst and kicked to the surface. The life ring hampered his stokes, but they would need it when he reached them.

Oh, God, let me get there in time. How long had they been out there? Were they still afloat? He couldn't take time to look. His legs kicked efficiently, his hands slicing through the water. What if he didn't reach them in time? What if he couldn't find them when he got out there?

Visions of the night Bailey drowned flashed through the dark caverns of his mind. He remembered treading the water, calling Bailey's name. He remembered studying the surface for some sign of his brother and finding none. He remembered the despair and shock that followed.

It occurred to him he was in the water for the first time since that night. His fear of losing Sam and Caden had superseded his fear of the water.

He lifted his head, drawing a deep breath, and looked for them over the gentle swells. He caught sight of Caden's orange cap and Sam's wet hair, and relief washed through him. Caden flailed, and Sam went under. He remembered reading in the paper the summer before of a rescuer who was drowned by a panic-stricken swimmer.

Terror propelled his body forward. *Hang on, Sam!* He'd give his life for them in a heartbeat. He was still fifty yards off, a lifetime away for anyone fighting to stay afloat.

He could sense when he passed the point where the ocean

moved toward shore. His speed increased, and he made better time. The undertow was strong, assisting his progress.

Lifting his head to draw a breath, he saw Sam above water again. They were only several yards away now. "I'm coming!" He put his head down and plunged forward.

The last few yards seemed agonizingly long. Finally, his fingers touched something and he came up. Caden grabbed onto him first, and he wrapped an arm around her. She gasped for air, sobbing. "Grab on, Sam." She must be relieved to have Caden's weight removed. He didn't know how she'd stayed afloat at all.

Sam grabbed onto his life vest. Fear glazed her eyes, and her breath came hard and fast.

He removed the life ring from his shoulder and put it over Caden's head. "You're okay, sweetie," he said between breaths. "Lift your arms and hang on to the preserver. You'll float. I've got you." He helped her get the preserver on, having to pull one hand at a time off him and thread it through the hole. "Hang on to the sides, Caden." The words were unnecessary; she grabbed the ring in a death clutch.

Landon reached underwater and untied the soggy strap of his life vest. When he'd worked the knot loose, he slipped it over his head and put it over Sam, then wrapped the strap around her waist and tied it securely. Sam clutched the vest with white fingers. Her body stilled, and she rested her head against the cushion.

Landon let go and kicked to stay buoyant. Caden's sobs had quieted to shuddering breaths. He looked between them. "Everybody okay?"

Caden's arms trembled and her teeth chattered. "H—how are we going to get back?"

The terror on her face broke him in half. He pulled her to him, pulled Sam to him, and held them there, careful not to put his weight on either of them. Sam leaned on his shoulder, and he set a kiss on the top of her wet head. He could have lost them both. If he'd been a little later, if he hadn't looked for them, he would have lost them forever. The thought was a knife straight to his heart.

His legs began to fatigue, and he knew he'd let them rest as long as he dared. "Okay, girls, here's what we're going to do." He pulled back and spoke with confidence. "We'll swim parallel to the shore to the end of the riptide, then we'll swim in." He grabbed Sam's life vest. "Grab Caden's ring so we stay together." Sam did as he asked.

"Ready?" he asked.

They nodded.

The three of them began their trek down the shoreline, swimming slowly as a chain, but Landon used his strength to pull them along. Sam kicked as much as she could but needed frequent breaks. He imagined her legs must be shot. His own were beginning to burn.

He kept his face in the water, using large strokes and drawing breath when necessary. After what seemed like an hour, he turned them in gradually, at an angle to the shore. His fingers, clamped on Sam's vest, were a knotted spasm, and his lungs burned from lack of oxygen, but he kept going. He could tell by their progress that they were finally free of the riptide. Survival was only a matter of persistence now.

Sam began kicking harder, seeming to sense the end of the ordeal, and Caden also showed a renewed burst of energy as they neared shore. When they approached the end of a dock, Landon let his feet sink below him and felt the blessed sensation of solid ground. His feet sank into the silt.

Sam, too, stood upright, and they walked Caden in until she could stand. As they left the water, Caden's legs wobbled, and

Landon wrapped an arm around her, keeping her upright until they reached the shore.

There, Sam and Caden fell on the grass, eyes closed, chests heaving, seemingly heedless of the sand sticking to their faces. Landon lowered himself beside them, taking deep gulps of air. "Everyone okay? Caden?"

He touched her shoulder, and she turned toward him. Twilight had fallen, and he couldn't see well enough to read her expression. "I'm . . . okay."

"Sam?" He laid his hand on her wet head, and she nodded.

He lay back against the grass and dragged in air as fast as he could. His girls were safe, and that was all that mattered.

Thirty-three

Sam lifted the covers and let Caden slide between the sheets. Her hair, still damp from the warm bath, fanned out on the pillow.

Sam pulled the quilt to Caden's chin, then laid her hand against her daughter's forehead. "You all right?"

Caden closed her eyes and nodded. Sam watched her for a moment, the realization that she'd almost lost her daughter hitting her like a hurricane-force wind. She ran her fingers down her cheek, and Caden suddenly opened her eyes.

"I'm sorry, Mom." A tear ran across her face and down into her pillow.

"Shhh. It was an accident." Caden had explained as Landon carried her home that the ball blew off the pier. She jumped in to retrieve it, but the ball moved a little farther away, and before she knew it, she was being pulled off her feet. It was a miracle she was able to get to the ball, or she never would have made it until Sam saw her.

"Not that," Caden said, turning toward Sam. "I'm sorry about how I've been acting. Sorry about what I said to you today." Her face crumpled.

Sam sank onto the bed, reaching for her, and Caden came into her arms. Her skin smelled like the generic raspberry soap Sam had bought at the Stop & Shop, but her hair still held the scent of salt water. "It's okay," Sam whispered.

She'd take Caden any way she could get her. Her daughter could fight with her, give her attitude, and tell her she hated her if she wanted. It was enough that Sam could feel the smoothness of her skin, could feel the weight of Caden against her.

She tightened her arms around her daughter and felt the dampness of Caden's tears through the oversized T-shirt. "I love you so much, baby." When was the last time she'd said the words? When was the last time she'd held Caden?

Why, Sam? Why has it been so long? The answer had been deep down in the place where she hid her pain. It rose to the surface while they were on the water, when the fear of losing Caden hit her full force, like a rogue wave.

But the fact was, the shadow of that wave had been towering over her a long time. The fear that she might lose Caden. That it was dangerous to love her too much. Because one day Caden might not be there to love. And what would become of Sam then?

Caden's arms loosened, flopping to the bed, and she fell back against the pillow. "I'm so tired."

Sam ran her palm across Caden's cheek, drying the tears, and brushed the wet strands from her face. "I know. We'll talk in the morning."

The morning. When they would leave. The past two hours had been like a bubble of time suspended outside of reality. What had happened on the water held significance, and Sam knew Landon's rescue affected much more than their survival. She just wasn't sure what.

She stood, her legs wobbly from fatigue, and pulled the quilt to

Caden's chin. Sam flipped off the bedside lamp, and darkness washed the room.

"Mom?" Alarm laced the word. "Will you stay with me?"

Sam sensed Caden's hand fumbling for her through the darkness. She'd planned on a warm bath and a shampoo to rid the smell of ocean from her hair.

It could wait until morning. "Sure." She walked around the bed and got in, pulling Caden close, her back spooned into Sam's stomach.

"'Night," Caden whispered.

"Good night, Caden." Sam nuzzled the top of her daughter's head with her chin and tucked her knees up inside of hers. In that moment, she remembered something. Sam had been six and came home from kindergarten sick. Her mom tucked her into bed and lay down with her. Sam remembered her mother's warmth against her back, the security of her closeness. Sam didn't know what had happened to change her mom; maybe her dad's death was to blame. But her mom had loved her in her own way.

Had Sam done any better? She had stayed with Caden, present in body but absent in spirit. In her own way, she had abandoned her daughter too. Emotionally, she'd been absent since the day Caden was born. Her soul grieved at the realization. So much time lost. How many regrets would she have had if today was her last day? If it was their last day? Caden never would have experienced being fully loved. Sam had told Landon her glass was empty, but Caden's needed filling now.

Her arms tightened around Caden, holding her daughter snuggly against her chest. Tomorrow was a new day, and change was possible. She had a second chance to be the kind of mother she wanted to be.

Sam's eyes stung, a foreign sensation. *Nothing will stop me from loving you, baby. You'll see.*

She closed her eyes and drew in fresh oxygen, appreciating that simple act as she never had. How terrible it was to struggle for breath. To take a gulp of air, not knowing if it was your last. She thought of Bailey and hoped he hadn't suffered that night. She hoped he'd been unconscious and unaware when he slipped into the water.

Sam's mind spun back hours before to when she spotted Landon on the water. She thought she was seeing things, but he was there. Like always, he was there. Her salvation. Just when she thought it was too late, that they were going under for the last time, he scooped them up and saved them.

Had she even thanked him? If not for him, they would be dead. The thought made her shudder. They owed him their lives, and she hadn't even thanked him. A knot clogged her throat. She'd been so mean to him, pushing him away, hurting him, and still, he stayed close.

Sam shifted her aching ankle slowly, trying not to disturb Caden. Her daughter didn't budge as she moved, so Sam turned onto her back, her muscles protesting. She was going to be a mess in the morning. She'd probably set her ankle back three days, and she wondered if she'd be able to work come Monday. She didn't want to think about Monday, or even tomorrow.

Outside, a loon called, joining nature's orchestra. She opened her eyes and stared into the darkness. Caden's form was still, and Sam knew she was sleeping by the steady sound of her deep breath.

Although her own body was limp with fatigue, her mind whirled like the relentless wind. The night song outside her window beckoned her. She slid from under the covers, moving slowly and quietly. When her weight left the mattress, she checked Caden. As tired as her daughter was, she'd sleep soundly and until late in the morning.

The wood floor was cold against her bare feet, and bits of dried sand stuck to her heels as she limped through the living room. She unlocked the back door and stepped onto the porch, leaving the door open so she could hear if Caden called.

The night smelled like roses and salt and fresh grass. The loon called again over the buzz of insects, and a wave washed the shoreline as if trying to shush the creatures.

The wind whispered through the screen, drawing her skin into gooseflesh. She wrapped her arms around herself and stared into the darkness of the night. A thin veil of clouds shrouded the moon, dimming its light.

Sam looked toward the east, two doors down where Landon lived.

Landon. As sure and steady as the tide. He'd been there when others abandoned her, he'd been there after she hurt him, he'd been there when she needed him most.

And you didn't even say thank you. Sam's feet urged her in that direction. She had so much to say.

But it was late and his lights were off. Besides, she didn't want to wander so far from Caden. She turned and hobbled toward the nearest chair.

A distinct sound reached her ears, cutting through the nocturnal noises. A quiet thud, like something hitting wood.

She walked to the screen door and opened it, then set it gently back in place. Her tired legs wobbled as she took the porch steps. The grass was soft and cool against her feet, tickling her bare toes with their fringe.

The thud sounded again, and she followed the echo down the

slope of the yard, listening through the lullaby of the water stroking the shoreline. The wind lifted her hair from her shoulders and made the hardware on Miss Biddle's flag ping softly, a cymbal for the night song.

Sam stopped at the water's edge, listening. The sound she heard had ceased, but a shadowy movement down the pier caught her eye. She stepped up onto the boards, her eyes fixed on its end, squinting through the darkness.

Her feet carried her down the pier's wooden length. Halfway there, she recognized the shadow as a person. Another two steps and she saw the form was lying down, hands clasped behind the head, feet hanging over the end.

Landon. Her racing heart flipped over at the sight. For a moment, she wondered if she'd conjured him up out of need. But when she blinked, he was still there.

Not wanting to startle him, she whispered his name as she approached.

At the sound, he jerked upright and turned toward her. "Sam."

She limped down the pier and lowered herself beside him, easing her sore ankle over the side.

"What are you doing up?" he asked.

She tucked her long shirt under her and settled her hands in her lap. "I'm not tired." The sounds of the night, the feel of Landon beside her began to soothe her mind.

"How's Caden?"

Changed. Just like Sam. "Sleeping soundly." A breeze blew across the bay, carrying the scent of his musky soap. "What are you doing here?"

"I couldn't sleep." Then, as if realizing he hadn't answered her question, he added, "I wanted to be closer."

Sam looked at him then. The heat from his eyes warmed her all over. "I never said thank you," she whispered.

"You don't have—"

"You risked your life for us. Without a thought of your own fears."

"I did what anyone would have done, Sam."

"Shut up and let me say thank you."

The corner of his lip tipped up, but he remained quiet.

Words would never be enough to express how truly grateful she was. Still, she said them. "Thank you." The moon's curtain must have lifted, because light played on the ridges of his face. "You're supposed to say, 'You're welcome.'"

His eyes roved over her face. "You're welcome."

Sam's hands trembled as if it were their first date. But they'd never even had a first date. She felt her lips twitch and turned away, looking out toward the horizon where the dark sky met the black sea.

"What?" he asked.

She looked at him, then lifted her palms, gesturing around them. "This. Us. How many times do you suppose we've sat here on this pier?" A seagull, out past its bedtime, called out, its shriek echoing across the water.

"Dozens. Hundreds." He smiled as if remembering.

They'd grown up out here on the bay. It had been her escape. *He* had been her escape. And then she'd left him, left the island, without leaving word for him. And when she came back, she did nothing but hurt him more.

Sam thought of Bailey and how her mistake had cost him his life. Had robbed Landon of his brother. Regret swelled in her, almost unbearable. If only she could go back and do the night over again. "I'm so sorry about Bailey."

He squeezed her hand. "You already apologized," he said softly.

Her eyes burned. "Is that enough?" It didn't feel like enough. Not even close.

He touched her chin with his fingertips. "It is for me."

All her mistakes oozed like sewage into her mind. Her silence after Bailey's death, her dalliance with Tully, the way she'd told Landon about Bailey only to push him away. The shame of it made her skin heat. How could he forget what she'd done?

"I've hurt you so much." And all he'd done was love her back. "But I intend to make it up to you." She let her face betray her feelings. She couldn't have stopped it if she tried.

"You already have."

The love she saw in his face gave her every assurance she needed to take it one step further. "Do you think I could change my mind about that question you asked before?" Her courage scattered like grains of sand in a storm.

The corners of his lips tilted. "It's a woman's privilege."

Sam touched the crest of his cheek, then traced the edges of his jawline to the cleft in his chin. His skin was warm and rough against her fingers. She felt a stirring inside for more. More than just a whisper of a touch. Much more.

He leaned close, and his mouth closed over hers. Sam's skin blazed, burning all the way to her heart, where Landon now resided. What had she done to deserve this man? His claim came back to her. "*Love isn't earned, Sam. It's a gift.*"

A gift she would accept. She'd be foolish not to. She let her lips linger on his until he pulled away, but only so he could hold her. Sam wrapped her arms around his back and nestled against his chest. His shirt smelled like sunshine and fresh air, and the tenderness of his hand against her face made her feel cherished. *I could stay here forever.*

She felt his chest expand then deflate with his breath.

"It's not so bad here, is it, Sam? The cobblestone streets, the warm breeze, the smell of the ocean . . ."

She listened to the steady beating of his heart, felt the warmth of his flesh against hers, and closed her eyes on a sigh. "No, it's not so bad."

His fingers threaded through her hair. "I'd follow you to Boston if you wanted."

Sam smiled against his shirt. "No." She still had work to do, coming to grips with her past. But it was something she needed to face for her own good. And Caden's. Where better to do it than here? With Landon at her side.

For a moment, fear crept in and rattled her. Sam grasped the material of his shirt, and she pulled herself close to him. "I'm still afraid," she admitted quietly. "Just so you know."

He tightened his arms around her, the strength of them making her feel safe. "It's okay to be afraid," he said. His hand pressed her cheek, holding her against his heart. "I'm not going anywhere. I love you, Sam."

His words seeped into the empty space and remained there. It was a start. "I love you too," she whispered, relaxing in his arms, choosing to believe, choosing to surrender. One moment at a time.

Reading Group Guide

1. From the beginning of the story (and even before that), Sam pushes Landon away because she is afraid to love. What are some of the things Sam does to keep Landon at a distance? What are some of the things people do to push God away?

2. What are some of the things Landon endures in his efforts to pursue Sam? How has God pursued you?

3. Sam's abandonment and the difficulties of her childhood caused her to make decisions that caused others pain. Do you live with regrets related to things you have done? Things that have been done to you? How have these things impacted your relationships? How can you break the cycle?

4. Sam was willing to settle for much less than Landon had to offer. What are some of the things we settle for? Why are we often willing to accept so much less than God wants to give us?

5. Sam's biggest fear was being abandoned. How did that fear affect her relationship with Caden? What is your biggest fear, and how has it impacted the way you live?

6. Sam felt she wasn't good enough for Landon because of the harmful things she'd done in the past. Have you ever felt that way toward God? What does Psalm 103:12 say about our past transgressions?

7. Sam's stepfather made claims that repeatedly played like a tape in her head, influencing her choices. What cruel or misleading words were said to you as a child that still influence your choices or attitudes? How can you change these destructive thoughts? How can you use words to positively influence others around you?

8. Landon told Sam that his love was a gift, not something to be earned. Why is it sometimes hard for us to understand that God's love is a free gift with no strings attached?

An Interview with Denise Hunter

Thomas Nelson Fiction: Tell us a little about yourself. How did you get started writing?

Denise Hunter: I'm a Midwestern girl, married to a wonderful man, and I have three terrific boys. When I was a child, my mother took me to the library regularly, and I was introduced to the world of fiction. In my elementary years, I wore out our school library's Laura Ingalls Wilder books, and throughout my middle school years and into high school, I always had my nose in a book. (Still do—just ask my husband.)

In my early twenties, I began to wonder if I could write a novel. I had two of my children at that time, and when my grandfather became very ill, we were told he was going to pass away soon. I visited him in the hospital, and as I watched him lying on the bed, I recalled the many things he had done for Christ during his long life. I knew he'd lived a full life with few regrets, and I wanted to be able to feel that way when my life drew to a close. On my long drive home, I decided I was going to stop wondering if I could write a book and just do it. I wrote my first novels during my children's nap times.

TNF: What was your inspiration for writing *Surrender Bay*?

Denise: My earliest vision of the story was simply about best friends who fall in love. The story evolved as it brewed in my head for almost a year and as I brainstormed with my writing buddies (authors Colleen Coble, Diann Hunt, and Kristin Billerbeck). But *Surrender Bay* truly took on a new dimension when the Thomas Nelson staff suggested making the romance in the story a picture of the romance between us and God. The story grew, bit by bit, from there, with lots of brain-racking, hair-pulling, praying, and rewriting.

TNF: There is no overt Christianity in the story. Why did you write it as an allegory?

Denise: I love the way Jesus told stories. His parables made His listeners think for themselves and draw their own conclusions. In His story of the prodigal son, Jesus never said, "Listen, folks, the father in the story is God, and the prodigal son is you." The son never had a "come to Jesus" moment; he simply returned to his father and was welcomed home with open arms. Jesus required the listeners to draw the connection for a reason.

An allegory allows us to see the familiar in a fresh and powerful way, and that's what I hoped to do with *Surrender Bay*.

TNF: What would you like readers to take away from this story?

Denise: I hope readers walk away from this story with a fresh view of the way God pursues us. I hope women find comfort in the kind of love He has for them, the kind that never fails, the kind that puts our sins as far as the east is from the west. "He will never leave you nor forsake you."

TNF: Nantucket sounds like a beautiful place to visit. Did you go there to do research?

Denise: Nantucket is a lovely island, a truly unique place. My family went with me for a brief visit so I could do some research as part of our vacation last year. I was so inspired, I sat on the beach and wrote the first pages of the story while my kids and husband frolicked in the water. The quaint town, the history, the cobblestone streets, and the people really make this an ideal setting for a novel.

TNF: Is *Surrender Bay* part of a series?

Denise: Yes and no. *Surrender Bay* is the first of four books that will be set on Nantucket, romance novels that will reflect the attributes of God listed in Zephaniah 3:17. The books will feature different characters, though, and stand completely on their own. I'm hoping they'll necessitate another research trip to Nantucket.

Acknowledgments

With grateful appreciation to all the people who had a hand in making this book happen: Amanda Bostic and all the wonderful people at Thomas Nelson. What an amazing group of talented people! I'm so blessed to be a part of your team. Agent extraordinaire Karen Solem. Erin Healy, who makes me look like a better writer than I am. My awesome brainstorming friends, Colleen Coble, Diann Hunt, and Kristin Billerbeck; I can't imagine doing this writing thing without you. BarlowGirl, whose song "I Need You to Love Me" inspired me time and time again during the writing of this story. Jim Bell and Cara Putnam, for their help concerning legal matters. Denny and Joy Geiger for help on research. Thanks to my husband, Kevin, and my boys, who had to put up with deadline madness and edits on the way home from vacation. You are a blessing from above!

the Convenient Groom

The next Nantucket Love Story
from author Denise Hunter

AVAILABLE EVERYWHERE

MAY 2008

AN EXCERPT FROM
The Convenient Groom

*Dating is like shopping for a garment. Everything
looks great in the display window. Once inside
the store, some of the dazzle disappears.*
—Excerpt from *Finding Mr. Right-For-You* by Dr. Kate

The red light on Kate Lawrence's cell phone blinked a staccato warning. But before she could retrieve the message, her maid of honor, Anna Doherty, waved her pale arms from the beach, stealing her attention.

Anna's smooth voice sounded in her headset. "Kate, can you come here? We've got a few glitches."

"Be right there." Kate tucked her clipboard in the crook of her elbow, took the steps down Jetty Pavilion's porch, and crossed the heel-sinking sand of the Nantucket shoreline. In six hours, thirty-four guests would be seated there in the rows of white chairs watching Kate pledge her life to Bryan Montgomery under a beautiful hand-carved gazebo.

Where was the gazebo anyway? She checked her watch then glanced toward the Pavilion where workers scurried in white uniforms. No sign of Lucas.

She approached Anna, who wore worry lines as naturally as she wore her Anne Klein pantsuit. Anna was the best receptionist Kate could ask for. Her capable presence reassured the troubled couples she ushered through Kate's office.

Right now, Anna's long brown hair whipped across her face like a flag gone awry, and she batted it from her eyes with her freckled hand. "Soiree's just called. Their delivery truck is in for service, and the flowers will be a little late. Half an hour at the most."

Kate jotted the note on her schedule. "That's okay." She'd factored in cushion time.

"Murray's called and the tuxes haven't been picked up except for your dad's."

Bryan and his best man had been due at Murray's at nine-thirty. An hour ago. "I'll check on that. What else?"

Anna's frown lines deepened and her eyes blinked against the wind. "The carriage driver is sick, but they're trying to find a replacement. The Weatherbys called and asked if they could attend last minute—they were supposed to go out of town but their plans changed."

Kate nodded. "Fine, fine. Call and tell her they're welcome. I'll notify the caterer."

"Your publicist—Pam?—has been trying to reach you. Did you check your cell? She said she got voicemail. Anyway, your book copies did arrive this morning. She dropped this off." Anna pulled a hardback book from under her clipboard. "Ta-da!"

"My book!" Kate stared at the cover, where the title *Finding Mr. Right-For-You* floated above a cartoon couple. The man was on his knee proposing. Below them, a colorful box housed the bold letters of Kate's name. She ran her fingers over the glossy book jacket, feeling the raised bumps of the letters, savoring the moment.

"Pam wants a quick photo shoot before the guests arrive. You holding the book, that kind of thing. You should probably call her."

Kate jotted the note. While it was on her mind, she reached down and turned on her cell.

"Ready for more great news?" Anna asked. Her blue eyes glittered like diamonds. The news had to be good.

"What?"

"The *New York Times* is sending a reporter *and* a photographer. They want to do a feature story on your wedding and your book."

Fresh air caught and held in Kate's lungs. Rosewood Press was probably turning cartwheels. "That's fabulous. They'll want an interview." She scanned her schedule, looking for an open slot. After the reception? She hated to do it, but Bryan would understand. The *New York Times.* It would give Kate's initial sales the boost it needed. Maybe enough to make the best seller list.

"Here's the number." Anna handed her a yellow Post-It. "That tabloid guy has been hanging around all morning trying to figure out who the groom is. I told him he'd find out in six hours like everyone else. The rest of the media is scheduled to arrive an hour before the wedding, and Pam's having an area set up over there for them." Anna gestured behind the rows of chairs to a square blocked off with white ribbon.

"Good. I want them to be as inconspicuous as possible. This is my wedding, and a girl only gets married once, after all."

"One would hope." Anna said. "Is there anything else I can do?"

Kate gave her sideways hug, as close to an embrace as she'd ever given her assistant, her fingers pressing into Anna's fleshy shoulder. "You're a godsend. I don't know what I'd do without you."

"Oh! I know what I forgot to tell you. The gazebo. It should have been here by now. I tried to call Lucas, but I got the machine, and I don't have his cell number."

"His shop's closed today, and he doesn't have a cell." The man didn't wear a watch, much less carry a phone. She should've known better than to put something this crucial in his hands. Kate checked her watch. "I'll run over and check on it."

The drive to town was quick and effortless, but Kate's mind swam with a hundred details. She jotted reminders on her clipboard when she stopped for pedestrians, occasionally admiring the cover of her book. She called Pam for a quick recap about the *New York Times* reporter, and by the time she hung up, she was pulling into a parallel slot on Main Street in front of Lucas's storefront.

The sign above the picture window read "Cottage House Furniture." On the second floor of the Shaker building, the wooden shingle for her own business dangled from a metal pole: "Kate Lawrence, Marriage Counseling Services." She needed to remind Lucas to remove it; otherwise he'd leave it hanging for another year or until someone else rented the space.

Kate exited her car and slid her key into the rusty lock of the shop's door. Once inside, she passed the stairs leading to her office and walked through the darkened maze of furniture to the back, where she hoped to find Lucas. She bumped an end table with her shin. *Ow!* That would leave a mark.

The high-pitched buzz of a power tool pierced the darkness, a good sign. "Lucas?" She rapped loudly on the metal door with her knuckles. The noise stopped.

"Come in."

She opened the door. Lucas Wright looked up from his spot on the cement floor at the base of the gazebo, his too long hair hanging over one eye. He looked her over, then turned back to the spindle and ran his thick hand over it as if testing the curves.

"Aren't you supposed to be at the beach?" he asked.

Kate crossed her arms. "I could ask you the same thing."

He stood, agile for his size, and backed away from the gazebo. Sawdust from the floor clung to his faded jeans and black T-shirt. "I was just finishing."

"You were supposed to be there an hour ago. The gazebo needs to be put in place before the sound system, and the florist has to decorate it, and there are people waiting to do their jobs."

He faced her, looking into her in that way of his that made her feel like he could see clean through her. "Today's the big day, huh?" Putting his tool on his workhorse, he dusted off his hands, moving in slow motion as though he'd decided tonight wouldn't arrive until next week.

Kate checked her watch. "Do you think you can get this down to the beach sometime today?"

Walking around the piece, he studied it, hands on his hips, head cocked. "You like it?"

For the first time since the week before, Kate looked at the gazebo—the white lattice top, the hand-carved spindles, the gentle arch of the entry. At the top of the arch, a piece of wood curved gracefully, etched with clusters of daisies. The gazebo's simple lines were characteristic of Lucas' work, but she'd never known him to use such exquisite detail. The piece had an elegance that surpassed her expectations. He did beautiful work; she'd give him that.

"I do. I love the etching." She sighed. Just when he irritated the snot out of her, he did something like this, caught her off guard. She always felt like she was tripping down the stairs when she was with him.

Focus! "It needs to find its way to the beach. Pronto."

"Yes, ma'am." His salute was unhurried.

Before she could offer a retort, her cell phone pealed and buzzed simultaneously, and she pulled it from her capri pocket.

"Hello?"

"Kate?"

"Bryan." Turning away from Lucas and toward the door, she eyed a crude desk with a metal folding chair that bore countless rusty scratches. "Good morning." A smile crept into her voice. It was their wedding day. The day they'd planned for nearly two years. "Did you sleep well?" She hadn't. She'd rumpled the sheets until nearly two o'clock, but that was to be expected.

The silence on the other end, however, was not. "Bryan?" Had she lost the signal?

"Um, Kate, did you get my message?"

There'd been a blinking red light this morning. She'd assumed it was Pam's voicemail and hadn't checked. Suddenly, she wished she had.

"No. What's wrong?"

"Are you sitting down?"

"No, I'm not sitting down. Just tell me." An ugly dread snaked down her spine and settled there, coiled and waiting.

"I'm on my way back to Boston," he said. "I left a message this morning. You must've had your phone off."

Kate's stomach stirred. She stared at the wall in front of her— a pegboard with a zillion holes, metal prongs poking from it, tools and cords everywhere. "What happened?" Some emergency, maybe?

What emergency could trump our wedding?

"I can't marry you, Kate."

The words dropped, each one crumbling under its own weight. The stirring in her stomach intensified. "That's not funny, Bryan."

It was a terrible joke. He'd never been good with jokes. His punch lines left you leaning forward, waiting for the rest.

"I'm in love with someone else."

Pain. A huge wooden spoon, tossing the contents of her stomach. Her legs wobbled, trembling on the wedge heels of her sandals, and she clutched the cold metal of the folding chair. "What?" Was that *her* voice, weak and thready? Someone had vacuumed all the moisture from her mouth, sucked the air from her lungs.

"I'm so sorry," Bryan was saying. "I know this is awful. You don't deserve this, but I can't marry you. It happened slowly, and I didn't realize what was going on until recently. I tried to put it out of my mind, but I just can't. And I can't marry you knowing how I feel. I'm so sorry, Kate."

"What?" It was the only word her mind could form at the moment.

"I know there's no excuse. I should have told you before now, but I thought it would go away. I thought I was just having cold feet or something, but it's more than that."

"We've been together for *two years*, Bryan."

It was a stupid thing to say, but it was all she could think of. Memories played across the screen of her mind in fast forward. The day they'd met in line at Starbucks in downtown Boston when Kate had gone there for a conference. Their first date at the Colonial Theatre. The long-distance courting and weekend visits. The e-mails, the phone calls, the engagement, the book. It all whizzed by, coming to a screeching halt here, at this moment. Here, in Lucas's dusty workshop. Here, in front of the special gazebo they were to be married in.

"I've already called my family and told them. I know there's a lot to do, and I'll help any way you want me to. And then there's your book . . . I'm so sorry."

Sorry. You're sorry? She pictured the precise rows of white chairs, the tent being erected as they spoke, the photographers.

The *New York Times*.

She closed her burning eyes. Everything would have to be cancelled.

At that thought, humiliation arrived on the scene, sinking in past the pain of betrayal. The weight of it pushed at her shoulders and she grabbed the hair at her nape. *Think, Kate! This is no time to lose it.*

"Stop, Bryan. Just stop and think about what you're doing. Maybe you're letting your issues with your parents' divorce affect your decisions. This kind of fear is perfectly natural before a wedding, and maybe—"

"No, it's not that—"

"How do you know?" She forced reason into her tone. Used her soothing voice—the one she put on when things got heated between one of her couples. "We love each other. We're perfect for each other. You've said it a hundred times."

"There's something missing, Kate."

She wobbled again and steadied herself with a hand on the chair. *"Something missing"?* What was *that* supposed to mean?

As her mind grappled with that seemingly unanswerable question, she felt a hand at her back, leading her into the chair. She was sitting, her head as fuzzy as a cotton candy machine, her emerald-cut engagement ring blurring before her eyes.

"What do you mean there's something missing? The only thing missing is the groom. For our wedding that starts in five hours. *Five hours,* Bryan." Now she felt the hysteria building and took a full breath, nearly choking on the way the oxygen stretched her lungs.

"I'll help in any way I can."

"You can help by showing up for our wedding!"

Her mind ran through the list of people she'd have to call. Her dad, the guests, her publisher. She thought of the money Rosewood Press had spent on this elaborate beach wedding. They'd flown in friends and family from all over the country, paid for the photographer, flowers, caterer, the wedding attire. Kate had only wanted a simple wedding, but with the release of the book, the marketing department had other ideas. *"An elegant wedding and a surprise groom just as the book releases. Think of the publicity, Kate!"*

A knot started in her throat and burned its way to her heart.

"I'll always care about you," Bryan said.

The words fell, as empty as a discarded soda bottle on a deserted beach.

Enough.

The adrenaline coursing through her veins drained suddenly, leaving her once again weak and shaky. She couldn't talk to him anymore. She wasn't going to break down on the phone, wasn't going to beg him to come back. It wouldn't accomplish a thing anyway. She'd heard this tone of Bryan's voice before. He was a man who knew what he wanted. And what he didn't want.

And he didn't want Kate. She suddenly knew that fact as surely as she knew tomorrow would be more impossible to face than today.

She cleared her throat. "I have to go."

"Kate, tell me what I can do. My family will pitch in too. I want to help fix things."

She wanted to tell him there was no fixing this. There was no fixing her heart or the impending collision of her life and her career. Instead, numb, she closed the phone, staring straight ahead at the holes on the pegboard until they blended together in a blurry haze.

He was leaving her. The man she loved was walking away. This wasn't supposed to be happening. Not to her. She'd been so careful, and for what? A hollow spot opened up in her stomach, wide and gaping.

Instead of the headlines reading "Marriage Expert Finds Her Mr. Right," they would read "Marriage Expert Jilted at the Altar."

Kate had never considered herself prideful, but the thought of facing the next twenty-four hours made cyanide seem reasonable. How could this be happening? To her, of all people? She'd written a book on the subject of finding the right mate and had managed to find the wrong one instead. By tomorrow the whole world would know.